BACKSTAGE PASS

—

Eric M. Todd

Frank Weimann

Elliot L. Hoffman

—

BPI

Backstage Pass Incorporated
New Jersey
MCMLXXXIX

BACK

A
Non-Performer's
Guide to

STAGE PASS

Rock 'n' Roll Touring Careers

Ref
ML.
3795
T57
1989
cp 1

This is Volume I of a series of four volumes. Watch for Volume II, a Non-Performer's Guide to the Record Business, from the Studio to the Store; Volume III, a Non-Performer's Guide to Motion Picture Careers; and Volume IV, A Non-Performer's Guide to Television Careers.

The opinions expressed by the interviewees in this book are their own and do not necessarily reflect the views of the editors, the publisher or the authors.

The vintage backstage passes reproduced on the cover of this volume are from the historical collection of Dave Otto/Otto Entertainment Graphics and are used by permission.

Library of Congress Cataloging-in-Publication Data

Todd, Eric M., 1958-
  Backstage pass.

  Contents: v. 1. A non-performer's guide to rock 'n' roll touring careers.
  1. Rock music — Vocational guidance. I. Weimann, Frank, 1954-   . II. Hoffman, Elliot L., 1930-   . III. Title.
ML3795.T57   1989   781.66'023   89-6692
ISBN 0-9622231-0-7 (v. 1)

Manufactured in the United States of America.
First Edition.

Dedication

❦ To all the talented, hard working and ambitious people who have made the Rock 'n' Roll touring business into an exciting, profitable and booming industry;

❦ To their teachers, lovers, wives, and friends who allowed them and often encouraged them to find useful careers backstage;

❦ To the people we interviewed and the ones we couldn't get to this time;

❦ Most of all, to youth, to the readers who are now dreaming, as we did not so long ago.

We hope that the examples and the advice they find in this book will make those dreams come true.

BACKSTAGE PASS

Putting a Rock 'n' Roll tour out on the road and keeping it there requires a well trained army. As in a real army, some of the soldiers work on the front line and others do their jobs back at the base. Until the tour is over and everybody is "at ease" there must be lines of communication, supply lines, transports, engineers, specialists, patrols and reconnaissance.

Every army has its heroes, both sung and unsung. Some are out front and some are behind the lines, but every one of them has his or her job, place and expertise. Every job is important and everyone in the organization makes a difference between a successful tour and a failure. Nobody is unimportant and no one is unnecessary.

While the experienced producer of a concert tour has choices as to the people he will select for his "army," he learns after a while that some are better than others. That means that there is always room in the field for good people, people who will work hard, loyally and efficiently, realizing that they can be as important to the "star performer" on his tour as the drummer or sound technician.

The work isn't always glamorous or exciting. Many of the people in this book will confirm that fact. Sometimes it is just lonely and difficult to do what has to be done to make a tour work right all the way through to the final performance. But the people who have made their careers "backstage" are, for the most part, happy that they made the choice and proud of their abilities and achievements. We have assembled profiles of many of those people, each of them among the top of a particular field of work. For most of them, the rewards are both financial and emotional. They love their work and the people they work with and are proud to be part of an artistic and creative world. But each of them started out as ordinary people, wondering what to do with their lives and how they could make themselves useful and happy in the course of earning their livelihood. The story of what it took for each of them to do what it is that he or she does, how they got to where they are and what they do now that they've gotten there is inspiring. It is also instructive. Their stories and advice may change the ambitions and the lives of those of you who are now able to see inside their careers. We are proud to present their stories and to offer their guidance to ambitious young people everywhere who are thinking of a meaningful career in the entertainment world. We look forward to seeing many of you taking over these roles in the future and making good use of your "BACKSTAGE PASS." Good luck. See you soon.

The Authors

Table of Contents

66I *sat down once to figure it out. We play about 80 to 120 cities on a world tour — maybe two-thirds of the year I'll be out on the road. After a while, the bus is the only place I can call home — and if it's big, beautiful, comfortable and has everything I can think of, the tour doesn't seem so long.* **99**

Ian Hill
JUDAS PRIEST

Tour Bus Contracting
Jay Adams

Picture yourself walking into a room decorated with classic brass decor, lots of leather, and perhaps some exotic lizard skins on one of the walls. As you walk along a little further you notice beautifully displayed artwork with color coordinated chairs and couches and a magnificent state of the art stereo system. Is this the living room of someone who belongs on the Lifestyles of The Rich and Famous? Well, not quite. We are inside an ordinary touring coach that Jay (Jay Boy) Adams has recently transformed into a customized work of art.

Although Jay Boy has been around the Rock 'n' Roll industry for a long time, he pretty well backed into the business of entertainment transportation and the customizing of touring coaches. "Since the time that I got my first guitar at age 15, I had wanted to be a professional musician. There was a group of older guys in town, who formed a band and asked me to join. That was the first job I ever had. At the time, those guys were playing fraternities, a few club shows and that sort of thing. I played in that group for three years until I went to college at North State Texas University when I was 18. While attending college I continued to play and really started to go for it on a professional level after signing with a manager in Houston. A few years later, I got a record deal with Atlantic and recorded two albums. I toured for a period of about 10 years. During that time I purchased a coach for my band to use while travelling. When the time came to go into the studio to rehearse for the third album, I had an opportunity to lease the coach to another of my manager's acts. Before long, I was ready to go back out on the road again, but the coach was still leased to the other band. So, I just bought another one. This happened to me on three different occasions. I would come off the road, and while I was taking a break I would lease out my coach. I wound up with four busses. I didn't plan it that way at all. I was too busy running a band, trying to write music and perform.

"As a professional touring musician, I wasn't putting the meat on the table. It was definitely the rentals from those coaches that were doing it. One day as we were preparing my tax return, my accountant suggested that I should look at this from the standpoint of a full time enterprise. He pointed out that I was making a lot more money on the coaches than I was performing. So I took a real hard look at it and decided that I should give leasing coaches 100% of my time. That was 10 years and hundreds of tours ago.

"We've worked with a lot of great acts including Dire Straits, ZZ Topp, Ratt, Night Ranger, Krokus and the Monkees. In fact, the most challenging project that I ever had was the Monkees. They were three individuals getting together after a very lengthy break. They just didn't know each other anymore. They were friends in a close knit operation in the 60's, but had grown 20 years apart. Everyone wanted a different piece of equipment, and they all wanted the best. It was both a large tour and a long tour. There were also a lot of different individuals involved in putting the tour together. Ultimately, they ended up with six coaches on the road. I had to watch it very closely because they wanted things done right, and were very demanding about their needs.

"Generally, the way we do business is that a band will come to us with requests for certain size coaches. People want either a six, a nine or a twelve sleeper. Let's say a band with four or five members and a tour manager would probably want a six sleeper. If the guys are strictly business and don't take any guests on the road, they might order a large rear lounge and only six bunks. Our floor plans are set up to handle three, six, nine or twelve bunks and these floor plans can be changed in a matter of half a day because our bunks are all convertible. They're built in modules and they are nut and bolted together rather than screwed and glued to the wall.

"If a tour manager calls me up with a special request, I can give him pretty much whatever he wants. From day one our coaches are planned as twelve sleepers. If you want a nine sleeper, we merely take three bunks out and replace them with either a large closet or a couple of comfortable chairs. Should you call with a request for a six sleeper, we simply take two stacks of bunks out and bring in a couch or two chairs, maybe even a desk for the tour manager or an additional closet. There are so many combinations that you can do and we do them all in a day at the very max."

Jay Boy's hiring standards are tough: "I look for someone who is willing to follow me around like a puppy for however long it takes to see how I want things done. This person must realize that 'it can't be done' does not exist in our vocabulary, because it must be done. I want someone with good sales attributes and who is willing to work very hard. This is a 24-hour a day job. I suppose that really applies to just about any part of the music industry. You must live, eat, sleep and dream this business. I'm always looking for a person who is very well rounded and who can be trained for this business. I would rather have someone come to me cold, without any experience, than to have someone come to me who has the type of experience that I don't want. Also, I've found that experienced people are going to do things the way they've always done them, and not the way that I want them done.

"Now, the shop is a totally different story. In a shop employee, I'm looking for someone with perhaps a little architectural experience, maybe a few courses in that in college, and good practical field knowledge from the standpoint of cabinetry. I want people who are excellent craftsmen. They have got to be able to work with plastic and formica. It's necessary to be a good cabinet maker. If you are not a good cabinet maker, you can't build a quality coach.

"Transportation is one of the most important parts of the touring industry. You can bet that every famous rock star has spent endless hours in a bus. A bright future lies ahead for the skilled technician. This is a good opportunity to help your favorite band travel in style."

3

> **❝ G**et me there on time/
> **Get me there in one piece/Know where you're
> going/Know how long it'll take/Keep the bus clean/
> Keep the bus working/Keep track of your road
> float/Look out for the posse while I fly the band/
> Keep your mouth shut/Listen to me/Laugh a little/
> Chill out/Stay straight/Be Cool/Get with the pro-
> gram. Or you're over. ❞**
>
> **Sean Carasov, Road Manager
> BEASTIE BOYS**

Tour Bus Driving

Rick Barretto

Getting the performers and technicians from city to city in a major tour is a major operation. Most tours depend upon comfortable, well-designed busses to take them around the country, often to as many as 80 different cities on a single tour. The man in charge of each bus has a heavy responsibility and his job requires special knowledge and experience. Rick Barretto is one of the best drivers in the world of Rock 'n' Roll.

I suppose you could call Rick Barretto the Ralph Kramden of the entertainment business. Born in Uruguay, South America, Rick's been a bus driver in the world of entertainment for 19 years.

Rick worked several years for a transportation company in New Jersey called Domenico Bus Service. This introduction to the entertainment business occurred when Domenico began providing service for many Broadway shows. One day, a principal in the business started a Rock 'n' Roll company called Quonexions and asked Rick if he would be interested in joining him. The possibility of working with a variety of bands intrigued him and Rick said yes.

"The first Rock 'n' Roll transportation band that I worked with was The Outlaws in 1976. Since then I've worked with REO Speedwagon, Kenny Loggins, Earth, Wind and Fire, the Bee Gees, Whitney Houston and Mick Jagger." When there aren't any rock tours out on the road, Rick sometimes handles professional wrestling venues.

"For the most part these guys are a lot of fun. Similar to a concert tour, the wrestlers travel from city to city, the good guys with the bad guys."

Getting people to a certain place by a certain time is the number one priority of a professional driver. "My responsibilities are to have the bus serviced and cleaned before every trip, pick up the band at the designated time and place, and give them a safe and comfortable ride. This may sound silly, but you've got to know where you're going. I cannot risk blowing a gig by getting lost and not delivering the band to the venue on time."

To help Rick provide a comfortable ride, there is a touring bus that will knock your socks off! Instead of rows of seats on each side of the aisle — behind this driver's seat you'll find a lounge with a television set and a VCR. Next to that, the state-of-the-art stereo system. As you walk further inside, (on the wall to wall carpeting) you'll notice a couch, dinette set, chairs, refrigerator, microwave, trash compactor, wet bar, bathroom, and central air conditioning. All the way in the back are bunks, 9 or 12 of them, and a well equipped rear lounge.

Rick suggests that before you try to get involved as a driver for a Rock 'n' Roll bus company, get all the bus driving experience you can. "You have local groups like the YMCA, CYO and others that provide transportation for their members that go on trips together. In the summertime there are countless summer camps, Boy Scout outings and other organizations that may provide you with the opportunity to get that necessary experience. Incidentally, most touring companies that handle entertainers require that the driver be at least 21 years of of age and have a clean driver's license.

"The only advice that I can give someone about becoming involved in this business is that you have to realize that you're out there to do a job, not to party with the passengers. While the guys are having a few beers, staying up late, entertaining some pretty girls, whatever — I regret to say that the driver cannot participate. Your

5

responsibilities won't allow that. This isn't like most other jobs that if you oversleep and get to work a half hour late, everybody just laughs it off — if you do that in this business you're going to have to look for another job."

Scenic & Lighting Design

Leroy Bennett

It takes technical skills and experience to design the lights for a show and make them work the way they should. Leroy Bennett's skills are one important reason why Prince's concerts are so exciting. He learned his trade from the bottom up.

You know how difficult it is to get tickets for a Prince concert, right? Even after waiting in line for a couple of days you're still not sure if you can get a decent seat. Leroy (Roy) Bennett remembers the first tour that he did with Prince, which was cut short because of poor ticket sales. "It's hard to believe, but it's true. It was a very brief tour due to the lack of attendance." A positive outcome of that tour for Roy was that he and Prince had developed a tremendous rapport. In fact, Roy ended up being hired as a regular employee. But getting to the right place at the right time wasn't quite as easy for Roy as it sounds.

When Roy was in ninth grade he worked with the high school band loading the gear and acting as the lighting director. "Even as a kid, whenever I heard music I always saw pictures or some kind of

7

images. Immediately after high school, I worked with a band in Washington D.C. for about a year and a half, setting up band gear, but primarily concentrating on the lighting for their shows. After a couple of years I left the band and went back home to Rhode Island to work for a lighting company as a technician. It provided my first tour, my first road experience. The band was Boston. The year was 1978.

"When I started working at the lighting company, I was the lowest man on the totem pole. I did all the dog work as a technician. Most of my work consisted of coiling all the heavy cables and doing all the patching. But, I was learning and gaining valuable experience. When an opportunity to do tech work at a higher level with the Zenith Lighting Company arose, I was prepared. Although I was hired as the second man on the crew, I quickly moved up to crew chief. A big break occurred when Zenith got an account that already had the lighting designed, but found themselves without a lighting director. My boss asked me if I would like to be the lighting director for a young artist who called himself Prince. Naturally, I said, 'Yes.' As Prince's popularity skyrocketed, my status in the business grew as well. It was solely through my experience with Prince, that I've been approached more and more often by a number of bands. I've gotten the opportunity to work with Duran Duran, Queen, Bon Jovi and Black Sabbath among many others.

"My job requires me to meet with the artist to figure out the concept of the show. Usually, I start off by designing the set which, depending on the size of the show, could take anywhere from two days to three or four months. It depends upon the complexity of the show. The next step is the lighting, which I also design. It's at this point that we put the lighting out for bids to different companies for fielding and leasing the lights for the show. Next, we go into the rehearsals. I usually bring an assistant because (in most cases) I don't go out and run the show myself. The assistant director and I go through all the visuals for each song to make sure everything is satisfactory to the artist. I sometimes go out on the road with the tour for a week or two to make sure everything is running smoothly. The normal work day on tour for me is about twelve hours.

"When a considerable length of time elapses and I haven't been out on the road, I miss it because I really get a rush out of doing live performances and feeling the vibes of the crowd. It really is an incredible high when you get an immediate response to your art. This isn't to say that there aren't anxious moments.

8

"There were some real close calls with Prince. On the Sign Of The Times tour, we had a faulty wire motor, which actually allowed a neon sign to self-destruct during one part of the show. There's a safety switch attached to the motors that lowers and raises a neon sign during the show. The safety switch malfunctioned and didn't stop the two motors when they had gone far enough, so the motor continued pulling the cable up. As a result the steel cable snapped and completely shattered the plexiglas that encased the neon sign. The next thing I knew, the plexiglas went flying everywhere and a good hunk of the sign came crashing down onto the stage. It just missed the head of the keyboard player (Bonnie Boyer). Fortunately, the rest of the sign was still held up by its electrical wire even though both steel cables had snapped completely.

"Our crew being the outstanding professionals they are, took care of it very efficiently. Although it seemed like hours, it was actually only a minute or two before everything was under control. The crew was all over the trussing and lights, and the show went on as though nothing had happened.

"If you want to be a lighting technician the best thing to do is to get some hands-on work. Some knowledge of electrical work is helpful. There are some terrific high school and trade school courses that you can take that would benefit you immensely. Another idea is to seek employment in a lighting company's shop. You'll learn how to actually package tours. That is, you'll become competent to set up the lights and put all the proper bulbs in the lamps for the lighting design itself. That's a great way to start off, because you are not put in a hot seat while you're still learning about lighting. You'll learn the equipment's limitations as well as its capabilities. In addition, you will learn not only how something works, but how to fix things that don't work. Once you've gained that shop experience, you very well may be ready to go on the road.

"The great thing about this business is that even if somebody doesn't have a particular skill, but is eager to learn, they will often be given a chance. A great attitude and a good sense of humor are two important attributes to have if you want to succeed on the road. Most of the people who go far in the business have a terrific attitude and outlook on life."

9

> **❝ If you've got the talent to be a headliner, someone who knows how and what to tell the media about you can move your career months, maybe years ahead. ❞**
>
> **Oscar Cohen, President**
> **ASSOCIATED BOOKING CORP.**

Publicity

Howard Bloom

What can a good writer do in Rock 'n' Roll? The answer is Public Relations. Howard Bloom wrote the book **Ten Ways To Organize a Boy Scout Troop** *and portions of* **The Boy Scout Field Manual on Stalking and Tracking.** *These days you can sometimes catch him "spreading the news" about some of Rock's biggest stars.*

Howard Bloom describes public relations as the art of getting media exposure. Bloom, founder and President of The Howard Bloom Organization is truly a PR star himself. He has worked with such giants as Prince, Bette Midler, Hall & Oates, John Cougar Mellencamp, Billy Idol, George Michael, Kool & the Gang, Run DMC, Lionel Richie, Billy Joel, Paul Simon, Peter Gabriel, and Diana Ross. He has also handled special projects like Simon & Garfunkel's Reunion Concert, Farm Aid and films like Purple Rain and Stop Making Sense.

"Our job is to get our clients newspaper, magazine, television and certain limited forms of radio exposure. Rather than buying 30 seconds of ad time on Entertainment Tonight, we call their programming people to convince them that we have a story that is going to be interesting to their viewers. If we are successful in having them cover the story, we may get 30 seconds or even a minute on the show. Therefore, instead of paying a $100,000 fee or whatever it costs to advertise we get the same exposure without the price tag. To be a good publicist you must see things through a journalist's eyes. In order to get Entertainment Tonight to cover your story, you must think the way a journalist thinks. Look for the kind of hook that they look for in a story. In effect, you're a surrogate journalist."

Howard didn't start out to be a Public Relations giant. After graduating from high school he went to college in Oregon, but soon dropped out to pursue the "spiritual realities" of life. After three years of adventure he decided to finish college at NYU. "In the summertime, prior to my sophomore year, I made a list of 100 employment agencies that had something to do with writing. My writing skills were quite strong, thanks in part to a high school teacher who swamped us with writing projects. Well, the first 98 agencies turned me down. Number 99 was the Boy Scouts of America. Ironically, I had been thrown out of the Scouts as a kid for failing morse code. Nevertheless, I wound up writing several publications for them before going back to college.

"At the request of a professor at NYU, I became the editor of a literary magazine. Although I wasn't enamored with literary writing, it provided me with a crash course in publishing. Upon graduation I knew I wanted to be involved in some aspect of the media. I visited one of the artists who had helped me with the magazine and we decided that since both of us were broke, I would go around with his portfolio and try to sell his work before I went to Columbia graduate school. A short time later I notified Columbia that I would not be attending that fall after all. The first year we made about $50 a week. The second year, however, we had become the leading avant garde commercial art studio in the country. Among other projects, we were the art directors for National Lampoon, doing graphics for ABC's seven FM stations, a film for NBC, book covers for publishers and lots of work for magazines.

"We were in business for several years before I began to feel exhausted by the long days. So I said 'goodbye' to all the artists and went off to write for Circus, one of the top Rock 'n' Roll magazines in the world. At first, I didn't know anything about Rock 'n' Roll. I had grown up listening to Bach and Beethoven. In fact, I hadn't even heard rock music until I was 19 years old. I wasn't familiar with the background of the artists. I didn't even know their names or anything. It was an understatement to say that I had a lot to learn. At Circus I worked 7 days a week and 12 hours a day because I had two jobs to do. The first one was to edit the magazine and the second job was to learn what Rock 'n' Roll was all about.

"The publisher came to me at the end of the year and told me that sales were no higher after my first year, but that they were no lower either. For the next 12 months the magazine increased dramatically in circulation in every single issue. Over the course of the next year the magazine increased 211% in circulation and money began to pour into the magazine. Seymour Stein (President of Sire Records) heard about this kid who was locked in a windowless closet over at Circus, who seemed to be some sort of money machine. He asked if I would go over to Gulf & Western. G&W was a distributor for 14 record companies in those days. He offered me exactly the amount of money that I had wanted to get from my publisher, so I accepted. With that, I moved over to Gulf & Western to start a public relations department with no more experience at it than I had with editing a magazine, running an art studio or organizing Boy Scout troops. With help from a hardworking staff the department turned out to be very successful.

"We were getting lots of publicity for artists who hadn't been getting recognition before. Both the company and the artists were doing very well as a result of our efforts. A year later, ABC came along and bought all of Gulf & Western's holdings. They fired everybody in the company except me. When they told me that I couldn't keep my staff, I resigned. In no time, a Vice President flew in and put a blank piece of paper on my desk. He said, 'okay, fill out the names of the staff members whom you want to keep, the salaries you want for them and the salary you want for yourself.' With that, I gave myself and the staff members all modest raises and we became the Public and Artist Relations Department for ABC records.

"One day Seymour Stein walked into my office and said, "Shmuck, if you're so smart, why don't you have your own company? That was a tricky question because I'm not very athletic, I'm not very good looking, I'm not very coordinated and I really have very few claims to any kind of value in life. The one thing that I like to think about myself is that I'm smart and he had just told me that I was a dumbbell. Based on the fact that I didn't have my own company and driven by Seymour's golden words, I started the Howard Bloom Organization."

When Howard hires people these days he looks for someone who is articulate. "To be a publicist you have to be able to speak well, to tell a good story and to speak factually. It's important to be able to write. Also, I need a person who would rather be on the telephone morning, noon or night, than breathe, eat or sleep.

"It's not what courses you are taking in school that counts as much as the job experience you've been able to get. How do you get your foot in the door to get job experience? First of all, you have to be humble. If you have to be an intern for free, then be an intern for free. If you have to be a secretary or receptionist, then be a secretary or receptionist. Don't hold out for the job that's going to put you on a higher level immediately, because you are not going to get it. Let's face it, everyone's looking for people with experience. If you have to put in six months as an unpaid intern, or six months as a receptionist, you will begin to acquire the necessary skills and you will begin to get valuable experience.

"I, too, want experience. Finishing school is important, but a degree in public relations could very well be a drawback. It's my belief that you're taught academic things in school that often bear no relationship to publicity in the real world. The things you learn after the classroom have more relevance to public relations than do your academic pursuits. We have our own training program. Our people start out as receptionists, with the goal of moving them from receptionist to publicity trainee, from publicity trainee to associate publicist, etc. You have to be willing to work hard for a while as a receptionist and at a very low salary. It seems to be menial work, but we promote from within. In this way, we're able to give our employees excellent on-the-job training necessary to succeed in the public relations field."

> **66** **The** size and scale of everything about a major Rock 'n' Roll show these days rivals any spectacle there ever was. Our audiences are entitled to a production they've never seen or heard before. It's natural for every tour to try to surpass the one before. **99**
>
> John Wetton
> *ASIA, KING CRIMSON*

Staging

Mike Brown

For over 25 years, Mike Brown of Grandstands, Inc. has designed and installed portable staging and grandstands for a wide range of events all over the country, providing seating for as many as 100,000 spectators. His client list sounds like a Who's Who of Rock 'n' Roll: Jethro Tull, Bruce Springsteen, the Rolling Stones, Fleetwood Mac, Aerosmith, Boston, Cheap Trick, Bob Dylan, Elton John, Foreigner, Journey, the Police, and Queen.

"Usually a promoter or production company will contact us to see if we can accomplish a particular effect in their staging. Some groups want to hide the sound wings of their staging while others like the bare look and dress up the stage only with lighting. For instance, Bruce Springsteen's Tunnel of Love tour was a totally dark look, with lighting used on the front of the stage on either side (where normally speakers would be) to accent the stage. Our expertise includes structural platforming and support systems. The David Bowie people wanted a gold scaffold, which they lit very artistically for a very nice

14

looking final effect. All the scaffolding was painted gold. The last time The Rolling Stones toured they had a brilliantly colored scrim (cloth fabric) to mask the scaffolding behind it. The Eagles' Hotel California tour had their album design on their scrims, which provided good masking for the scaffolding.

"To design the staging we first must get the size requirements. Once we determine that it's possible to meet the band's needs, we send out the plans so that the production people can see if there's anything else they may want. Then we figure out the local labor costs, where the set is going, how often it's going to be used, how much supervision for on-site work is required, and the personnel we'll have to supply at our end. Sometimes as many as 4 separate units are needed to leapfrog ahead on a tour that is packed tight with dates one after the other. With more than one unit, we can be taking down one stage in one city while we're setting up another one someplace else further ahead on the tour.

"The artist's production people are usually very creative, but we have unique liability for our staging that has to do with the integrity of the structure that supports the sound and lighting equipment overhead. Roof truss grids are usually suspended by steel cable, mounted to motors over the group and often portions of audience. There has been some tremendous weight escalations in that area. We used to provide a structure that would safely hang 6,000 pounds. Some knowledgeable production people say that any more than that is ludicrous and shouldn't be allowed. However, I know of at least three acts that have gone as high as 30,000 pounds of weight and one that even topped 40,000 pounds, hanging over the audience. This is why we send a qualified roof technician to look after the interest of every client. In fact, we have had as many as 12 experts helping with a single project.

"Our permanent staff is over 50. We have peak periods in the summer and slows in the winter. We have people working all year round with all the indoor and outdoor acts. However, most arenas have their own in-house staging. It is a judgment call on the group's production to say whether or not they want to utilize their own staging. Many times the band pays for the staging whether they use it or not. Elaborate staging is a luxury with a real cost factor. That's why some bands have gotten it down to having one stage which can follow the band out of the venue and beat the lighting people to the next show.

"The US Festival (1983) was the biggest stage ever designed and built. In fact, I believe it's listed in the Guinness Book of World records. The average stage is about 80 feet wide. Next to the supports on each side of the stage there are usually sound wings, 40-50 feet wide. In the case of the US Festival, however, there was an area, a huge rainbow design, which was about 400 feet! For the Rolling Stones tour in '81, we also did a huge installation, a Diamond Vision screen 30 x 20 feet high and 80 feet off the ground."

Mike describes the stage as "the entertainer's home away from home." It's his theory that if he doesn't feel comfortable, his act may not come across as good as he had hoped. The reason for the artist requesting specific amenities for his stage is that he needs to feel a sense of intimacy with the audience through that staging, and some continuity of his surroundings whenever he has to perform. "The people who hire us are able to afford these luxuries and have earned this right. After all, there aren't many people who can draw crowds of up to 60,000 for one show."

Here's what Mike says about getting into the field today: "I think that the staging end of the entertainment industry is a terrific entry level job. The actual construction of the staging is a manual labor job which is a transitional step to something better in the business. There are also clerical, design and drafting jobs in staging. Construction jobs require you to have some basic knowledge of the tools and other equipment used in the erection and dismantling of the stage. You'll also have to be quick and efficient. The staging crew get to the job first and they are the last to leave the venue. It also takes muscle and perseverance. We are very proud of the fact that many of the people who have worked for us as truck drivers or crew chiefs have gone on to other jobs, some of them even being successful production managers. The normal transition is to come out of staging, learn a lot and go into a service field as riggers, stage managers, or road managers.

"The good people pass through this aspect of the business and go on to even greater responsibilities."

Pyrotechnics

Pete Cappadocia

A pyrotechnician is like a private explosives expert. He makes the bombs, smoke and flames that some shows use, but he keeps it all under control. It took years for "Pyro Pete" to learn how to do this and to perform his special effects for Judas Priest, Kiss, Metallica and many others.

"Pyro Pete" Cappadocia is an extraordinary pyrotechnician. Pyrotechnics are the fire or flame devices, crash sounds, air bursts, and anything (legal) that bangs, cracks, fizzes or smokes during the staging of a concert. In very simple terms, "Pyro Pete" designs and operates safe special effects for Rock 'n' Roll shows. "A band will come to me and say this is going to be our stage set and what can you do to enhance it."

"Pyro Pete" is responsible for the legendary display of pyrotechnics that Kiss used during their spectacular stage shows. For those of you who had the opportunity to see Kiss in concert, Pete's work should be an exciting memory. As Eric Carr started going

17

into a drum solo the lights would dim. The drum riser, in the shape of an army tank with a big gun, would move towards the front of the stage and begin a series of turns panning the audience with the gun. Smoke would billow out of the tank's exhaust stacks. "Special speaker cabinets were hung along the regular PA's so you couldn't tell which were real and which ones were fake. The design of the phoney cabinets was precisely the same as the regular PA cabinets except that instead of having speakers in them, they had air bursts extended from the bottom." An air burst is a charge that goes off in mid-air and produces a sparkly, glittery fallout for about 15 to 20 feet.

In addition to the air bursts, smoke charges were attached to the inside of the cabinets and the grill cloths were wired on with big hinges and springs. All of this was hung up with retaining cables so that "the whole thing could just fall apart and hang there." Although they looked as if they would fall into the audience at any moment, they were firmly secured by the heavy cables.

As Eric continued playing his drum solo on top of the tank, the turret's movements from side to side would increase in speed. After a dramatic build-up, the tank would move over and point towards the speakers and Eric would stand up on the drum turret and point his finger towards individual speakers. The special effects cabinets would then explode, as though Eric had commanded them to do so. "Pyro Pete" used a dozen flash charges in the gun barrel to give the effect even greater realism.

"I make everything modular so all the components actually plug in and fit properly in the other pieces. This goes back to something I learned in set design while at Hofstra. We were taught how to make things that fell apart in such a way that they could be easily put together again. It would take about 45 minutes to put in the pyrotechnics and to fly the cabinets using the modular pieces for each of the Kiss shows. This would be virtually impossible to do if the 'breakaway' parts weren't reusable."

Pete's typical day starts with the laying out of all the pyrotechnic material. The first job is to hook up everything that "flies" (is suspended overhead) to the lighting trusses. It's necessary to raise everything off the floor so that the crew can start setting up the stage. Before the cabinets are fully raised overhead, the air bursts are attached. After all the cabinets are hoisted in place, and the gun loaded with flash charges, it's on to the ground effects.

Cylinder devices (flash pots) are placed on stage. On command flash pots will emit multi-color powder flashes at designated times during the show. Large steel tubing loaded with fast burning powder (concussion mortars) are the last effect to be prepared before showtime.

Some of the bands that "Pyro Pete" has worked with most recently are Judas Priest, Metallica, Def Leppard and AC/DC. With only a limited amount of experienced and talented pyrotechnicians on the scene, Pete's in great demand. For example, he missed out on an Iron Maiden Tour. "I've worked with Iron Maiden for years, but because of a conflict in my schedule with AC/DC, I was unable to do the Maiden thing. Right now, the guy who's on that tour got the gig because I couldn't do it. I phoned him up and asked him if he wanted me to give the Maiden people his number. So, he's doing the Iron Maiden tour, which has been a regular client of mine for the last couple of years. Sometimes you must look at these things from a business point of view. Iron Maiden is only good for a total of four or five months, therefore it was a choice between eleven months work with Judas Priest or only four or five months of income.

"A lot of tours are looking for technicians. If you're going to be doing special effects, you really need to have some sort of background in pyrotechnics, at least on the college level. If you participate in a good theater department in high school, you will be semiprepared for the business, but you really need more experience than that to go on the road. Because of the tremendous cost involved with touring, the only people who go out on the road are the most qualified and trusted pyrotechnians." Pete suggests you start at the bottom. "Generally, the promoter provides people to unload trucks and move equipment. In fact, it's probably a good idea to try to be a part of the local stage crew. It will provide you access to people in the business who may be able to help you.

"The best suggestion that I could give anyone is to get into a school that has an active theater department. This will provide both classwork principles and hands on experience. It will help you obtain a working knowledge of basic production terminology, such as: upstage, downstage, stage left, stage right, house left, house right, etc. There aren't any college courses that specifically teach special effects, but classes like set design will be an integral part of the whole picture. Special effects are something that you actually have to work with and learn from others. Eventually, by using a lot of imagination you can devise your own techniques.

"When I was in college I took courses in construction and stage props. The same goes for the lighting courses that were available. Actually, it wasn't until I went to college that I got really involved with special effects, per se, but I had always been active in theatre productions. Thanks to a friend at Hofstra, I got a summer job that's never ended. During my third semester, I was asked to help out on a Plasmatics show—just moving equipment and assisting the band's pyrotech. Well, one thing led to another and I ended up going on the road with the Plasmatics for 3 years. For the first couple of years I was an assistant, but was asked to take over the special effects duty when the other guy left the tour. When the Plasmatics broke up, I went out successively with Def Leppard, AC/DC, Kiss, Judas Priest and so forth. It's been like a 6 year spring break.

"All of my friends think this job is like a dream come true. It probably is, to a certain extent. I get to travel all of the time and to do what I want. I'm even looked after while I'm on the road. My hotel bill is taken care of. I'm paid a per diem and I get a nice salary besides. As long as I do my job well, I'm going to be able to continue this life style. It's a lot better than having to go to a 9 to 5 job every day. For me, this job provides a lot of freedom. I'm responsible for getting the show off and for making sure that it's done safely. As long as I do that then anything else I do, say or even what I look like is not going to be important.

"Having been out on the road for so long, I've made friends with a lot of band members. I enjoy hanging out with them because they're really nice guys. I've even gone on vacation with some of them and I've even been invited to stay over at their houses. I suppose that my friends back home would consider that the most fantastic part of my job. But it takes a lot of preparation and hard work to get there."

> **❝ An artist's dream is to be in that place and time in your career when you are surrounded by trusted friends who also happen to be wise and loving advisors. ❞**
>
> **Roberta Flack**

Tour Management
Amy Polan Clarke

Amy Polan Clarke has managed every tour for the Grateful Dead, from start to finish, since 1976. "I book the venues, make all the deals, contend with every settlement, go on the road with the band and take care of all the financial matters for them. That's a pretty full time job."

Amy Polan Clarke is also the Vice President of Monarch Entertainment and oversees its video production department. Amy has produced several long form music videos, including Lou Reed performing live in concert and was involved in Rock Influences, a very successful series on MTV. "Rock Influences was a series of shows that focused on particular genres of music, say, for instance, Progressive Rock for which we shot a concert with Jethro Tull at the Capitol Theater. Sometimes we used live footage intercut with interviews and archival footage of people that influenced that particular rock group."

Although Amy has these two distinct jobs, she's probably done everything else that there is to do in the company. She still pitches in to settle or cover a show and has never slowed down, even though she is now the Vice President of Monarch. Amy's relationship with Monarch and its President, John Scher, goes way back. "I knew John in high school. I was working at a travel agency and he was in college when he produced his first local show. All of our friends worked the shows and it was very loose, just sort of a fun thing to do. I continued to work full-time at the agency and part-time at the shows. I did the guest lists, secretarial work, whatever needed to be done. He would dictate letters over the phone to me at the agency and I'd type them up on his stationery. In those days he would pay me in lunches."

Amy finally went to work for John full-time a couple of years later. "My duties remained the same, secretary, bookkeeper, agent, whatever had to be done, but we were really an organization by then. John had started booking the Capitol Theatre and that was where a majority of our shows were held." Amy vividly recalls a day when work was piling up and John came in and said, "Let's hire a bookkeeper." In quick succession, Amy found herself hiring a receptionist and a bookkeeper. As the staff continued to grow Amy made her way up the ranks.

"I have never done much of the booking. I've been more an administrator of the company, dealing with the bands, the settlements and what-not. With the Grateful Dead it's a unique and separate kind of situation, where I'll do just about everything. We don't 'manage' them, but we 'tour manage' them and co-promote all of their dates everywhere, except on the West coast (where they really don't need us). The entire process begins with picking the part of the country where we would like to start the tour and then how many days at that venue. I work with all of the local promoters where we're going to play. We try to figure out the expenses of each particular place and the profitability to the band. Once that's determined, I'll present the whole thing to the band and they will either accept what we've done or make some modifications. Once the dates are confirmed, we write to everybody (it seems to be a hundred letters) to explain that they are a unique band and require special care.

"Rather than promoting our own dates all over the country, we prefer to work with a local promoter in each area. After all, he has working relationships with people at the venue and can get the best advertising rates in that area. It's important to have a local middle man. The Grateful Dead is a band that is fortunate to have a lot of people who have followed them. The 'dead heads' will buy out every date on the tour, so you've got a kind of carnival atmosphere in the parking lot before each show. It's wonderful, but it presents a special situation that the promoter has to be ready for. Security can be a problem. There are often a lot of people milling around outside of the venue. We've had minor problems with this in some of the downtown locations where there's no place for the kids to hang out outside. Promoters will whenever they can, make a 'camping area' in the parking lot. We've had some very beautiful and warm scenes in some places where kids set up tents and sell things. These days it's rare to see a well behaved mass gathering of people wearing tie-dye, long hair and no shoes, except at our Grateful Dead shows."

Amy believes "It's more difficult to get into the business these days than when I started. We learned as we went along. The artists were also learning their way. The touring business was just beginning and wasn't fully recognized as a money making activity. Therefore, we had the luxury of being able to make mistakes without getting fired. I remember the days when settlements with a band meant giving them a box office statement and handing them a check based on the deal you had negotiated. Today, every expense needs to be documented and sometimes settlements turn into a war zone and can get very heavy."

Amy feels that she was at "the right place at the right time" and that it's generally more difficult to enter this part of the entertainment industry today. Amy recommends getting an education. Courses in Business Management would certainly be helpful and there are also courses that teach you about the music business. Perhaps the most beneficial aspect of going to school would be the opportunity of working on student activities committees where you might get something very similar to an apprenticeship for a promoter.

"It may be tough to break into the business, but for someone with persistence and determination, a position is always waiting. Anyone who is willing to start out as a clerk or secretary, work hard and learn from others has a chance to move up in the ranks. I've found this to be a very non-sexist business, with opportunities for qualified women in all areas of the industry. I know female lighting directors, booking agents, truck drivers, etc. There is nothing to prevent a woman from succeeding in this business.

"This is a very exciting business, There is none other that can be compared to it. Where else can you be in an important position of real responsibility and still wear jeans to work? No other industry can give you that indescribable sensation of standing on the side of a stage and hearing the roar of the crowd when your co-workers step on stage and do a show that you helped put together. You become part of one big family when you travel. On the road you work hard, deal with problems and adversities and succeed together. Best of all, you make friends and share experiences and a camaraderie that few people will ever know."

66 When I first saw a huge battery of those remote control lights, the first thought I had was that my band's performances are going to have to get even more phenomenal to keep up with the excitement those lights can create all by themselves. **99**

Ernest Chapman, Manager
BLACK SABBATH/JEFF BECK

Robotic Lighting

Zeb Cochran

Computerized robotic lighting is a specialized field that has developed dramatically over the last four or five years. This has come about with the invention of the VARI-LITE^tm and other automated lights that can be moved by remote control, fast and in any direction. They allow you to instantly change color, intensity, even the beam size.

Zeb Cochran spent weeks in preparation for going out on the road with Van Halen. "For literally 2 months I listened repeatedly to tapes of their old albums and live performances to get an idea of where the music needed to be highlighted." This homework was essential to Zeb, who's expertise is doing computerized robotic lights for concerts. "These new lights enable you to 'position' lighting where you're not necessarily using the movement to dazzle the senses, but rather using it to build full color washers that don't move on stage," says Zeb.

Zeb has worked with artists as diverse as Michael Jackson, Motley Crue and Amy Grant. "Amy Grant is probably the most wonderful person I've ever worked with. The same goes for her husband (Gary Chapman), who also plays in the band. From the management to the band roadies, they make up a simply amazing organization. Whenever you tour with Amy, everyone makes you feel like part of one big family. On days off we would go out to parks and have barbecues and play baseball. It was one of the most rewarding experiences that I've ever had, and it was great fun to be with them."

Zeb's biggest challenge up to this point was the Monsters of Rock tour. "This was a very exciting project because it allowed me to do something that was never done before. We took a sky tracker (a large rotating searchlight type of spotlight) and a computer controlled yoke, which gave me complete control of the unit. This enabled me to pan 360 degrees and I had 20 color changers, each with 16 different colors at my disposal. With this control I was able to point at anybody or everywhere. The truly amazing thing was that when doing outdoor stadium shows, not only was I doing lighting effects for the 100,000 kids sitting in the audience, but at the same time it could be seen in the sky, ten miles around the venue.

"The hours that you're required to put in are long and hard, however you're well compensated for your work. The longest I've been away was probably the Scandal/John Waite tour, when I had no days off at all. I finished a tour with Missing Persons in L.A., and flew that same night to New York to begin work with Scandal for three months. Because of my heavy touring schedule, I miss almost all of the important holidays. Holidays don't mean anything to you when you're on the road. Weekends have no value. The only thing that matters is numbers. It's the 12th, 13th, 14th. The day of the week is completely irrelevant. It doesn't make any difference to you whether it's Tuesday, Wednesday, or Saturday. It's inconsequential."

Zeb warns young people that "it's tough to break into the business. My youngest brother tried to get in for the longest time. His tenacity finally paid off when he got a gig as the fifth man on the lighting crew on Motley Crue's last tour. He started out making $500 a week.

"If you don't live in a major metropolitan area, it makes it even more difficult to get into this business. I'm living proof of that. It took me ten years to get where I am today. There is very little opportunity in areas that are without major arenas. If you're serious about becoming a part of this business, my advice to you is to get involved as a stage hand. Learn everything you possibly can in school by taking lighting classes or even theater management courses. College alone isn't going to be the ultimate answer because you need practical application. I know a lot of roadies who have degrees in microbiology or business administration. My suggestion is to take that information from the classroom and combine it with your experience as a stage hand. It will then begin to mean something.

"Once you have a little bit of experience, start knocking on doors. Make a weekly habit of calling on the people in the business who can help you, promoters, lighting companies, sound companies and anyone else connected to the music business. Never refuse an opportunity to work. Your persistence will eventually pay off. When that company needs someone they're sure to remember your name."

Concert Promotion

Ron Delsener

Ron Delsener did his first shows out of his parents' house. "I used to go to the circus and even as a teenager I would go to see shows on Broadway, then I'd come home and try to imitate the same performance in my basement. My sister and some other kids would be the stars of the show and I would be the producer." Since those days, he has produced and promoted virtually every major Rock 'n' Roll artist in the world.

Ron Delsener once worked for a marketing firm that promoted college concerts with Ford Motor Company sponsorship. All Ford wanted was to have one of its cars displayed on campus. This simple deal allowed the school to produce rock shows for very little money. "At that time, a friend of mine who worked at an advertising agency asked me to come up with a promotional idea for Rheingold Beer. A co-worker sitting next to me, Hillie Kristal (owner of CBGB's in New York City), suggested that I do something with Central Park. And that was it. I visited the Park's people and found out that I could rent the place from them. They considered me a concessioneer, just like the guys who sell hot dogs. They didn't consider it to be a cultural event, like the opera or philharmonic. Therefore, they made me pay a pretty stiff rental. But Rheingold put up the money and said that I should sell the tickets for only a dollar. Actually, their first thought was to make it free, but then they reconsidered, figuring that it might attract the wrong type of crowd." What a bargain! For one dollar New York audiences saw The Who, Jimi Hendrix, Otis Redding, The Stones, Cream, Elton John, Janis Joplin, the Doors, you-name-it. Delsener became a hero.

Delsener has since promoted hundreds of concerts, but the dollar ticket became history. He has also promoted dozens of benefits like No Nukes, with Bruce Springsteen, Jackson Browne, James Taylor and a lot of others. One of the highlights of Ron's career was when Simon & Garfunkel got together again after many years and gave a free concert in Central Park. Some of the money necessary to produce the show was provided by a record company, a jeans manufacturer, from the sale of tee shirts and the majority, from Paul Simon, himself. As a musical event, it was a tremendous success.

Thinking back to the early Rock 'n' Roll shows in Central Park, Ron remembers driving some of the residents of Fifth Avenue and Central Park West crazy: "We used to do two shows in one night. For instance, Led Zeppelin would go on at 7:30 and 10:30 PM. We would have to clear out the first crowd and then fill up again. Sometimes when it took a little longer to clear the first show, people in line for the second show would throw things and get surly, but we were pretty lucky that we never had a riot." The security force that kept these audiences under control consisted of only a dozen of Delsener's men plus about 15 to 20 city policemen. "About 8,000 people would be seated in the Wollman rink, but 20,000 people were sitting outside on the grass; they could have come over the wall at any time. It was always very tense, like living on the edge, at every concert."

There have been some odd pairings of performers, mismatches which proved to be disastrous to the headliner. Ron recalls a couple of such evenings: "One time Bruce Springsteen appeared when he was still a local band and opened for Anne Murray in Central Park simply because we thought he was great, but didn't have any other venue for him. It was okay with Anne's manager, but the only problem

29

was that Bruce was so fabulous that he demolished the crowd. Anne is a great star, but it was tough for her to follow, particularly since everyone walked out after Bruce's set. Another time: We had a a folk singer cancel as the opening act for the Rascals, so they gave me a $100 band called the 'Jimi Hendrix Experience.' All I knew was that they said he could play the guitar with his teeth. Hendrix came out and blew everyone away. The people in the audience who brought their children had their mouths hanging open because they couldn't believe what they saw Hendrix doing, I think he actually got his guitar pregnant that night."

In 1980, New York City decided that they didn't like what was going on at the concerts in the park, so Delsener had to look elsewhere. He found Pier 84 in Manhattan and has been presenting shows there ever since in conjunction with the Miller Genuine Draft Series. Although the shows are well-attended, Ronnie says they are still more or less a labor of love. "The venue is a little out of the way and although the music is great, the place doesn't really provide the greatest amenities for either the artists or the audience."

Ron uses many different venues. For example, a few years ago, the word was spreading that the Jones Beach Theater on Long Island was taking bids to rent out their space. "I went there with commitments from many top acts and was awarded a contract to promote shows. Right from the start the venue was a huge success. We opened with Eric Clapton for two nights. Jones Beach continues to work very well. Most acts like to play there in the summer because of its excellent facilities. Originally, there was a moat between the stage and the first row, but it prevented the artists from seeing the first 20 rows of the audience and they didn't like it. I invested 400K into building a deck out over the moat. It's been well worth the investment because Jones Beach has become one of my most popular venues with a seating capacity of 10,400 people."

In addition, these days Delsener books virtually all the shows that play at the Garden State Arts Center (an outdoor amphitheater) in Holmdel, New Jersey. Some of the acts who have performed there are Billy Idol, Julio Iglesias, Diana Ross, Stevie Nicks, The Beach Boys, The Moody Blues, Frank Sinatra, and Liza Minelli. He also books all the pop contemporary events at an 11,000 acre state park called Waterloo Village in North Jersey. Anyone who's attended a show at Madison Square Garden, Nassau Coliseum, the Palladium

Theater or the Beacon Theatre realizes that Ron has promoted some of the greatest spectacles in the history of live entertainment.

The role of the promoter can be described like this: The promoter puts up the money for the show. "We take a show, guarantee an act, say $100,000, for itself and we agree to pay all costs. That includes expenses like advertising, stage, sound, lights, insurance, ushers, security, cleanup, backstage catering, even dressing room furniture. We take the whole risk. If the show is successful, we make a profit. If nobody comes, we take the loss. Although their deals with most artists put a ceiling on the profit we are allowed to make (usually 10 or 15% of what the act earns), there is no limit on the amount we can lose."

Ron admits that it's very difficult to break into the business these days. However, if you've booked or promoted acts when you were on the college campus or had some background in an agency, there's a chance. Those activities help you to get to know some of the booking agents and managers. That can be a tremendous opportunity. Generally speaking, many of the acts playing college campuses are on the verge of breaking into the big time. If you've dealt with them on behalf of your school, this can give you a real advantage later. Ron adds candidly: "If you were not a college booker while attending school it's going to be really rough to break into this business. The only other way would be to come up with an unusual idea that nobody else has ever thought of, but that's not very likely."

Ron, however, says that there are other ways to get into other parts of the business. "Take a job performing even routine or clerical duties for an established agency. You will learn about the business from the inside and get a good idea of what an agent's life is all about. Keep in mind that many companies promote from within. Another avenue to explore is to try to get a job at a record company, doing anything and work your way up. This is a business where people can move around a lot, from one job or company to another. If you keep your head up you just might see an opening one day that is exactly what you're looking for."

Lighting

Carol Dodds

---

*Very often in a live concert there is little or no scenery.
Therefore the lighting is the sole element available to enhance the
artist. Reduced to its simplest terms the touring lighting designer is
the visual director of the live performance. This is especially true in
the larger venues. Bands rely on the lighting to provide an added
dimension of excitement or spectacle for their audience. This differs
greatly from theatrical lighting, where you don't want the audience
to be distracted from the actor's performance.*

Carol Dodds is, without question, among the most respected
lighting designers in the entertainment business. Her success began
with her first show, a huge rock extravaganza with over 40 bands that
included America, Joe Walsh, Bachman Turner Overdrive, The
Eagles, Marshall Tucker, REO Speedwagon, Ted Nugent, Lynyrd
Skynyrd, and Bob Seger. Since then she's worked with acts as
diverse as Weather Report, Kiss, Rush, T-Rex, Aerosmith, Blood,
Sweat, and Tears, Jeff Beck, Linda Ronstadt, The Bee Gees, Heart,

Bob Dylan, Joni Mitchell, Marvin Gaye, Tammy Wynette, Lynda Carter, Cameo, Queen, Miles Davis, the Go Gos, Todd Rundgren, Barry Manilow, the Talking Heads, Mister Mister, Hiroshima, Sheena Easton, Kenny Loggins, Dan Fogelberg, Roger Waters, Michael MacDonald, ToTo, and most recently she was the video director on Bruce Springsteen's Tunnel of Love Tour. That's quite a résumé!

The design process itself is multi-faceted. The first thing that must be done is to formulate the "concept" of the tour. These preliminary meetings are strictly informational. "We'll go over the concept or script in great detail. Of course, the budget must be taken into consideration. Next the idea must be submitted to the artist for approval. I'll work out some design concepts which we will bounce back and forth until we arrive at a satisfactory arrangement.

Then it's down to tons of paperwork and drafting to hone the ideas into a concrete plot for the equipment supplier. Once the mechanics have been worked out the implementation of the design begins. It's called preprogramming and takes place prior to rehearsal. Everything must be fine tuned by the final rehearsal. By the time the first audience arrives, the process has taken months of work.

Like many others in Rock 'n' Roll, Carol had always been interested in the entertainment business. "My mother was an actress and I remember watching her on early television. It was the directing aspect of acting that fascinated me, which is probably why I ended up in designing. I tend to look at the overall view rather than isolated portions of a performance."

While on a summer break from a Masters program in lighting and technical aspects of theater, Carol came to New York and got part time work at two different lighting companies. "From that point forward I've worked in the lighting field.

"It was very tough in the beginning because I was the low person on the totem pole. Each day was an early morning drive to the show to set up all the equipment and to make sure that it worked well during the show while the lighting designer was operating it. I suppose you could have considered my job at that time to be the second or third electrician, but it was more like a stagehand. Gradually, I was given more and more responsibility. It seemed that every day I was able to take one more step up the ladder working my way up from the bottom.

"On a typical show day we load in early in the morning. The time is set by the production manager. A number of teams are set up to do the show's lights, sound, set and bandgear. Each department is responsible to tune it's own system.

"My job is to perform the focus and systems checks. By the time the show is ready to start I've already prepared myself to coordinate the operation of my boards, handle rigging cues, direct the follow spots as well as any extra controls that are used in the show for additional lighting or effects. For concert productions this job is comparable to combining designer, stage manager, and head electrician in a theatrical application."

Although Carol has done literally thousands of shows, every project has its inherent challenges. "The technology in the field has taken the leaps that audio took years ago from very basic equipment to the very techno-intensive. You must continually update your information to keep on top of the latest innovations. Going through these changes as they happen is quite fascinating. At the present time I'm into computerized systems that we use in even the simplest of shows. Programming is used in control, movement, color, patterns or special effects."

However, opportunities have always seemed to be available in lighting. Carol admits it is getting much more competitive than it used to be. "Primarily, touring is now being treated for what it is—big business. It's a business for professionals. There are many established designers, however, much of the work goes only to the top designers in the field. The best attitude to take is that you have to 'pay your dues'. You need to know your craft, have some business acumen and gradually build up a résumé. Perhaps the best approach would be to start at the bottom of the lighting industry and supplement your work with lighting or computer courses." Carol thinks that for some people college is the answer. "While working towards your degree, actively participate in theatre or concerts at school. Once you establish a base, contact designers or even local promoters and apply for any job that's available. Getting a position as an assistant or apprentice would be ideal.

"It's certainly very difficult to keep friendships/relationships going when you travel a great deal. I've only been able to keep up acquaintances with people who are attuned to this craziness. Relationships are tough to maintain, but there are alternatives to the ordinary. This depends primarily on the personalities involved. It is impossible for a woman to have a family and do this type of work. On the positive side you're able to travel places and meet people that you've probably only dreamed about. Things must be kept in proper prospective as it's not as romantic and glamorous on the road as it sounds. You'll find that life revolves around work rather than family."

> **66** *In this business, one gets a true sense of the old saying, 'time is money.' If my trucks don't show up on time, it costs my artists thousands of dollars. Therefore, I'm willing to pay a little more for reliability and cooperation. I want truckers who are willing to help with the load, if that's what it takes to get the show up on time. The only prima donnas in my organization are the artists.* **99**

> **Bill Siddons, Manager**
> **CROSBY, STILLS & NASH**

Entertainment Trucking

Tom Duncan

Not only are you driving a $100,000 vehicle, but you are carrying another $100,000 to $500,000 worth of equipment and it has to get to the show on time. The entire show rests on your shoulders. Without that band equipment, there's no show. You have to do what is necessary day in and day out, with little more than a phone call a day from your boss as guidance. That's a driver's reponsibility in a nutshell.

Tom Duncan's company, Stagecall, provides transportation for entertainment companies. Tom: "To be specific, we do not involve ourselves in moving human bodies. We don't move the bands. We don't move roadies. We don't move people. We only move equipment. We've commited our efforts and resources to something we understand (and do well) instead of trying to do a little bit of everything.

"The primary quality that I look for when hiring new employees is someone who has an almost pathological sense of punctuality. You need to grasp that concept. Because punctuality is all that I'm providing. Being on time, that's it. The cost of creating a show from scratch is so high that any tardiness from the people who are responsible at the very beginning, which means the truck being there on time, begins to impact the client in a negative way. Obviously, it can't be tolerated. Above all else, I need people who will take it almost to the point of being a fetish.

"If a guy has been a superstar for 4 years and is ten minutes late, he's not going to be dismissed. Very often clients develop a relationship with my drivers. They know what I expect of my drivers. Sometimes they even intercede between me and my drivers when there's a problem. For example, we'll hear from the client: 'Listen, your guy was late, but I talked to him. You've got to give this guy another chance!' Or the client may tell us that they don't want anybody else, so don't even think about firing him. Obviously, the client's opinion is going to hold a lot of weight because they're paying the bill. However, the one thing about which the client's opinion is not taken into consideration, is when the problem is related to drug or alcohol abuse.

"A lot of infractions that can be dealt with on a strike 1, strike 2, strike 3 philosophy cannot be managed that way with drug or alcohol problems. It's simply one strike and you're out. One single incident can adversely affect my relationship with a client. I can't afford to allow that to happen.

"This is a self-starter type of job. You have to be an individual who can work with almost no supervision whatsoever. Also, you have to understand that you're taking on a tremendous responsibility.

"Generally, the drivers are not required to unload the trucks. Often they will volunteer, however, just to make sure that the truck is packed in the safest and most efficient manner. Drivers are expected to dress neatly. Don't presume that because you're in the Rock 'n' Roll business that you can show up in a torn t-shirt and levis with holes in them. First impressions are still important, and we expect to see our drivers dressed respectfully. We don't expect suits and ties, but certainly the way they dress conveys a sense of what they're about."

Stagecall stresses professionalism in every detail, from clean trucks to the latest equipment. The 45 and 48 foot tractor trailer units incorporate air-ride. "Air-ride suspension for all our trucks sets us apart from general trucking. The suspension of the truck is the most critical thing in the physical aspect of moving equipment properly. Only air-ride provides the kind of ride that's necessary for the equipment to arrive in the same condition as it left.

"The end result is, that we work with some of the biggest bands in the world. Some of the jobs are very challenging. A recent Pink Floyd tour probably was our most difficult project to date, because of the time constraint between the shows. During the first three weeks there was tremendous mileage between each venue. The drivers were under severe pressure to make deadlines. All of the logistics had to be done in practically micro milliseconds in order to make everything happen as planned. They did a great job under tremendous pressure. Some of our other major jobs were with Genesis, the 100th Anniversary of Coca Cola, and Michael Jackson. The Coca Cola project was the biggest project by far — thirty-four trucks in and out of Atlanta!

"When someone asks me about getting into the business, I feel obligated to point out both the pros and cons. For one thing, the industry is going to form you. You're not going to form it. Anyone who thinks he's going to get into Rock 'n' Roll trucking and come up with a lot of shortcuts to change the way work is done, is in for a real rude awakening. This business is known for its long hours and extended periods of time away from home. There's never any sympathy for someone who says, 'Look, I've been away from my wife for 10 weeks. We've got these two days off in New York. Can't I fly home for a day?' The answer to that questions would probably be 'NO.' It's likely that there will be a production meeting the next day that requires everyone to be in attendance. You're expected to work hard and to stay with the program as it exists. You don't get things your way. This is not Burger King. You do things the way production has to be done, whatever it takes. If it means staying up for 48 hours, then you stay up for 48 hours.

"On the positive side, I think if you drive a load of, say, dog food from New Jersey to California, that's a job well done. However, when you get your bills of lading signed you look at the guy who just signed them and you realize that he really didn't care that you got there on time that day, or that you might have gone through hell to deliver that dog food without being late. All he cares about is that he got his dog food. 'Now, get this truck out of sight fast so that the next one can

38

come in!' But when you work for a rock band it's different. I drove for Billy Gibbons of ZZ Top. If he had some special equipment that hadn't yet had a road case built for it, he would bring it to me and ask if I could carry it in the truck with me. Billy did that because he trusted me. He made me feel that it was very important to him that I was the one carrying his equipment. I knew that the show was important, because 100,000 kids would go to hear him play! I also know he's a great guitar player and the fact that he entrusts me with his guitar has a big effect on my sense of self-esteem. In other words, he appreciates the person who makes sure all of his stuff gets there. It really gives me a good feeling. That's the difference between that load and the dog food. How can you place a dollar value on something like that? You can't say, 'I'd rather take the dog food, because I can make $1,000 a week and I can only make $600 a week in Rock 'n' Roll.' That's just meaningless to a guy who feels a strong sense of self-worth because of a job well-done.

"Our insurance requirements make it necessary that our drivers be at least 23 years old. This may be an advantage to young people interested in a trucking career because it gives them plenty of time to get driving experience. I suggest they try to work in and around the transportation business, maybe start out servicing trucks or busses. That will do two things: (1) you'll learn a lot about solving problems, which will help when you're out on the road and have a breakdown, and (2) it will give you a chance to drive the vehicles. Even if you drive for only 100 feet, you'll begin to get a feel for it. Before you know it, you'll be making deliveries and gaining the valuable experience of self-confidence that will lead you on the road to Rock 'n' Roll."

66 When you reach for your guitar for the next number, it better be in tune, plugged into the amp and no more than two feet away — in every city, every night. 99

Jerry Harrison
TALKING HEADS

Guitar Technician

Jon Dworkow

Someone has to see to it that all the musical instruments on stage are working properly and will do so throughout the entire tour. These days Bon Jovi depends upon one particular man to make sure that his amplifiers and guitars do whatever he wants them to do. But don't call Jon Dworkow a "roadie." He's a lot more than that.

When Jon ("J.D." to his friends) Dworkow was in junior high school he worked with a local organization called the Youth Adult Council of Westport, CT. This was a civic association that held a summer series of concerts each year. Among the bands that performed there were the James Gang, Buddy Miles, Stewart Copeland's (first group) Curved Air, Edgar Winter and the Byrds. J.D.: "I got involved because I was able to see the shows for free and was allowed to hang out back stage. I always helped unload the trucks, but the reason they let me hang around the office was because I would do everything, from putting up posters to picking up tickets."

Inspired by these concerts, J.D. took guitar, trumpet and piano lessons. Exposure to music at an early age helped him develop a

40

good ear, something that has helped him to get where he is today, taking care of the guitars, amplifiers and stage equipment for Jon Bon Jovi. "My job with Jon is to have his guitars tuned and set-up properly when he's on stage and to make sure the equipment is in the best possible condition."

The piano and the trumpet studies ran out of steam, but J.D. continued learning all he could about playing the guitar. A neighbor, Charlie Karp, was quite a talented guitar player, who eventually toured with Buddy Miles and Jimi Hendrix. Once J.D. was out of high school, Charlie would take him along on his local gigs. After the Buddy Miles tour, Charlie formed his own band called White Chocolate and began playing bars. J.D. started wrapping up cables for him and helping the band load their truck. Before long it turned into a full-time job and gave Jon his initial experience in working on guitars and amplifiers. Then White Chocolate (now called Dirty Angels) was asked by Aerosmith's road manager to pick up the last leg of the Aerosmith tour. "I remember we just jumped into the truck and drove non-stop, New York to San Antonio in about 26 hours." That was Jon's first professional tour.

"It happened so quickly. I mean, we were the opening act on a rock tour, but we drove our own truck and all of that stuff. Having done 8 shows on the road with Aerosmith we got a taste of it, but we didn't get a real sense of it. Triumphantly (or so we thought), we came back home. But, playing the bars again was a real letdown. Yet, I didn't think about changing jobs. I was going to stick with this thing because it was my first job in the business and we all had that romantic notion that we were going to be rich and famous. However, that dream never materialized and the band broke up."

J.D. worked with another local group, the Simms Brothers Band opening on the U.S. tour for Peter Frampton. "We got to see some of the good stuff, but we were doing all the driving while they were sleeping. I enjoyed seeing America, but it was a difficult way to do it." Once the tour ended, the Simms Brothers also went back to playing the bars.

Determined to work with bigger acts, J.D. asked for help from a very good friend of his, John Regan, the bass player on the Frampton tour. It was because of Regan's recommendation that J.D. got a call from Frampton's tour manager. "I was told that they were looking for new blood and they were excited about the fact that I was very much into my job." J.D. joined the crew in the summer of 1980 and went to South America later that year, touring Brazil, Argentina and Venezuela.

"We had just finished doing two shows in Venezuela when the police attacked the crowd and the crowd was taunting the police. It was just really ugly. It became so violent that we had to fly out early without the band's equipment. Now, we had been traveling with that equipment as 'excess baggage' on flights for months. Ordinarily, I would have had to stay with the gear, but the authorities wanted to get us all out at the same time. As fate would have it, the plane that was carrying the equipment crashed. Tens of thousands of dollars worth of guitars, drums, and amps were destroyed. It was terrible, but I suppose it could have been much worse.

"My job with Peter lasted 3 more years, then I briefly worked with Joan Jett and the Blackhearts. Then I got a phone call from a friend of mine in the business saying there was an opening with Billy Idol." J.D. called Idol's road manager to set up an interview and a short time later went to work for Billy Idol. The Rebel Yell tour lasted about ten months and the rock world saw the rise of Billy Idol. "My responsibility was to both Billy and Steve Stevens. Their guitars had to be tuned and in their proper places on stage, and I had to do all the routine maintenance necessary to avoid problems during the show."

At the conclusion of that tour, J.D. was introduced to Tom Marzullo (production manager for Prince). Prince was going out on tour in November and even though J.D. was tired, within three days he was in Minnesota getting ready for the rehearsal. Prince's Twin Cities Tour was like nothing J.D. had done before. It went went back and forth between three different venues in the Minneapolis-St. Paul area. Setting up, breaking down, moving across town, setting up again, rehearsing, and breaking down again. "We rehearsed everything from the show to loading our trucks. We had eleven trucks at the time and around 50 people in the crew. I just loved it. The money was good and the music was great, but as the Prince tour wound down, I left to work with Billy Idol once again."

In April of 1985, JD went into the studio with Billy and stayed there taking care of the guitars for the next 18 months, except for a month off to work on LIVE AID. "I'm very proud to have been a part of that." When J.D. rejoined Billy in the studio, he remembers that there were great vibes in that facility. The Stones were doing their Dirty

Work album in the same studio. "They would be coming in during the night to record, while we worked during the day. But, we were there for so long that we would see other record projects come in, finish, and go out. The thrill of working in the studio definitely wore out after the first year.

"Without question I was married to this whole situation in the studio. We eventually finished 'Whiplash' and went out on the road, finishing up in New Zealand and Australia. Later in the year, I worked with Billy in his home in LA and set up a studio for him."

As J.D. sees it, people get involved in the entertainment business for a variety of reasons; some are frustrated musicians, others think it's their vehicle to stardom and there are countless other reasons. "If your intention is to get involved in the business to be a superstar, to hang out with rock stars and do drugs and feel like you're part of the Beatles, then you've really got to reexamine your priorities and decide whether it's something you really want to do. If you want to be a musician, then be a musician. If you think the greatness will rub off on you by mere association, it's not going to happen. You are not the main attraction; what you are doing is a subordinate action. It takes a weird breed of animal to become a 'roadie.' I despise that term because it sounds condescending, but on the other hand to call us technicians is somewhat patronizing. There really is no official term for us. We just work. We go out there because we love to be around the Rock 'n' Roll music and we find the alternative life style very appealing.

"For the most part we have an incredible sense of loyalty. We're like a good hunting dog, always there, loyal and dependable. This trait is something that you don't learn in school, although I firmly believe that you should go as far as humanly possible with your education. My parents were very disappointed by the fact that I didn't go to college. I'll sound like my parents for a second, but by not going to college I've limited my alternatives. If I ever wanted to, or had to do something else, I'm not trained. I don't have the basics. I feel it's important to have a college degree because it shows that you can stick it out, if nothing else. I avoided going to college because I didn't want to take on the responsibilities. I just didn't want to deal with it at all and so I took that famous 'one year off.' It's been 16 years since I've been out of high school. I suggest that anybody who wants to be anything in this world, not just in Rock 'n' Roll, get a complete education.

43

"There are added benefits of going to college. Many schools put on a lot of concerts. That's a good place to get involved with the crews and to get a taste of what the work day is like. Set-up starts at 7 or 8 in the morning, show time is about 8 o'clock in the evening, and then you break down the show around 11:00. So, that's what the work is about (real glamorous, huh?). Don't fool yourself by thinking that it's not hard work. It's tedious at times, too, because like other jobs you tend to do the same thing over and over.

"Once you've decided that this is what you want to do, you must consider what it's like on the road. The work load is extremely heavy, make no mistake about that. It takes a lot of concentration and it's quite strenuous. As strange as it seems, the way you unwind is going to dictate whether you're going to make it in the world of Rock 'n' Roll, or not. You can't go to the bars and get completely polluted or do grams of blow and expect to perform up to the professional level of work that is demanded. If you get involved with people who don't care, that's one thing, but that's not a situation that you're likely to find. The professional groups in this business care a great deal. If someone is depending on you to be coherent when something breaks on stage, you've got to have a clear head to know how you're going to fix it. You can't allow a performer to get embarrassed in front of his audience due to an equipment failure for which you're responsible. You need to be in control of all of your senses. You've got to figure out what the problem is and deal with it without people knowing. That's the main concept. We're supposed to be the invisible men. We're not supposed to be on stage. The best rock shows are those in which you don't see any of the crew people on stage.

"An aspect of the business that has become rampant in recent years, has been the abuse of cocaine. In some instances, cocaine was used as a form of introduction by the weasels in the business, who would have no other way to meet certain entertainers. Their only function was to supply cocaine. This has proven to be an extremely destructive force. Speaking from personal experience, it nearly ended my career in the business. Experimenting with drugs didn't allow me to concentrate on my work. About five years ago I made a conscious decision to eliminate drugs completely. Many years before that at the time I was using drugs, you were distrusted if you didn't do them. Now, it seems to be the opposite way around. If someone uses drugs, everyone else seems to stay away from him. When someone's work slips because of drug use, it has to be dealt with. Often, they simply get replaced. I'm very much against drugs — period. But, I can't preach it. People have to make their own choices."

66 *A great booking agent, especially if he or she is working with a great manager, can make the most of every oppor-tunity that comes along in an artist's career.* **99**

Julian Lennon

Booking Agency

Bill Elson

An experienced booking agent like Bill Elson, acting for many of the top artists in the business, can help build the career of a new artist or sustain the success of an established artist. This depends upon the deals he makes for that artist and the promoters to whom they are introduced. That is why he represents some of the biggest names in Rock 'n' Roll.

What roads do you have to travel to be able to go from getting John Brown a gig at a 200 seat coffee house to booking INXS at sellout arena concerts throughout the nation? Bill Elson's trip literally took him from a small town outside of Chicago to Los Angeles to New York City to Chicago and back to New York. Today, Bill is considered to be one of the driving forces behind the hugely successful International Creative Management (one of the top 5 booking agencies worldwide). Although he had a real flair for marketing, it took him five years of uninterrupted education to get a degree. "I'm not a good student to say the least and I spent every other semester on scholastic probation."

In his third year of college Bill started going to a lot of the coffee houses in the Chicago area. Bill recalls fondly: "Coffee houses generally had a capacity of some 200 or 300 people. This provided a sort of intimate form of entertainment. Usually a single performer was accompanied by a backup musician but for the most part it was simply an individual showcase. The intimacy of that kind of initial entertainment experience has very much been a contributing factor to the fascination that I hold for this business. There is something about listening to an act perform in an environment where you can see them clearly and know that they are singing for you specifically as a member of this small group. Live entertainment in such a setting is a phenomenon that is very different from that which most people experience today.

"When you go to see a concert for the first time, it's likely to be in a setting where the size and scale of the physical environment restricts you from having an interaction with the band. It's more like you're witnessing the show as just another person in a vast audience. People like Springsteen and some of the other great entertainers cut through that and even though they play stadiums, the most awesome quality of their performance is that they have personalized it for their fans. The individual in the audience feels that the performer is playing just for him or her."

The Beatles' arrival in America had a dramatic effect throughout the country on all forms of music. Particularly hard hit was folk music. At the college Bill was attending, it shut down the entire folk music scene. Also, popular entertainment was moving out of small venues into large arenas with the advent of the electrified music of the English bands. "One of my first promotions was to hire a local folk singer whom I liked a great deal to come out and perform at the school library auditorium that held about 100 people. The school was supposed to underwrite the peformance, but at the last minute there was a mix up in the administration and the school backed out of the concert. I ended up bankrolling the show myself. My roommate and I sold tickets for one dollar each. We made $65 at the end of the night which not only provided an exciting experience for me but made me want to do more shows. The last two years of my education were spent running a small buy and sell concert agency that operated on a regional basis out of a phone booth in my dormitory.

"After graduation and a few attempts to continue booking bands on my own, I ended up getting a job in the Chicago office of the

Agency for the Performing Arts. APA happened to represent some great psychedelic bands which were still completely unknown. I found myself booking Jefferson Airplane, the Doors, Janis Joplin and virtually all of the important psychedelic era acts. I worked out of that office for about a year enjoying a certain degree of success. I even got a $50 raise which brought me up to $175 a week.

"I was briefly moved to the west coast, but it was my first time far away from home, and it was difficult for me to adjust. After a year or so back in New York, I showed my gratitude to APA for investing in my educational experience by leaving them for more money at a job in Chicago. I got my just reward by being fired from the new job nine months later and was out of work for three months. Then Premier Talent offered me a job that was very timely in more ways than one. Not only did I need the job, but it turned out that Premier was representing all the major acts of the British invasion. I stayed with Premier for the better part of seven years before going to General Artists Corporation, an agency that was eventually purchased by my current employer — ICM."

The first thing a booking agent does is to call promoters around the country to arrange and negotiate concert locations and revenues for a particular artist. The agent must organize the tour on a reasonable geographic and scheduling basis. "Let's say that Robert Plant is out on the road, you don't want him to do too many shows in a row and lose his voice or too many miles apart so he can't make the distance between venues. The agent must also try to keep a certain distance between competing shows. I try to advise as to the advantage of playing one building over another, where to start touring and where to end the tour. If you're touring from November all the way through spring, weather is a factor. You try to get some of the northeast out of the way prior to the harsh weather, and because that's where the population density is the greatest. Then you go south and west as long as you can, avoiding the bad weather, but balancing the effect of freezing temperatures on the need to play major population centers as early as possible." For their services, agencies like ICM are paid 10% of the earnings of the band excluding t-shirts and other merchandise.

"The big break for me was doing that folk concert at St. Procopius College. Everybody liked it and I made money. In this business, as in any other, if you respond to it and it gives you a real jolt

48

of excitement, that's the path to follow. If you go into it just to make money, you probably won't ever be happy with your life. Some of the most miserable people I know in this business — miserable to deal with and miserable in terms of their own peace of mind — are people who made a lot of money but can't stand what they do. The really successful people in this business simply love what they are doing. I work probably 60 hours a week for no other reason than that I love what I do. Through years of hard work I'm now in the position of representing some of the greatest bands in the world. However, if I were booking acts into a Holiday Inn I could still deal with that. The point being that it's not the money that motivates me. There isn't enough money in the world to make it enjoyable for me to do something I hate.

"The first time INXS came to America they didn't know the east side of New York from the west side and just played small venues. A year or so ago they sold out Radio City Music Hall three times in about an hour! There is satisfaction in that. So, if you represent a particular act and are determined to be an agent, make sure you're really committed to that band because you love working for them and believe they deserve to succeed. Make sure the reason isn't because it gives you a chance to stand next to someone who plays a guitar and attracts good looking chicks, or that it's simply a way to make money. Booking is hard work and if you don't like it there is no other reason to spend 50 or 60 hours a week doing it. You can probably make more money selling bonds or driving a cab. The best advice I ever received was, if you just work hard and do good work you can't help but make money. I didn't believe it then, but I now know it to be true. Making money becomes a lot easier once you find what you want to do most because then the money becomes unimportant. What matters is becoming the best you can be at what you're doing. Then, when you're really good at it, the money will find you. If you like what you are doing, don't give a damn about how much you're getting paid for it and just be happy to be doing it."

> **66** **T**here's a special
> place in Rock 'n' Roll for carpenters who can build
> sets that look spectacular but come apart quickly
> and in small enough pieces to get them on the
> truck and ready for the next night's show. If you
> think of it as building a house that you take apart
> every night, you will realize what kind of skill and
> expertise is involved. **99**
>
> **David Fishof, Producer**
> **DIRTY DANCING, MONKEES,**
> **AMERICAN BANDSTAND TOURS**

Stage Carpenter

Leo English

Leo English is now a well known stage carpenter, but he didn't get involved in the entertainment business until he was 27 years old. He had been doing a variety of other jobs after college. One day, a friend who owned a production company asked Leo to help him with some stage work for local bands in the Santa Cruz area. That was it.

Starting out as a stagehand (even at that age) meant learning everything from the ground up. Leo recalls that it entailed doing set ups, loading trucks, emptying trucks, and anything else that needed to be done. Eventually, he heard of a job opening with FM Productions, a company then owned by the legendary promoter Bill Graham. Leo has been employed as the head carpenter at FM in San Francisco for the last 12 years.

The responsibility of the head carpenter is to coordinate the unloading of the truck, and erect the sets before the performance. If the set requires moving parts, Leo must make sure that they move the way they should and on cue. After the concert, the set must be dismantled and reloaded into the truck. Ordinarily, all of this means supervising a crew of about ten men.

A typical day for Leo and his crew on tour begins between 6 and 8 in the morning (depending on the size of the show). The work day can last until 4 a.m. the next morning. "Long days are pretty typical of most road shows, including the last Pink Floyd Tour. In additon to Pink Floyd, I've done two tours with the Rolling Stones, David Bowie, Billy Joel and the Cars. While working with Bill Graham, I did several hundred other shows.

"The longest stretch I have been out on the road was nine months. That was with David Bowie. One of the highlights of the last five years has been getting the opportunity to work in 22 countries. Another one that immediately comes to mind is rigging Mick Jagger to fly overhead. Very often in the shows that I work on there are moving pieces. In this case working directly with Mick was really great. He is truly a nice guy. Mick would come down during the middle of the night to make sure things were going okay. He pretty much knew all of the crew (about 150 people) by their first name.

"One of the best people I have ever worked for was Billy Joel. He's really quite an interesting man. Billy treats his crew better than I have ever seen anyone treated on the road. He not only travels with the crew, but eats with them as well and makes sure that everything's first class. He's right in there with us."

Leo is often asked by teenagers how they can get into the business. Here's how he answers them: "One of the best things that I can recommend to high school students would be to first get involved in local school plays. Begin by building set pieces on that level. This will provide the kind of experience that is critically important. You'll learn a lot about stage managing, set construction, and lighting. In addition, you will see that your efforts can make a difference. Although I'm an exception to most rules, I started building sets for high school plays and continued to do the same sort of thing through college. Hands on experience is the best way I know to learn anything. I gave my daughter, who wants to do what her dad does, the same advice.

"As far as courses are concerned, drafting is definitely a bonus. Drafting, mechanical drawing, or an electronics course would be very good. Many of the technicians have taken courses at trade schools.

In fact, electronics is becoming more and more an intregal part of the business. There are so many devices that are controlled electronically that having that edge could very well mean the difference between getting hired or not.

"Another avenue to explore is joining a Union. The main one is called IATSE which stands for the International Alliance of Theatrical and Stage Employees. While I'm non-union and considered a part of management, there are benefits to being in the union. One of them is money. Some of the guys who work for me make a lot more than I do working union jobs (but I would still rather be the boss.

"To work in entertainment you have to really be dedicated. There are times when it gets pretty lean, because it is subject to the whims of artists, who often decide to change touring plans at the last possible moment. So, instead of being out on a 6 month tour, you get stuck at home with very little to do. On the other hand, this is one of the few businesses where there are no limitations because of lack of education. If you've got a good head on your shoulders and you're really devoted, there are still a lot of opportunities to grow.

"A word of caution, traveling is very hard on relationships. It's my belief, however, that the rewards far outweigh any sacrifices you make. You have to be sure that this is what you want to do because it can get real discouraging sometimes.

"When I hire someone the first thing I look for is to see whether or not the applicant is making eye contact. When someone looks at me straight in the face, it tells me that they have some confidence in themselves. The next thing I look for is kind of a gut feeling. If I feel good about them, I'll give them a shot. Then I just watch their skills and how they work. They don't have to be all that experienced, but they do have to be able to pick things up quickly. That's basically it. I'll give just about anybody a shot, but the eye contact and the confidence is really important."

Box Office Management
Paula Esposito

Do you have a passion for order? Are you so organized that all your clothes are arranged alphabetically or by color? If so, you might make a great Box Office manager. Paula Esposito of Monarch Entertainment: "I have close to 30 shows on sale right now, and you really have to learn how to do two or three things at the same time. It takes an extremely coordinated person to do this job, because every ticket is money for which you are responsible. This job has helped me to become one of the most organized people on the whole planet."

If you think it's just a matter of selling tickets, listen to this. Prior to a show going on sale, the box office manager must contact the band's management, record company and about a dozen other people connected with the show to determine exactly who will be invited as guests of the show. "The building office personnel are notified as to how many guest tickets we will need and of any special requests that the band has made. Such requests would be for a specific location,

53

certain rows or particular sections. I'm responsible for distributing those tickets. If the band doesn't ask for specific seats, I have to decide exactly which tickets they are going to get. In addition, I have to make sure that I have enough other tickets to cover Monarch's own needs. This can be more difficult than it sounds because you never know how many important people are going to be in the area at the time of each show. Even if you had some idea of the number, you wouldn't know how many people were going to request tickets for the concert.

"Concert tickets normally go on sale four to six weeks prior to the event. Ticket requests are made right up until the night of the show. On the evening of the performance I take the band's tickets and go to the venue. I'll also write out their guest lists. The number of tickets that the band gets can be anywhere from 100 to about 750 tickets. Once the show is over, I have to account for each and every ticket that we give out. The breakdown is rather simple, but what complicates matters is that we usually have about 30 shows on sale at the same time. This is especially troublesome if you have a couple of stadium shows, as we generally do during the summer.

"I'm responsible for thousands of dollars every day. Since we have so many shows, it seems as though we never slow down. We try to handle most of the tickets through mail order because it's a lot easier for us. If we were to have people come and pick them up, we would have to stop working every five minutes to accommodate the customers. The amount of paperwork involved is tremendous. Every ticket that's sent out must be recorded in case it's lost in the mail or stolen. Checks also have to be recorded just in case they bounce. Given the amount of tickets sold, you can imagine the stacks of paperwork that can quickly pile up around us.

"Our staff of five people put in a phenomenal amount of hours each week. Our boss, John Scher, is the number one promoter in the country. The total number of shows we have done in the past two years is incredible, so everything we do is extremely fast paced. My personal life has suffered greatly from this. The amount of time that has to be put into this is unbelievable. Of course, working Saturdays and holidays doesn't help build great relationships. Actually, I rarely answer my phone at home, because I get hundreds of people asking for tickets. Our work week is Monday to Saturday, and if there is a show on Sunday, we work. A typical Saturday finds us at work early in the morning and leaving around midnight. At the end of September through the beginning of October last year, we were putting Pink Floyd shows on sale on Friday, Saturday and Sunday. During this stretch I worked 27 days in a row, 8 or 9 of them being 16 hour days."

Paula started her box office career at a punk rock club in Passaic called Hitsville. "It had live bands seven nights a week and it was done on the club level, so I was able to get first hand experience. As an assistant manager I learned exactly how a show is run because I had to prepare everything. Whether it was having to call to order extra equipment, or if the house PA didn't work, I had to get it fixed. It even got to the point where I was doing the lighting, catering, working the box office, maintaining the guest list for the band, and paying them as well.

"I was very lucky because Hitsville was in beautiful downtown Passaic, a half mile from the infamous Capitol Theatre. The Capitol used to have shows that were over by 11:00. Since we were a rock bar that stayed open until 3:00 a.m., the people who worked at the Capitol would come down to the club afterward and I got to know many of them quite well. Towards the end of the Hitsville run, one of the girls who worked at the Capitol theatre box office asked me if I wanted to do some part-time work for her. I was putting in fewer and fewer hours at Hitsville, so the offer was very much appreciated. With that, I began working at the Capitol Theatre for John Scher."

About six months later one of the people who had worked in Scher's box office left and Paula was asked if she would fill in until they could find a replacement. "Well, weeks turned into months and here it is several years later, and I'm still working for John."

Here are Paula's words of warning for anyone considering a job in the box office of a major promoter or arena. "The stress level at times is virtually unbearable. I'm sure that it's unhealthy for anyone to do this for a long period of time. An annoying aspect of this job is when someone starts calling me 10 times a day about a show that is still six months away. To quickly satisfy that type of person, I have developed total recall. I can have a guest list that is 20 pages long with 50 names on a page and I'd be able to tell you if John Smith was down for Pink Floyd tickets. Through this job I've been able to learn how to recall names and how to memorize things in general. I probably know thousands of people by their names.

"This job was easy for me because I started at the very bottom. It didn't take me long to work up to my current position, which is about as far as I can get in this part of the business. I'm pretty lucky being in the New York area, because it keeps me so busy. There are times when work is great fun and other times that I can't imagine anybody wanting to do this for a living. Before I leave the business, I would like to go on the road with a band, just one time. Naturally, it would have to be with someone I like, because I don't believe I could listen to the same band over and over, night after night, unless it were U2. Initially, I really liked going to the shows, but after you've done it 400 or 500 times you don't want to go anymore."

66 ***O****nce you've seen a great laser light show, you can never forget it. It's like 'Flash Gordon goes Rock 'n' Roll.' My personal suspicion is that the chaps backstage working on that fabulous laser equipment are from outer space — light years ahead of the rest of us.* **99**

John Entwistle
THE WHO

Laser Operation

Daniel Ferguson

Like many other people who work behind the scenes at rock concerts, those who operate and design the laser portions of the show are under enormous pressure. Although their segment may only last a few minutes, that time is pressure-packed and may have taken five, six, even seven days of rehearsing to make everything come together.

According to Daniel Ferguson of Laser Design, "It's the smell of the grease-paint and the roar of the crowd that makes this job worthwhile and gives you a sense of satisfaction. I think the toughest part of my job is the pressure of having to pull off the actual effects perfectly, night after night. Hearing the applause of the crowd relieves that pressure and makes me want to go through it again for the next show.

"We do laser light shows for big extravaganzas and even for small trade shows. We set up equipment and project images on screens and we bounce laser beams off mirrors positioned throughout an arena or ballroom. We have the capability to do full color animation or simply write names with our lasers. We also design custom graphics and logos to project. If a client would like his own logo projected, it first has to be digitized in the studio. Let's say, it's the Coca Cola logo or the Run DMC logo; they send us an 8 by 10 piece of artwork and we have to manually transfer the logo with a light pen into our computer which instructs the scanners how to make the different images. With another of our effects we can create shapes over an object or a person to highlight them. Our lasers produce tunnels, squares, rounds, triangles, and star-shapes. We can do a 'lumina' which is an effect like swirling clouds or a 'rhinestone ball' which is like shooting out a field of stars. In addition, we can run fiber optic strips, take the sheathing off and use it like neon to wrap around the set, cars, or motorcycles; it's like bendable neon. We can also send the laser through a fiber optic and project the beam out the other end at another remote location."

Ordinarily, it's very difficult to break into this business, but Dan was lucky. His story goes like this: In high school and college Dan always had the desire to go into the entertainment business, but never thought he would find his place in the laser area. "I worked as a roadie for a band years ago just hauling equipment and setting it up. That's when I got my first taste of the excitement surrounding Rock 'n' Roll."

Dan planned to get a college degree but he ran out of money to finish his education and needed a job. "I finally got one with a video company in Hollywood that was sharing space with a laser company. Eventually I got laid off by the video company, but the next day the laser people asked me to work for them." Dan got his first on the job training out on the road, on a major tour with Electric Light Orchestra in 1976. Lasers have been his life's work ever since.

The first thing Dan does before each show is an on-site survey. "This is necessary," he says, "because it takes water to run the laser. Therefore, you have to go in before the show actually starts and look at the venue. There are several questions that you must ask yourself. Where are you going to hang the mirrors? What electrical power is available? Where are you going to position the laser? How far away is the water hose from the actual laser position? The laser is a very high temperature piece of equipment. It gets up to about 360 degrees. In order to keep it cool you must run water through the laser and around the tube itself. The glass tube will contain either argon or krypton gas, which determines the color of the beams. This water cooling process keeps the glass from breaking or melting down."

"The laser beam is actually hot enough to do damage to the eye itself. A direct beam in the eye can cause temporary blindness. Laser shows have changed over the years. When we first did laser light shows, some people were putting dangerous beams into the audience. Because of that former practice, the use of lasers is now strictly controlled by the government. They do not permit any stray beams to go into the audience." That's why, after inspecting all of the logistics in the venue itself and determining whether he has enough power, Dan has to notify the U.S. government what he's going to do. "Every two years you have to apply for a variance, which is like a license. During that same two year period of time you must notify the federal government and (sometimes) the state that you are going to perform a laser light show in their state. It's constant communication with the federal people."

Dan has recently worked with Run DMC and New Edition. "We've also done all types of trade shows for Merrill Lynch, Cadillac, and Toyota. We did a big Fourth of July party at Tampa Stadium last year and a Halloween show at Knotts Berry Farm in California." But all this work has its negative side for Dan. "I'm often on the road for my birthday and virtually every holiday. I get to spend most Christmas Days with my family, but not New Year's Eve. Usually, I'm doing a show that night. If you're single, you always lose girl friends when you come back and sometimes even wives. It's hard to keep a good relationship with some of your good friends because you are gone so long and you come back to find that they've changed. It gets lonely out on the road. I always enjoy coming back to my own place. It gives me a better sense of security."

Dan says this about getting into the field: "There are classes that can teach you about using lasers, but it's a completely different ball game when you get out there on the road trying to set up a show every day. While a trade school could certainly teach the basics about lasers and design, there isn't any trade school that can teach about touring. My pet peeves are hotel rooms, living out of a bag, and putting up with terrible meals. Usually I get heartburn on the road and have to carry around a bunch of Rolaids. You have to make those sacrifices and you have to be away from your friends and family for long periods of time.

"You can't help asking yourself every once in a while, is it worth all that? You want to know my answer? You better believe it is."

> **66 When you spend
> money and energy trying to get yourself the best
> equipment to perform with, you don't want to
> wonder if it's going to make it through the tour.
> We're talking about getting bounced around on
> trucks and hauled on and off stage. I don't know
> who it's rougher on, guitars or guitar players. 99**
>
> *Graham Parker*

Travel Cases

Coy Frisbee

*You may have noticed cases or boxes on the side of Bruce
Springsteen's, AC/DC's and many other concert stages. It's in those
boxes with wheels under them that the production companies and
band members store their gear. The cases are designed not only to
protect the equipment but to allow it to be easily rolled into trucks.
They're normally constructed of specially laminated plywood
joined with aluminum rivets on the side.*

Coy Frisbee designs and builds most of those travel cases
these days, but his first job in the business was moving equipment
around for a friend's band. "We worked weekends and maybe a
couple of nights a week in local high school auditoriums and CYOs. I
never really got to the bigger bands. What happened was that a
record company expressed interest in three of the guys in one of the
bands that I was working with, so those guys left the group to form a
new band. They released an album that never really sold well and
they just opened up for bigger acts all over the country. It became

61

tiresome after a while, so I decided to try to make a job out of something I'd done for a long time, which was building cases for band equipment. It allowed me to be home and to still stay connected to Rock 'n' Roll at the same time.

"My idea was to come up with the Mercedes-Benz of cases because they had become cheaply made and poorly constructed. I had used the mass produced cases and they continually fell apart or presented other problems. After a couple of years of thinking about going into business, I took the plunge. My research consisted of my personal experience on the road and the tearing apart of a couple of different brand cases to see what I could learn from them. I just started with much better materials, strictly the top of the line."

Coy soon discovered that he opened up a completely different market. "The other case companies primarily sell through music stores. Let's face it, there are thousands and thousands of music stores across the U.S. Although my company, C & D Cases occasionally does sell to the music stores, my market is direct to the bigger bands in the business. Not only can they afford to buy top of the line cases but their heavy travel schedule dictates a need for better quality. Everybody had the same problems that I had when touring and it seemed natural to me to supply them with better quality cases. This philosophy appears to be working out because everyone has been coming back for additional cases and spreading the good word at the same time.

"All our cases are hand made. The basic necessary skill is carpentry. The case is actually made from scratch with the skills acquired from high school mechanical arts and woodworking shop classes. We look for people with common sense along with the ability to read a ruler and use tools both properly and safely. We provide the plans and our people are expected to be able to follow them precisely.

"Building cases is perhaps the most laid back job in the entertainment business. This job isn't a grind as most jobs are when you're touring. The industry in general is filled with people who really like their work and are getting paid for doing what they love to do. However, it can be stressful when you get an order on short notice. Sometimes a band decides to tour and will need cases in three days. This is an almost impossible task, but we manage to do it anyway by putting in ridiculous hours. We've learned to expect the unexpected. What a great way to make a living!"

> **66** **I**n professional wrestling we got some of the same things you got in Rock 'n' Roll. Like Cyndi Lauper and a great bunch of stage hands. Those stage hands are tough, but sometimes they get confused and forget which night it is, yours or ours. So what if once in a while they try to smear body oil on a guitar player — or bring out a piano stool for Andre the Giant? Nobody's perfect. **99**
>
> "Captain" Lou Albano

Stagehand

Arthur J. Giegerich

Arthur J. (A.J.) Giegerich started working in Rock 'n' Roll as a part time employee in New York at the legendary Fillmore East. "A friend of mine happened to be down there just before it opened and told me that they were looking for some help. So, for a whopping $10 a night, I became an usher."

After the Fillmore closed, A.J. began working at the Academy of Music (also in New York), which was later known as the Palladium. This lasted until promoter John Scher offered him a job as the head of security for the Capitol Theater in Passaic, New Jersey. During the course of his eight year career, A.J. resigned his security post to become the head of the Capitol Theatre stage crew.

To broaden his work experience, A.J. decided to go out on the road. "I toured for the next five years as Barry Manilow's head carpenter. When Barry went into the studio, an opportunity came along to do a brief tour with Linda Ronstadt. Thanks to John Scher, I was able to go out with the Grateful Dead for an extended tour. While on a break I got my union card and began to do some work at the Meadowlands Arena in Secaucus, New Jersey. I was fortunate to be there when the facility first opened because it enabled me to eventually quit touring and work full time at the Meadowlands."

Technically, A.J. works for the Meadowlands Local 642 of the International Alliance of Theatrical and Stage Employees (IATSE). Local 642 has a contract with Meadowlands to supply labor. "Performance Magazine has voted Meadowlands the 'Facility of the Year' several times in a row. It's really a great place to work. Once an artist is booked to play Meadowlands, the band's production manager will let us know what time in the morning (usually 8:00 a.m.) they'll need manpower. At the same time, we're notified of the type and amount of workers that are needed."

A.J.'s duty as the head carpenter is to oversee the setup. "During most shows we'll typically use four truck loaders, one forklift operator, two electricians and twenty grips. However, each show is unique. For some smaller shows, we may use six guys to set up the stage, the next show may take twenty men or, we'll have an outdoor show that requires 100 laborers.

"The work schedule usually begins around 7:00 a.m., when part of the crew comes in to start building the stage. That takes about two hours. At 9:00 a.m. they'll ask for, say, four truck loaders, four riggers, two ground men and eight grips. 'Grips' is a generic term for stage hands. At this time, the prerig and advance work is done. Around 11:00 a.m. 20 more guys may come in do the bulk of the work. They'll work until 5:00 p.m., at which time the crew will be cut back to four department heads and ten grips. Following a dinner break is the show call. This is usually done a half hour before the concert. Then the people who are going to run the spotlights and the deck hands for set changes, all come in to do the show. Normally, the show call is a lot smaller. You may have 40 people setting up the show. However, less than half of them will work during the actual performance. Once the show is over, we'll bring back 40 or 50 people for the load out.

"Although I've been doing this job for quite some time, it's difficult to predict just how long it will take for load out. For example, Crosby, Stills and Nash had three trucks and it took us four hours to load them. Two weeks later we did Def Leppard. It took us three and a half hours to load their eight trucks, including their staging. The biggest show that we ever did was Pink Floyd. The band came in with eight trucks of equipment alone, i.e. not including a dozen or more trucks of just staging, and it only took us three and a half hours to load them. This clearly demonstrates that there is no correlation between the amount of gear an artist has and how long it will take for load out."

A.J. has this suggestion for young people: "Perhaps the easiest way to get your foot in the door is during the load in. There have been plenty of instances of someone showing some initiative by just showing up and asking for work. We've utilized many inexperienced guys to unload trucks or help set up the stage. If you're interested in working, it certainly doesn't hurt to come down and ask. All it takes is somebody with a lot of common sense because you'll be able to tune into the roadies. The most difficult part of the job for a newcomer is to understand the flow. The roadie already knows the order of things that have to be done and is accustomed to giving instructions to the house crew. Anybody who can see the total picture and plays a heads-up kind of ball game can do it.

"Show some interest in learning. Display a willingness to run errands or learn how to use certain tools. The more you learn, the more valuable you become. Versatility is a key thing throughout the entertainment industry as far as continuing to get work. Make every effort to become acquainted with a new trade. Develop your basic skills. Ascertain how to run a spotlight or a camera, or even how to operate a laser. Each additional skill increases your future value.

"It helps to make friends. It's like working anyplace else. The union is really secondary. It's a bunch of guys who work together. They perform with a lot of team work. I've worked both union and non-union. Unions are a good thing because they guarantee the promoter a reliable, well-trained work force at a reasonable rate. The promoter not only gets quality work, but also knows in advance that he's getting what he's paid for."

According to A.J. there are strict rules of behavior backstage. "Believe it or not, there is certain protocol that must be followed. Basically, you stay away from the artist. A successful stage hand doesn't come up and begin asking entertainers for their autographs. Certainly, there are moments when you speak with them. Leave those people alone and they'll come out and socialize with you. But you really have very little contact with them. They do their job and you do your job. You just don't intrude on their space. It's very rude and unprofessional."

Is A.J. satisfied with his career? Here's how he answers that question: "This is a terrific way to make a living. Live entertainment goes through phases and changes, disco one year and heavy metal the next. But, it's all music. Down on the floor you find out that there really isn't any difference. Our crew used to go like, 'uh oh, Iron Maiden'. Then Iron Maiden comes in and they've got really hip gear, very together guys, hip personnel. It doesn't matter who the act happens to be. You could hate an act like Barry Manilow. But, he may come in with the most sophisticated gear and the most together equipment. You can't generalize and put down heavy metal or Frank Sinatra. The music almost becomes secondary after awhile. You'll find that that the major differences between one artist and another will be the quality of their production and the ease of working with their crew."

> **❝If the lighting and stage effects aren't great at a show and don't add to the excitement, the audience might be better off listening to the concert on the radio and using their own imaginations. ❞**
>
> **Rick Wakeman**

Electronic Controls

Bob Goddard

Bob Goddard designs lighting and electrical equipment for a select few. "I'm not designing this equipment for a mass market. It's being designed to fit a particular client's needs and, in turn, to benefit their particular audiences. There are very few other things that I would want to do if I wasn't doing this. It's kept me going and I enjoy it greatly."

When Bob Goddard was a freshman at Syracuse University, his favorite professor left the school to become the technical director at N.Y.U. and to run their School of the Arts. "I decided to follow him down to NYU. The Anderson, an old yiddish theater down the street from the school, began having rock concerts. Someone contacted promoter Bill Graham and told him of all the activity in the lower east side and asked if he'd be interested in doing his own concerts at another theater down the street. It was an old derelict theater called the Loews Commodore. The next thing you know, Graham stepped in, renamed it the 'Fillmore East' and things started to take off from there. My friends and I walked in one day to see what was going on and began helping Graham's people out. One thing led to another and I got a job there. They were doing much more interesting things at the Fillmore than I was doing in school anyway. That was my entrance into Rock 'n' Roll.

"I was essentially a theatrical electrician for the Fillmore. We put the house dimmers together out of old parts we found in the basement the night before the club opened. In those early, legendary days of the Fillmore East we just waited around for things to start blowing up, so that we could try to fix them.

"Once we got the electrical system in good shape, I got involved working on the theater's sound and wound up spending most of my time that way. This gave me an opportunity to work with Hanley Sound, one of the first sound companies that really understood how to design a system for live Rock 'n' Roll. They were truly the pioneers in live entertainment sound. Working at the Fillmore and with all the people who helped out there taught me that you had to do whatever it took in order to make it happen.

"During this time, the Vietnam War was in full swing. Since I had left college I was now subject to the draft. Being a Quaker, I refused to fight and was labeled a conscientious objector. I served my military duty by working at NYU hospital as a technician doing cardiac monitoring and oxygen therapy. This left me with my nights free to keep working at the Fillmore.

"The Fillmore closed in 1971 just about the same time I finished my two year stint as a conscientious objector. I was a little exhausted, so I took a vacation to England. While there, some of my new-found friends from the Fillmore were trying to open a big Rock 'n' Roll theater (The Rainbow) in London. I stayed to work with them for about six months and decided to move over there permanently. So I came back to New York to pack up my things for the big move to London. While I was waiting for my work visa in New York and closing up my apartment, I got word from London that the Rainbow Theater had gone bankrupt. I unpacked my bags and here I am.

"I began to work with Bob See, who actually packaged the lighting system for the first David Bowie tour in this country, around 1972. He was looking for someone to design an electronic light dimmer control system and special consoles suitable for Rock 'n' Roll. Together we were able to build some useful things for his company. I've always been kind of a one-man show, doing small scale projects along the line. But recently I have expanded a bit. For years I resisted turning my company, Goddard Designs, into a standard manufacturer, and throughout most of the seventies I only worked with special clients like Bob See, The Grateful Dead, (Bill Graham's) FM Productions and a few choice customers and clients like that.

"I've done a lot of work over the last ten years with a designer-partner, Michael Callahan of Consolidated Edification, Inc. Most recently we created a control console for Cheap Trick that won an Industrial Design Award. The portion that I did was the electronics, which were quite sophisticated. (Incidentally, I hold five patents). The Cheap Trick sign had six lines of type repeating 'Cheap Trick.' They wanted to be able to flash any of the words, in any particular order. The sign started manually, simply by touch. All you had to do was run your hand around the panel and the lights would follow it on the sign. This panel also had a number of buttons that you could push in order to get specific functions, such as lighting up a whole line at a time or a whole column at a time or even one letter at a time. You could also record a rythym into its memory that would follow along in a syncopated beat. I designed what this board would do electronically and Mike Callahan designed the packaging."

Bob also had some of his automation equipment out on a recent Pink Floyd tour. "A popular feature at concerts are traveling lights. Normally, the lights just tilt, swivel and pan. However, Pink Floyd built 4 long aluminum tracks above the stage. Two tracks went across the stage, one over the drummer and one over mid-stage. They mounted a whole bunch of robotic lights on the trolley car or gantry crane. This enabled the lights to travel along the track, stage left to stage right, but they could also be raised or lowered just as easily. We've built similar automated systems that allowed scenery to travel on the same type of equipment for the Broadway plays Starlight Express and Anything Goes. We're now starting to sell these systems for industrial shows and other events.

"I never maintain a large staff, but the people I do generally hire are musicians or artists, people who are looking for part-time work and who'd rather do this than be a waiter or waitress. I may have 6 or 7 people working at one time. I look for someone with a lot of common sense, who pays attention to detail, and has good pattern recognition. This is not something that requires a lot of formal education. You have to be mature enough to take responsibility. Here I teach someone how to do 15 different jobs. The people who work for me can say that they never do the same job twice. It makes them feel as if they helped build the whole thing instead of just tighten a right hand bolt. For the electrical aspect of this job, you should have good math skills, some basic physics and preferably a good background in electrical engineering or computers. Right now, it very difficult to find people who can do software programming for me."

Bob warns potential entrants that "Any career in the music business is extremely hard to get into. People rarely go from point A to point B in this business. Career paths are constantly altered. I ended up doing something very different from what I started out to do. A few people get very successful while others fail miserably. If someone were to ask me if they should go into the business, I would say no, you're crazy, do anything else, but don't do this. If they were to persist, I would try to discourage them some more. If they come back to me and say, 'I don't care what you say, man. This is what I want to do with my life,' then I'd say, sit down and I'll help you. If you have the desire and you decide that this is what you want, that it feels right for you and no amount of discouragement will affect you — you'll probably succeed."

66 I *never want to think about the traveling part of the tour. I just wish someone could point me and my drums to the next town and get us there on time. The less it feels like traveling, the better I feel about touring.* **99**

Carl Palmer
EMERSON, LAKE & PALMER, ASIA

Travel Agency

Nicholas Gold

There's even a special kind of travel agent for Rock 'n' Roll who can set up the hotels and travel schedule for the army that must move each day to another town and stay each night in a different bed. It is their job to transport concert tours around the world and see that everybody has a comfortable new home every night.

Nick Gold works for a full service travel company in New York, but Nick is no ordinary travel agent. Nick is descended from a long line of drummers and although he's always been musically inclined, he never wanted to become a professional musician. Nick had been working in corporate travel when he suddenly learned that Supertramp needed extended travel arrangements. After a meeting with the band, they hired him to put their entire world tour together. "That was years ago and from that point it's been full speed ahead. In fact, I'm still working with Supertramp." Nick has worked with Earth, Wind and Fire, Stephanie Mills, Tiffany, Run DMC, Melissa Morgan, Full Force, Salt & Pepa, Taylor Dayne, David Bowie, AC DC,

71

Scorpions, Emerson Lake & Palmer and dozens more. He has also done all the travel arrangements for the 'The Fresh Festival,' a 1985 tour that had approximately 130 people on the road.

One of the most difficult projects that Nick ever undertook was the MTV Museum of Unnatural History, a seven million dollar museum display that has been touring the country. "It was like taking a mobile Hard Rock Cafe around the United States. This 'Museum on wheels' enabled the public to see some great Rock 'n' Roll memorabilia. The MTV Museum toured for seven months and it was a project for which the travel plans had to be made immediately, in one shot. One difficulty was that often the memorabilia would be displayed in shopping malls in the middle of nowhere and just finding a hotel nearby, required a great deal of research.

"Scheduling bands involves moving 20 or 30 people from city to city on a daily basis, making sure that the hotels are in place, and satisfying any special requests from the band members or the road manager. For example, the lead singer may want a particular temperature in his room or another artist may have another need that must be attended to. I must impress upon both the hotels and airlines the need to comply with these details. You have to stay on top of it and it can be very demanding. You're on call 25 hours a day, eight days a week. I'm a workaholic and there isn't anything that I don't like about the travel industry."

There is a difference between the typical travel agency and those who cater strictly to entertainers. "Instead of booking one or two airline tickets for a couple travelling to Disney World, I have to do a whole series of flights for 20 or 30 members of a tour going everywhere. The same applies to booking hotel rooms. Due to the fact that you're working on a much tighter budget, you have to negotiate a lot more, particularily with the hotels. Airlines won't give you a tremendous amount of room for negotiation, but the hotels have tremendous flexibility, depending on the time of year, market conditions and so forth."

There are many ways to get involved in the travel industry. Nick suggests contacting independent travel schools, both in the U.S. and England, that teach students the use of computers, geography, and how to read an Official Airline Guide. "The airlines themselves are another good source for training. Of course, there are the big boys in travel, like American Express, Thomas Cook, and Fosters. These particular companies have their own in-house travel schools. Then too, there are travel schools set up through universities and they are another good way to go. Any of this training can be an advantage in getting a travel career off the ground."

Here are Nick's thoughts about hiring new travel agents: "Personally, I look for someone who doesn't have many outside responsibilities. A person who's quite flexible and who'll adjust to the crazy hours that the travel business demands. I'm looking for someone who is maybe even a bit bizarre. I need somebody who is equally at ease wearing jeans and a tee shirt as he or she is in a corporate suit, should either need arise. It's necessary that our agents have fun doing their job. More than anything else, we need people who truly want to get into the industry to help make a difference and not primarily because they are star struck." However, Nick concedes that everybody in the entertainment industry is a little star struck, but he has "found in the past that some people only had the idea that this was one of the ways to meet stars. Their sole purpose in life was to go and meet people like Bruce Springsteen and Billy Joel. This travel work for tours was the way they thought they were going to do it. But the truth is that it only happens after you've worked hard, provided excellent service to many clients and earned your reputation in the entertainment travel business."

66 Great Rock 'n' Roll
*photographers make me nervous. When they look
at me I'm always sure they can see secret things —
like whose old man I was with last night or how I'm
sure I'm going to look like an unmade bed in any
pictures they take today. But you can't print
this.* **99**

ANONYMOUS

Photographer

Lynn Goldsmith

Somebody has to take the photographs you see on concert posters, ads and program books. It's a specialty that's also a form of art, all by itself. It's hard work and a long road to the top. Lynn Goldsmith has made the journey and is now one of the most respected entertainment photographers in the business.

When she was still in college, Lynn Goldsmith sang in a club band called the Walking Wounded. "We used to open for groups like Jimi Hendrix and Traffic, but there were internal problems and we broke up." After that, Lynn studied stage and screen directing at the University of Michigan. After graduating, she made her way to New York and was fortunate in landing a job at NBC. There she met a man named Joshua White who was then doing the Joshua Light Show for Bill Graham at the old Fillmore East. He needed help putting together a new projection system called "video magnification" and hired Lynn. He was the first to offer large screen projection for rock shows and Lynn's knowledge of TV direction was useful to him. "My job was to call the shots that were being projected on the screens behind the bands."

Soon another TV network, ABC, decided that there was a market for Rock 'n' Roll on late night TV and created a show called In Concert. They picked Joshua Television to dress up the show and Lynn found herself appointed as network director of Rock 'n' Roll TV. "We did a special with Grand Funk Railroad called Phoenix House. This was the first time they let me do the documentary portion of the program. I spoke to the band about an idea that I had to do a short film that could be used in movie theatres as a means of promoting the band and they went for it. We called it An American Band and they even followed it up with an album of the same name. When I look back, it seems that some kind of camera was involved every time there was an important step forward in my life.

"After the initial excitement wore off, I got incredibly bored with directing on television. All this time I had also been taking photographs of what was going on around me and that's what helped me move on. Part of my way of preparing for the television shows was to go out on the road ahead of time and take pictures of the act we were going to tape. Well, someone at a record company had seen some of those photographs and offered a thousand dollars to use them in an ad. When I hesitated (I was shocked) he raised his offer to fifteen hundred. The lights went on in my head and I realized that there must be something in this. So, looking back, that TV show was my ticket into professional photography. It was amazing to me that you could make money at something that you loved to do. This was so simple. Still photos to me were simply a partnership between me and my camera.

"I became associated with Sting early in his career when I did some work for the Police. Grand Funk's opening act was the Climax Blues Band and their road manager was Miles Copeland. The Police's latest release, Roxanne, had flopped and A&M was considering getting rid of them, but Miles believed in them and wanted some photos he could place. He wanted to make it look like the band was happening so the label wouldn't drop them. Anyone could have just gone in and snapped some pictures of that great looking band, but I wanted to try out some ideas and catch some of the national magazines with my pictures. I did a time exposure with fireworks that hooked into one of their songs. Newsweek loved it and ran it.

"Soon after that I was able to get the Police a half page in Rolling Stone. Several fan magazines followed. I would like to think that my small effort helped Miles turn A&M around. In any event, they decided to re-release Roxanne and this time it hit really big."

Lynn sees photography and music as closely related art forms: "Being a good photographer has to do with balancing things like light, feelings and mood, which is a lot like creating music. When I look through a lens I visualize exactly what I want to accomplish with that photograph. By knowing in advance what it is that you're going for, you have a better chance to make it happen."

She suggests several ways to become an entertainment photographer: "Most people try to break into the business by taking concert shots. Nowadays, it's difficult to get into a good position to shoot pictures at major shows without authorization from the band's management. You can't expect to shoot a Bon Jovi show without credentials. In addition, many bands put a three-song-limit on photographers. It takes time to be recognized, so the people that I photographed in the beginning were not very well known. But, they always were people that I respected as artists. I sought them out and frequently they became life long friends, like Iggy who was in the Prime Movers when I was in the Walking Wounded. If you want to shoot concerts, you'll need a couple of cameras that can take heavy duty knocking about. Other equipment such as a wide angle lens, long lens, and strobes are pretty important for capturing good photos. But that's expensive stuff; expect your initial investment to be close to $1500. Also, don't forget that every time you shoot a roll of film, process it and go to the lab will cost you close to $20."

"If I were just starting out and didn't have a portfolio of pictures to show anybody, I would contact a photographer whose work I admired and literally offer to be their slave. Tell them you'll work free, sweep floors, take out garbage, anything to be their assistant. Being a photographer's assistant is like going to school, only better. I've had a number of assistants throughout my career. The people who come to me from photo school usually seem to be very naive, but the street wise assistants learn very quickly and most of the ones I've had have been able to go out on their own more rapidly.

"For those of you who already have a portfolio, there are a couple of choices. You can approach the small magazines that are looking to pay photographers nothing, but will give you photo credits.

Credits may give you an easier entrance to photograph the world of Rock 'n' Roll. The second option is to go to the artist's management and show them your work. Tell them that you really want to work with their artist. Ask them to consider letting you do some pictures with the band for publicity purposes, that's not going to cost them anything to let you try. I used to write to artists whom I didn't know at all. I sent Frank Zappa samples of my work and told him that I really wanted to photograph him, that I would run it all around to the magazines and, in effect, be like a free publicist for him. He gave me a chance.

"A big part of my business is referrals. Usually one client will mention to another that I did good work. Other times, artists have gotten in touch with me, not because they say I'm a good photographer, but because they heard that I knew Bob Dylan. It is true that you are continually in contact with famous artists, but if that's why you want to get into this business then I guarantee that your art will suffer for it and it will all end up badly.

"There are so many different art forms you can pursue as a photographer. Album covers allow you to be very creative; today you also have video shoots in addition to still photographs, concert shots, newspapers and magazines. Here's what you should never forget: Keep your camera with you at all times. Practice your craft. If you want to be a Rock 'n' Roll photographer start out taking pictures of high school, college and bar bands. Offer to place them in local newspapers or magazines. This makes for a double win, since you and the band will get much needed publicity. Who knows, you may discover a band that you can grow with. Remember, whatever area you choose to work in, it's extremely important to get your portfolio together. It doesn't have to be a selection of famous people, just as long as the work reflects your point of view."

66 *Without a team of*
sound specialists and their state-of-the-art sound
equipment, one-half of what you came for just
wouldn't be there. **99**

Frank Dunnery
IT BITES

Sound Contracting

Bob Goldstein

There is nothing more important to an artist than good sound. If an artist walks on stage in a 20,000 seat facility and his very elaborate light show doesn't work, it's not necessarily the end of the production. There is almost always a couple of spotlights in the building that could function and still do the show. It wouldn't be as good, but they would still be able to do the show and nobody would ask for their money back. However, if the sound doesn't work the show just ends and that's it. The sound contractor has the ultimate responsiblity for all the people and equipment involved in producing that sound.

The sound contractor has the ultimate responsibility for all the people and equipment involved in producing that sound.

In the 1960's, Bob Goldstein played in a band called the Continental Rockers. "At that time there weren't any good bass guitar amps, so I decided to build my own system. Eventually, it became a pretty good sound system." Bob worked for a major electronics company throughout his freshman year at college and played music on the weekends. After one of his gigs, he got a call from someone who wanted to rent his sound system. Before long, his bass guitar amp was being rented out constantly as the sound system for discos.

"The rental business was so good that I formed Maryland Sound, a company that provided sound systems and DJs for parties and night clubs. We also did a lot of sound system installations. I was still playing music on the weekends, but making money with my equipment. There was a big event held during the summer on Pier 1 in Baltimore (now Baltimore's Inner Harbor area). Concerts used to be held from midnight until six o'clock in the morning—Friday, Saturday and Sundays. "As a result of renting out my sound system there, I was offered a job as a disk jockey at a popular club in Baltimore.

"A club owner asked me if I would work as a disk jockey in one of his upstairs rooms during the winter. A lot of big name entertainers performed in the downstairs room at the same club. Eventually, I became the house sound man for the downstairs acts. Roy Clair came through there quite often with Frankie Valle and the Four Seasons and I became friendly with them. Soon Frankie became my first account (he's still with me) and I quit my part-time job as a DJ to concentrate strictly on my business. Since that time I've gone on to work with most of the major touring acts over the last 20 years.

"There are several people responsible for getting the sound system to work to its maximum capabilities. The house engineer has to have an absolute knowledge of how the sound system operates. What the audience hears is the music that is created on stage delivered to them through the sound system under the control of the sound engineer. Generally, he selects the microphones used on stage for different purposes and for different groups. One vocalist might sound great through a certain microphone, yet another vocalist may not. The professional sound engineer also knows how to send the sound signal flow out of the house console to create whatever different 'effects' he wants to make the performance sound like the artist's album. Also, he needs to make acoustical changes in the room itself, so that the sound system works, to 'equalize' the room. The house sound engineer must take all that knowledge and use it to transmit to the audience what the entertainer does on stage and present it in the most favorable light.

79

"A monitor mixer has very much the same job. He has to have the same skills as the engineer, but instead of processing the sound through speakers for the audience, he processes it on speakers that play back the sound to the band. Every member of the band will have his own monitor speaker and own mixture of sound that goes to that speaker. A lead singer may want only his voice and the bass drum. The drummer may only want the bass guitar. A guitarist may want a composite of everything in his speaker. A monitor mixer has to be able to get a good sounding mix for each of them."

There are also sound systems mechanics that go out with the tour and have to know how the system works. The mechanics need to organize themselves by first setting up the speakers and all the equipment, plugging in all the speakers into the amplifiers, linking all the amplifiers in and connecting everything together at the house console. That same mechanic could very easily take care of a microphone or cable that goes bad or for that matter anything else that goes wrong.

It is tribute to Bob's ability to produce terrific sound that his client list is so diverse. "I've always enjoyed worked with Bette Midler. She's an extraodinarily demanding artist, who insists that the sound be perfect in every seat in the hall. She really pushes you to do a good job. We also have been with Hall & Oates, since the mid 70's and they too (along with their management), insist that the sound system be perfect. The same thing applies to Pink Floyd. David Gilmour and Nick Mason are very conscientious when it comes to the quality of sound in their shows. They both are very concerned with achieving high fidelity sound and their thorough understanding of sound systems has been most helpful. They push us to excel, and that's great. It's terrific working with such dedicated people."

Bob's work has taken him to some unique places. Pink Floyd on a recent tour even performed at the front gate of the Palace of Versailles, with the Palace itself acting as a backdrop. "There were 84,000 people there each night in a facility that never had a show before. Pink Floyd literally took over the entire city of Versailles."

Bob has had both practical and formal education in sound. He rates as outstanding a course he took at the Eastman School of Music at the University of Rochester, New York. "I would strongly encourage anyone who wants to get involved in this business to take one of those summer courses. I think Brigham Young also has a full audio course and so do some of the colleges that are a part of the University of California. Of course, there is the RCA Institute in New York as well. Once you obtain some technical knowledge, it would be a good idea to apply at a local sound company for some practical experience. Working in the shop would greatly benefit you in the area of troubleshooting as well as make you aware of all the advances in the industry. After working in the shop for a while, the company would probably send you out to small venues and gradually work you up to the big touring acts. Given all the technical advances in sound over the past several years, it seems that the future holds endless possibilities."

66 **M**aking a performer appear out of a puff of smoke is literally magic. Behind it all is, of course, plenty of careful planning, designing and construction. But it's all worth it if once our audience sees a spectacular opening like that they can never forget us. *99*

K. K. Downing
JUDAS PRIEST

Stage Illusions

Franz Harary

Girls, a word of advice — be nice to that nerd in your science class. He just may be touring with your favorite rock star in a few years. Magician/illusionist Franz Harary was one of those outcasts in junior high school. "Performing magic was a way to impress the friends you had and to make new friends. The weird thing about magic is that a lot of people who get into it become obsessed. It's a way of proving that they are as good as the next person. That's how I got into it, but then I got really intrigued by all of the psychology, the misdirection and what makes people think the way they do."

When Franz Harary was a little kid in elementary school he always participated in school plays, skits, singing, dancing, and anything else that would attract attention. "In junior high school I thought I wanted to be a musical comedy star; you know, singing, dancing, all that stuff. That's really what I pursued all through high school, getting heavily involved with music along with theater and dance. My persistence paid off and I was given a college scholarship to study classical voice. I went to college because I felt that I needed to get a well-rounded education.

"I continued to do magic throughout my four years of college. At the same time that I was studying to be a singer, I was creating illusions for the marching band and orchestra as well as for the ballet and opera at the University of Michigan. Michigan has the foremost marching band and the best opera department in the country with over 2,000 students in the program. It provided a great proving ground for trying out illusions for large audiences. With the marching band, I had 140 people at my disposal and it enabled me to come up with a lot of illusions that could be done on a field. Things like making the trumpet section vanish off the 30 yard line. Because Michigan is not really the hub of special effects or magic, there weren't a lot of people to talk to.

"What happened in those four years was that I came up with principles and theories that allowed illusions to be created that had never been successfully demonstrated before. After graduating from college in 1984, I went to L.A. because I had found out about the Jackson's Victory Tour through Entertainment Tonight. I tracked down the production manager and sent them a video tape of stuff I had done. He gave me the opportunity to set up illusions on that tour.

"The first gig provided a tremendous learning experience for me and I battered my way through the tour. It certainly had its trying times. During the tour we had designed everything inside the sound stage in L.A. When we got to the location outdoors, I found that I had completely forgotten about the winds. Perhaps I was a little overcome by the fact that for the first time in my life money was no object; I could design or build anything that I wanted.

"Consequently, I forgot all about the elements, which was the main thing that got me there in the first place. One illusion I designed for the show was to make Michael float up in the air and disappear. In Kansas City we had nasty winds that continued throughout showtime. Before I knew it, Michael was not floating up, but all over the place completely out of control. My heart stopped. That's it. My career is over. I was sure that I was on my way back home to Michigan doing banquets. But, I calmed down and figured out a way to restage it. We had Tito Jackson hold on to Michael at all times during the levitation. Fortunately it worked and the crowd loved it.

"From there I did a whole mess of stuff for Alice Cooper, demonstrating lights going through a person's body. In another bit,

Alice takes pieces of junk and garbage and builds them up into a robot. Suddenly, the robot comes to life, attacks and chases him on stage. Then Alice chases it up to a platform and breaks it apart into a zillion little pieces. For Kool and the Gang, I did an effect where I turned Kool's head 360 degrees. That got a real killer response from the audience.

"There's definitely a future in Rock 'n' Roll for illusionists who can design effects. You've got to love magic before you can even think about making a career out of it. Start in the library and research the history of the craft. Once you find a magic shop, you'll meet the local talent. They will help you if they see that you're sincerely interested. Work on tricks in front of any size audience. Do kids' parties, rotary meetings, county fairs, etc. You've got to learn all you can about lighting, staging, and basic set engineering. Courses in psychology will teach you how to manipulate people's perceptions, which is a big part of designing illusions. When your big break comes along, you'll not only have an understanding of the psychological aspect of magic, but will also be knowledgeable from a materials and structures standpoint. This will give you a decided advantage over other entrants in the field."

66 Rocky — *a complex man, survivor of riots at Long Beach and Grasshoppers at the Rainbow. Always there, sometimes mixing the sound from 3 feet under the board. Will turn it up to "11" if you ask him. Got more stories than J. D. Salinger. All bowed up with no place to go.* **99**

Mike D.
THE BEASTIE BOYS

Monitor Mixing

Kevin Holman

A monitor is a speaker that the band listens to as opposed to the sound that the audience hears. Some say mixing monitors is an interesting job — others say for 90 minutes a night it's the worst job in show business. You are definitely in the hot seat. You're on the side of the stage and if the artist doesn't like what he/she hears, boy, do you know about it in a hurry.

Kevin (Rocky) Holman got tired of all the B.S. from "so-called managers" who kept telling him how famous they were going to make him. Being a drummer with a band that never quite made it and didn't look like they would in the foreseeable future, Rocky quit. "Having become more than a bit disenchanted with the whole scene I started to work with some of the successful bands in the area. So, I humped gear, drove trucks, did some lighting and built speaker cabinets. From there, it was off to Hollywoood to live with some friends who had a band. The proverbial being at the right place at the right time happened for me and I moved up to bigger acts.

"While hanging out in L.A. going nowhere fast, I began hanging around at the Gino Vanelli rehearsals with a friend of mine who worked for him. As it so happened, the drummer broke his arm. I ended up with the gig. It lasted two weeks. At the end of the two weeks, they no longer needed me but we got along so well that they kept me on as the stage manager. It was on this tour that I met the guys from Audio Analysts. Shortly after being on tour with Gino Vanelli, I was hired by Audio Analyst for whom I have worked ten years as a monitor mixer for bands like Journey, Molly Hatchet, Loverboy and Billy Squire. Currently I'm on the road with Bon Jovi.

"A monitor mixer takes different instruments that want to be heard on stage by the various members of the band. For instance, certain drummers only like to hear the vocalist and maybe a bass player; others play off the guitar player. The monitor also acts as a reference point. It's a way for singers to pitch.

"What the audience hears is everything mixed together. If there's a group that's running 60 inputs into the house console, the crowd is going to hear a mixture of those 60 sounds all blended together. Whereas the monitor mixer may have 36 of those inputs that the band needs to hear. Most times the band doesn't listen to everything that's going through my board. Sounds that are utilized to enhance their music will often times throw somebody off.

"Many arenas provide a very poor environment for live music, consequently you can be standing right next to a guitar player and his amplifier may be running at 120 decibels, but you can't hear it. Therefore, the monitors must be positioned on stage so that they're pointing at the artists enabling them to play as a band."

Rocky recalls that you used to see big black wedge-shaped things laying all over the stage. These days, however, artists are hip to "the look" and so the monitors are often sunk underneath the stage. "This may be appealing to the eye," says Rocky, but it causes the monitor mixer to lose 30% of the capability of the box."

"A monitor console, any mixing console for that matter, can be rather intimidating when you first look at it. It's important to keep in mind that there are 40 repetitions of the same circuit on the input side and 16 repetitions of the same thing on the opposite side and you only deal with one at a time. One input can be sent to 16 different outputs. Each one of them looks exactly the same on the board. The wiring leading from the back of the board dictates where they will go."

Rocky has developed some extraordinary abilities: "You can whistle a frequency and I can tell you what it is. This comes from being in the the same environment every day and listening to feedback and other audio gremlins. Today, the new kids on the block all have frequency analyzers. It isn't necessary to recognize frequencies; all you have to do is look over at the display. But, then again, you don't know what you're hearing when something bothers you out there. You can't tell what the problem is until it feeds back to you, and then you rely on your experience to rectify the situation."

One problem for Rocky is that artists may complain about the sound on the monitor just as a way to blow off steam. "Perhaps they had a fight with their wife or girlfriend, maybe someone has a bellyache, your guess is as good as mine. You have to keep in mind that most times you're dealing with someone with a very sensitive personality." Handling those personalities is a very big part of the job.

"As far as advising someone on how to get into the business, hell, I had a great time driving Ryder trucks around all the midwest. A word of warning — for every good time I had there was a miserable night on a snowy road. Today, you can go to school to be a roadie. It's weird. There are schools and networks that you can attend. In fact, I know people who were hired from those sources. I do know that some of the major companies have hired people out of these schools. There's no school, however, that can teach you what it's like out on the road. That's something that you can only learn by doing it. The fact is that you must pay your dues to succeed in Rock 'n' Roll. Most people get their start by working with local bands and progress upward, there are no shortcuts."

"Once I decided to become a monitor mixer I knew it was just going to be a matter of time before I 'made it.' The thing that was scaring me was whether I would be able to hold out long enough on the money I had saved until I hit the big time. The frustration factor that builds up inside of you comes from chasing an endless amount of leads that never materialize. You just sit there after being away from home for months and you say to yourself, am I just reaching for it or what? Is this really going to happen? When it does finally happen you work twice as hard."

The typical day for the sound crew means going in at 8:00 o'clock in the morning and not leaving until 1:00 o'clock in the morning the next day. Rocky says, "You're constantly putting in 18 hour days in this business. You may get away from it for an hour or so in the afternoon, if you're a senior sound guy, but not if you're the fourth man on the sound crew. As the 'cable maggot' you better be there from load in to load out because if one of the older guys on the crew is looking around for you in the afternoon and he doesn't find you — watch out. You'll be the fourth man until they get sick of seeing you and then you'll be unemployed. But, if you can hack the long hours and the sacrifices that are necessary to make it, then come on."

66 When something
unpleasant and unexpected comes up on your tour,
an accident, a security problem, a promoter's bad
check or a broken down bus, the first call you
make is to your lawyer. If you've got the right one,
he or she will stay up all that night to worry and
you will be able to go to bed and sleep like a
baby. **99**

Bill Curbishley, Manager
THE WHO

Entertainment Law

Joi Huckaby

Lawyers have to adapt their training and skills to lots of different worlds. Joi Huckaby, as an attorney for a tour, must start worrying many months before the first concert and can't relax until after the final show. Here's how her role relates to the rest of the touring organization.

Joi Huckaby never thought she would ever be involved in the careers of people like Robert Palmer, Cyndi Lauper or Judas Priest. Like most young people who are thinking about the possibility of a career in law, Joi's early images of lawyers came from history books, television and mystery stories rather than from Rolling Stone magazine. She graduated with honors from a prestigious New England college and went on to Harvard Law School, where again she did brilliantly. In fact, she did so well that she was offered a job at one of New York's biggest and most successful "corporate" law firms doing high powered work in the department of mergers and acquisitions. But Joi had always loved theatre, music (particularly

Rock 'n' Roll) and dance. In fact, earlier in her life she had studied ballet and had dreams of a career on stage.

"The life of a Wall Street lawyer wasn't for me, even with the salary and generous benefits that go with such a job." She longed to be involved with creative people and began thinking about a change in career direction. Two years after she started her Wall Street career, the big break came when she heard that a New York firm (Beldock Levine & Hoffman) was looking for a top young lawyer to learn entertainment work and that they were particulary seeking someone with a top academic background and experience in corporate finance work. She applied and got the job, "an exciting chance to work under the direction of lawyers, who worked with such important artists as the Who, Yes, Robert Palmer, Roberta Flack, Cyndi Lauper, Jeff Beck and a lot of others."

Starting from her first day on the job she was made responsible for overseeing the negotiations between various managers and the suppliers of touring services, such as trucking companies, bus and equipment suppliers, sound and light companies, stage designers and the like. "I have to draft and review their contracts, monitor their work during the tour and deal with a lot of unexpected problems that come up on every tour." A large part of this work requires her to know about the merchandising business, an important and necessary part of every tour.

"Every relationship between the parts that make up the body of a tour must be described, written down and made into an agreement." It takes a special skill to write them so clearly and simply that they can be understood and followed by everyone involved. "Most of these contracts require you to understand what really happens on a tour so that you can describe on paper what each person is expected to do, what he can expect from all the others and what he will be paid for his work. It is now common for one of the performances on an important tour to be broadcast 'live' and sometimes one of our artists may decide to make a film or a television 'special' out of his performances on the tour." These are complicated arrangements and a lawyer's experience and skill are necessary. Then too, Joi says there are times ("thankfully rare") when someone in the audience gets injured by stepping on a broken bottle or is the target of a firecracker thrown by a foolish fan; but here the lawyer needs to do little more than put the claimant and the insurance company together in the same room for settlement.

The work of a lawyer during most of a well-run tour can be just "standing by." That means that while a client is out on the road, lawyers like Joi have to "know where everybody is each day of the tour and where they can be reached whenever necessary. Lines of communication must be left open 7 days a week. You must make yourself available at a moment's notice. You never know if the artist or someone else on the tour may need your help on an urgent matter." The kinds of call she dreads the most (but has to deal with) are those that involve accidents on the road. Such an incident occurred during a Judas Priest concert when someone in the audience threw a firecracker. "You know it's not your artist's fault, but you still worry about somebody getting hurt at a show that's supposed to be fun." Even though a good part of her work is done at a desk or with a pen or dictaphone, Joi says, "While one of our clients is on tour my mind is never completely off duty."

For the most part, lawyers rarely have to be on the road or at particular concerts, but Joi admits, "It's hard to do all the work and all that worrying and never see what it looks like when it comes together on stage." Like most other lawyers in the business, Joi makes it a point to attend the performances of her clients when they play in or near New York City. "Sometimes you meet backstage for the first time people you've been dealing with on the telephone and fax machine for months, maybe years."

Joi feels that she is extremely fortunate to be learning from the example of some of the most experienced attorneys in the entertainment industry. One of the senior partners in her firm "has been doing this since the days of Jimi Hendrix and was involved one way or the other in every big jazz and rock festival starting with the daddy of them all, the Newport Jazz Festival, back in the late 1950's right up through Woodstock, Watkins Glen and Live Aid. He's taught me that the most useful thing a lawyer can do is to worry about problems before they happen so that the problems never happen at all."

These days it seems that many more lawyers than ever before are interested in entertainment careers. "I don't blame them," says Joi, "but they ought to understand that you quickly realize that the important word in the name of the career is 'lawyer,' not entertainment. You must be the best lawyer you can possibly be to begin with."

The hours can be terribly long and the work, because it is entertainment, can often require your time and attention late at night and on weekends. Furthermore, you may often be working for clients who are still "on the way up" and can't begin to afford the kinds of fees that corporate lawyers charge on Wall Street. Unlike Wall Street, where the size of the fee is the measure of everything, an entertainment lawyer begins to measure his own success by the progress of his client's career or the success of a tour. "That can be the real satisfaction."

Joi would advise young lawyers interested in entertainment careers to "pay attention to high school, college and law school training, and do as well as possible so that the best schools with the best teachers will be available to you." The best jobs, she says, are often the hardest to get, "so you've got to bring all the qualifications you can when you're applying for one of them."

Before moving a lawyer into the area of entertainment, Joi's firm believes that lawyers must become skilled in general legal work, particularly litigation or contracts. "At the same time, however, they encourage me to spend several hours a week reading the 'trade' magazines and newspapers (like Variety, Billboard, Performance, Hollywood Reporter, etc.) so I can pick up a broad knowledge and vocabulary of the industry, including the new technologies, the new media and all of the other trends and developments." While entertainment law job openings are scarce, Joi feels that "keeping informed through the trades may alert you to new possibilities and ways to use your legal training and skills in the entertainment industry.

"Sometimes I sound like I'm complaining about having to leave word wherever I am so that people on the tour can reach me in an emergency," Joi admits, "but I'm not really complaining at all. In fact, I'm boasting that there are people out there who need me and want to be sure that they can find me on a few minutes' notice. It's a terrific feeling and I wouldn't trade it for anything."

> **66 The audience shouldn't know about all those rehearsals and sound checks you have before you open the doors and let them in. It's like an athlete or a magician does, you have to make something that's hard look like it's easy. 99**
>
> **Stanley "Buckwheat" Dural, Jr.
> BUCKWHEAT ZYDECO**

Studio Equipment Rental

Mike Johnson

Before a show goes out on the road it needs lots of rehearsal time and a place to do it in. For the big tours, a garage won't do. The people who operate rehearsal studios are specialists in seeing that performers have everything they need to get their shows ready for the road, including renting to the band much of the equipment and musical instruments for the engagements ahead. S.I.R., in New York and California, is at the head of everybody's list and Mike Johnson was responsible for getting it there.

Studio Instrument Rentals is a company that has production facilities throughout the United States. Although best known for renting band equipment and rehearsal studios, they also rent audio/visual and sound equipment as well as provide storage area to the working musician. When the company was formed in 1967 there weren't any companies that rented guitars, amps, drums, etc. — they just didn't exist. A music store in those days was mainly a record store that had some sheet music and a few drum sets, perhaps a few brand name amplifiers or guitars. Under no circumstance would they dream of renting out equipment to, say, Jimi Hendrix at the Whiskey A-Go-Go for one night.

1967 was an extraordinary time in the music industry and there was a huge need for rehearsal studios, which for the most part weren't available. Bands rehearsed in basements and living rooms. Getting a "studio" usually meant, at best, a dance studio with linoleum floors, no air conditioning and a vocal master P.A. Ken Berry and Dolph Rempp (the founders of S.I.R.) recognized this need and built a facility for rehearsals. Soon after it was built, Mike Johnson (now a partner) was rehearsing there with his band in the hope of making a record. When the group failed to get a recording contract everyone went back home except Mike, who stayed on to work with Ken and Dolph. He has never regretted for a minute having made that move. "Deciding to work for S.I.R. was a difficult decision for me. Being a musician was my first ambition, but after five or six years of starving, you start looking at other aspects of show business."

Mike began working at the San Francisco location in 1971. Like most people in the business he started out at the bottom. The first facility cost him $300 a month in a building with no air conditioning and held one studio. "I slept in the attic and must've worked 100 hours a week on the average. But, I loved it. I was young and it didn't matter how many hours I worked because I was having fun."

Even though this early branch of S.I.R. barely had enough equipment to fill an Econoline van, it was a still a 7-day a week, 24-hour a day job. Mike didn't mind living in the S.I.R. office, but he had to go to the YMCA for showers. "There was no money in it for the first year, but it really didn't make a difference to me. I was 18 and had the possibility of owning a piece of my own company, being my own boss and getting to work with some of the greatest bands of all time. It was very exciting. I had fallen in love with music when I was 12 years old."

For young Mike Johnson it was an incredible trip: "The first bands I worked with included the Doors, Jimi Hendrix, Grateful Dead, Janis Joplin, Cream, Led Zeppelin and Crosby, Stills, Nash & Young." They all had a need for rehearsal time and to rent equipment. Although they had their own equipment, it was never enough to cover all the venues that they were playing."

Mike left San Francisco about 1973 when S.I.R. opened a studio in New York. His first New York rehearsal clients were equally impressive: David Bowie and Barry Manilow. Aside from a major adjustment in lifestyle, Mike made a smooth transition into the New York market. Besides renting band gear to local bands, S.I.R. began renting to many European acts on both an extended basis for U.S. tours as well as just one or two dates that they might be playing in New York. In addition, S.I.R. expanded its services and started to supply small portable risers that could be used not only for local gigs, but for movie sets and musical TV shows. It was simply cheaper for a TV network that was flying a band in from Australia to play three songs to rent band gear from S.I.R. than to fly equipment roundtrip, paying for both the air freight and road crews. S.I.R. was soon providing the equipment and local transportation for many of the biggest shows on television.

"When I got to New York, once again I worked by myself, but eventually was able to hire one employee, then a second. Most days we were coming in at 8:00 a.m. and leaving at midnight. We did everything that needed to be done from setting up rehearsals to answering phones to going out to deliver pianos. We even had to clean the toilets and sweep the floors. The business continued to grow and as we became more organized we computerized our business. We programmed the computers to handle billing, accounts payable and accounts receivable, etc. Those computers, by the way, really helped us to do the volume of business that we have done in the past 15 years.

"Today, there are countless ways to get into this business. Most of the tour, road, and stage managers that I know started by humping gear or being a gofer. Often times, these same people were loyal to an unknown act, who made it big and they became successful along with the band. I'm where I am today because someone gave me a chance to prove myself. For that very reason I'm willing to give others the same opportunity. Basically, all you need is a good attitude, a driver's license, some common sense and a willingness to work for a low starting wage. Generally, I hire people with no experience. I would rather hire a young person with a good attitude who's willing to work hard and learn things the right way as opposed to someone who has bad work habits and who would go back to doing things their own way when I wasn't looking. I like working with young people. I'm constantly looking for them and I'm willing to give any honest, hardworking kid a chance. All I need him to do is be on time and work hard for me. I'll teach him everything he needs to know."

95

This kind of training at S.I.R. seems to be very effective. "Many of the top production people, road and stage managers, have come directly from my staff over the last 15 or 16 years. In fact, I know of 10 tours out right now whose top echelon people are former S.I.R. employees. It's not that S.I.R. is the only place to work. There are nightclubs, sound and light companies or jobs where you can learn to drive a tour bus. Even accounting firms need junior accountants, bookkeepers and other clerical workers. You can sometimes offer your services to an entertainment law firm, a management company or promoter and find that they need new recruits.

"You can also try to go to work for a recording studio. You'll start out by doing the clean up and helping to set up. The next step up is to be an assistant engineer and then the engineer. If you have talent, maybe you will be a studio manager. Promoters all across the country usually need three to four good technical people to assist the band when they come in. There are music departments at many universities that are starting to get very nicely organized where you may find work. There are a limitless number of avenues to pursue, so if you really have the desire to be a part of this business you can do it!"

> **"You wanna hear a real Rock 'n' Roll nightmare? — The Promoter forgot to pay his electric bill, the hall is packed and we go on in ten minutes."**
>
> **Joey Ramone**

Power

Paul Josewitch

Paul Josewitch's background is electrical and electronic engineering, but he got the idea to become a power expert after supplying a generator for a James Taylor concert in Central Park. Paul remembers: "James Taylor needed a generator to power his show. We saw more and more people producing sound and lighting packages, but not many companies providing true electrical services for these events. Through a natural growth process we've applied our thinking and designing to create this massive amount of electrical equipment that we use." Today, S.B.P. is one of the foremost power companies in the country.

Paul has since lent his expertise to Bruce Springsteen, Michael Jackson, Live Aid and even to Ronald Reagan. "We designed all of the distribution equipment for the President when he visited Russia. This clearly demonstrates that S.B.P. is more than just a power company; we are an engineering company as well. For the 1986 Statue of Liberty events, Paul estimates that they used over 200,000 feet of heavy duty welding cable (that's forty miles of cable) to power the event. "For a concert, we provide work lights and transformers to give both the sound and lighting companies the energy they need to put on the show. When Springsteen went overseas, we provided the transformers that we built specifically for overseas applications.

"We consult and provide the electrical end including designing electric distribution systems for all the performing arts. Our basic function is to provide power, by either creating or transforming it. Normally, a major act will contact us and inform us of their power needs. We go out to look at the venues and determine what power is available and what we have to supplement or modify in each venue to provide their required energy."

There are many different jobs available within a power company, sales staff, electricians, clericals, and engineers. Paul's engineers are particularily important to him. "They are responsible for designing and updating equipment to meet (and often establish) industry safety standards. Being an innovator, we are looked upon by different testing agencies because we are not using conventional means to create what we are doing. In other words, we're not buying extension cords that have been tested by X, Y or Z. We are actually designing the format to provide this energy for specific programs.

"Most of our electricians come to us with (at the very least) some technical ability, not necessarily technical knowledge. We can train an individual, but he needs both the ability to learn and the desire to succeed in life. We want people who really want to work to gain both an education and a bright future. We are not looking for the person who is merely looking to pay his bills for a certain period of time. Our company policy concerning 'substance usage' is strictly adhered to. No drugs or alcohol is permitted anywhere in the company's operations. Unfortunately, this is a major problem in today's world, but if you consume alcohol while working for us, you're immediately removed from duty.

"One of the biggest problems in today's high tech world of production is that there is always something that, often at the last minute, has to be added, moved, tested or modified. Because of the frequent changes in the production, a knowledgeable person must remain on location at all times. What distinguishes S.B.P. from others is that we are a power company that designs the specifications for all of the equipment we build. We have engineers on duty who take care of problems for other people who just say they're engineers. Our electricians are licensed by the state in which we operate and are members of associations statewide. They are kept abreast of both new and modified electrical codes, so that we remain on top of things at all times. A person can call me from anywhere in the world, explain their power problem and our engineering team can solve it for them."

For those seriously interested in a career with a power company. Paul says, "The best thing to do is go to some events and see who is doing the power for them. Become an electrical groupie and you'll find out what kind of production is going on and who is doing it. Then contact these people. Let's say, for example, our trucks (with eight inch letters) are parked outside a venue, why not write down our number and call us. Go to a show and spend some time not necessarily backstage, but at the back of the venue and see what's available. You'll notice a power company or a generator that was delivered by some company or another. Contact these companies and see if there is a position available. Volunteer to sweep the floors, if that's what it takes to get in at the ground level."

Paul's ideal applicant is someone who is a self starter and has a true thirst for learning. "You have to perform, continue to study, get to the venue on time, and stay constantly on the run. You have to be on location and take care of your clients. There are many sacrifices, long hours and low pay for starters. The concert industry itself is not known for being particularly high paying, unless you are the performer. In order to grow, you must put in long hours. This is not a nine to five job. If that's what you're looking for then my suggestion would be to work for an electrical company that does parking lot lighting. However, I find that most people prefer the excitement that the entertainment business provides. There's a certain trade-off in that you have to pay for it through the efforts of extended labor."

66 *The sound man is out front at the board hearing what the audience hears. What we hear on stage from our monitors is entirely different. An artist therefore has no choice but to entrust the most important element of his show — how he sounds — to that technician somewhere out there in the dark.* **99**

Robert Palmer

Sound System Technician
Michael Keifer

When Michael "Hoss" Keifer was a teenager, his best friend was a drummer in a garage band that went out on the weekends to do shows. "I would be the guy who would go with them and set up (for no money) just to be a part of it. For as far back as I can remember, even when I was in school — I was always hanging out with people who were musicians." Well, the musicians that Hoss hangs out with now are a little better known than his old schoolmates. They include a lot of Billy's with last names like Joel, Squire and Idol. Of course, you can throw in Journey, Tiffany and quite a few others as well.

Having done his thing in venues from Milwaukee to Moscow and virtually every big city and small town in between, Hoss has worked his way up to the big time. As an employee of Audio Analysts, he designs and sets up sound systems for concerts and operates monitor and house sound boards. "When I first started out, I was what we call a 'cable maggot.' The maggot runs all the cabling, all the electricity, all the power to the amp racks and all the speaker wires. That's quite a bit of work. Once that task is completed the sound people fly (hang) the PA in the air so the crowd in the back of the big arenas can hear what everybody is playing on stage."

The head of Audio Analysts, the company that employs Hoss, has this to say about him: "A million dollar sound system isn't worth a dime if a 50 cent part fails and your staff cannot repair it on the spot. We just don't put anyone out on tour with our systems. They have to be the best. Hoss Keifer has filled that bill on many tours."

In addition to getting ready to do a show each night, Hoss has to do the everyday maintenance. "On the road we usually have four guys working. One guy is a technician, one guy does cabling, one guy sets up system sound boards and one guy will mike the stage. We pretty much keep all the bases covered.

"Although there are times that I find more bad than good to say about the business," says Hoss, "it has afforded me opportunities that very few people will ever get. One of one big ones was the chance to go to the Soviet Union. Billy Joel performed in Russia and we were there for two and a half weeks. From the time of arrival the production staff was pretty busy all the time. In fact, we probably had a total of just one or two days off. Part of the reason that the work load was extra heavy was that part of the crew was made up of Russian soldiers. Naturally, they were inexperienced, which made the set-up take much longer than usual.

"I stayed in the Hotel Moscow which someone told me has 7,000 rooms. The hotel is huge, but the rooms are real dinky. They had tiny single beds and TV sets that got only one station. The funny thing was that the hall monitors spoke English. One day I needed some laundry done and the monitor told me to just give it to the maid and she would do it for me. That's exactly what I did and when I came home she had it hanging up to dry over my bathtub."

"Billy did four shows in Moscow and played for something like two and a half hours a night. The crowds were very reserved initially, then they really got into it. They loved it. In direct contrast to that excitement and exuberance was the fact that it was like living through the Great Depression over there. You would walk into these huge stores and they would only have four pairs of pants in the whole place. It was really weird and somewhat difficult to explain. It is very depressing. Plus, the people have a problem with body odor.

Perhaps it's because the water is green there. I mean you can't drink it or bathe in it every day like we're used to doing. There's nothing like the USA, I'll tell you that.

"The best way to go about getting into the business is to try to get on as a local stagehand. As an IA (the stagehand's union) local working in your hometown, you'll start learning a little about the business before you dive in straight ahead. That's the way we hire a lot of people. Of course, another way would be to hook up with a local band or nightclub and learn as much as you possibly can before going out on the road. The technical aspect of sound is gained primarily through experience. There are technical schools but working as a cable maggot would be a better choice because it provides first hand experience.

"One of the good parts about being on the road is that you get to see a lot of the country and you usually get paid well to do that. You can make some really good money and meet a lot of nice people. Bad features are the long hours and long bus rides, which are not fun. Most people think this job is a lot more glamorous than it is. What they don't realize is that it's a lot of hard work.

"When I got into this business, I was single. It was great travelling all over the world. Now that I'm married and have a daughter, it's tough to leave home for months at a time. If you're a young guy with no ties at home, here's some advice. Get out on the road, make a ton of money, meet nice people and a lot of women. But most of all, work hard and build a great career for yourself."

66 *From gruel at The Capitol to sushi at Giants Stadium, with a bottle of Dom or a 6-pack of Bud, Cy is the gourmet master of Rock 'n' Roll.* **99**

Frank Stedtler, Production Manager
MONSTERS OF ROCK 1988

Catering

Cy Kocis

Like an army, a concert tour travels on its stomach. The work and hours are tough and food "breaks" are often the only form of relaxation available. Cy Kocis runs a catering business that provides good, healthy food to touring bands on location.

A typical day starts around 7:00 in the morning (sometimes earlier) when the crews come in for breakfast. "Of course, this doesn't count all of the prep work the day before or the time you spend going to the market. We also serve lunch and dinner to the entire entourage as well as supply all of the dressing rooms. Normally the shows are over about 11:00 and we prepare light foods for the band. By the time we load up it's usually 1 or 2 o'clock in the morning. Then we go onto the next site when we are doing a tour.

"The meals we prepare cover all kinds of cuisine: Japanese, Chinese, Italian, French, Middle Eastern, anything. Sometimes people will make some unusual requests: specialty items like roast pig, or something like sushi prepared in their dressing room. If dinner

103

is American cuisine, such as steak, you may go through 30 pounds of meat in one particular meal. It always depends on the amount of people you are feeding. During an average show we usually serve dinner to 50–75 people."

Cy got his start in the catering business when a friend of his who was working for a rock promoter called and said they needed a backstage cook. "I used to cook strictly as a hobby and my friends all seemed to like it. When I was asked if I wanted the job I didn't know what to say. But, I thought — why not? I'll give it a try. I had recently left my job as a respiratory therapist and felt that this was as good a time as any. My first assignment was to feed 300 people working on a Pink Floyd concert. It was an outside show, which allowed us to barbecue the food. We had shrimp scampi, barbecued ribs and chicken, steaks, kabobs of vegtables and grilled swordfish. Fortunately, everything turned out well. The crew gave us a standing ovation! Later, the band marched over and stood in front of us and applauded. It made us all feel great!"

Among the artists who have enjoyed Cy's food while on tour have been Michael Jackson, Van Halen, Stevie Wonder, Pat Benatar and the Grateful Dead. "Michael had his own cook taking care of his meals back at the hotel. However, we would take care of that phase of his life at the venues. We would prepare anything that Michael wanted in the dressing room. Primarily, it was fresh fruit juices; he's a pretty straight eater and didn't want anything that unusual.

"There is a lot of interaction between the cooks and the band members. The kitchen is the place where people hang out, just like at home. Where does everybody hang out when you have a party? The kitchen.

"Carlos Santana and his band are wonderful people to work for. They're very friendly people and appreciative of our work. James Taylor never forgets to come back and say thank you. He likes to hang out after the meal. The Springsteen people were really nice too. The more you travel with a band, the more interaction you have with them. The kitchen becomes a sanctuary for the artist. On the Michael Jackson tour I had my own little private dining area so that certain people could get away and not have to worry about being bothered. That worked out real well. It's just nice to meet nice people.

"I have some promoters that I regularly work with at particular venues. When their shows come up, we'll get those gigs. Also, certain bands that come into town will ask us to do the show. The catering aspect of the music business is huge."

Cy observes that the business of catering for tours is growing rapidly: "There are a lot of caterers getting involved in doing the backstage work throughout the country. Some areas are still lacking a little bit, but for the most part, promoters are beginning to retain their own food people or hire local restaurants to fulfill their catering needs."

Cy believes that would-be show caterers have several ways to go: "In order to to get into the business it may be necessary to hook up with a catering or food service that works with a local promoter. Admittedly, it may not be all that easy to get direct access to the promoter. Therefore, this indirect approach may be your best bet. Standard cooking schools can teach you about cooking for masses of people. Often times I have to set up my own kitchen and bring it with me. Naturally, if you have the $200,000 to invest in a mobile kitchen — that's great. But, it's tough for most people starting out to get that much money going. If you decide that this is really something you want to do, don't be discouraged by the long hours or rejections when starting out. It takes time to get established and you get a lot of work through word of mouth and reputation. The main ingredient that you must put into your food is caring. Give a damn about what you're doing. It's the feeling that you put into the food that makes the big difference."

66 *It is impossible to predict what will happen in a concert environment from show to show, how a crowd may react on a particular night. But one incident, no matter how small, can do a disproportionate amount of damage to an artist, promoter or venue. A professional and experienced security company helps keep concerts running smoothly from before the time the doors open until the parking lot is empty after the show.* **99**

Rick Sales, Manager
SLAYER

Tour Security

Pete Kranske

Concert audiences can be huge. That is why there are now specialty companies that provide security, crowd control, ushering, ticket taking, parking and box office services. Some companies are local while others service many cities across the United States and employ thousands of people. Pete Kranske and partner Damon Zumwalt started such a company. Today, they are without question, the epitome of equal opportunity employers.

During the late 1960's there began to be a number of fights at the local dances in San Diego that appeared to be either ethnic or racially motivated. In order to deal with this problem Damon Zumwalt organized a group of young men from all different backgrounds, but well known in the area, to act as bouncers. The men he recruited were surfers, Samoans, Blacks, Caucasians and Latinos. According to Pete Kranske, "Damon got the leaders of all these groups together. They were real good squared away guys. These were the kind of people who were looked up to in their communities and he started this peer group type of security." One of the men he hired was Tyrone Young, an All-California athlete in both football and baseball as well as Mr. Junior World in body building. "All the young people looked up to Ty and so they didn't want him mad at them. When he would ask them to stop doing something, they would stop."

This concept worked so well that several local rock promoters called Damon to ask if they could use his staff to work at their concerts. A Los Angeles concert promoter (Steve Wolf) approached Damon about providing security at his L.A. venues. At this point Damon knew he was in business. He began to recruit UCLA students and that is how he met college football star Pete Kranske.

While growing up, Pete was always involved in athletics. A football player and wrestler in high school, he wanted to be either a football coach or an attorney after graduating. His first year of college was spent at Virginia Military Institute, but he transferred to UCLA following his freshman year. At UCLA, Pete not only excelled on the football field but was also an important member of the wrestling team. Pete got involved working on rock concerts as your "basic" security guy. "It just so happened that Damon and I worked well together and I was given more and more responsibility. A couple years later we entered into a partnership and have been in business ever since. Incidentally, besides providing services for rock concerts we also do the same for athletic events. For instance, we have done the last 12 Super Bowl games and in an average year we'll do 76 football games and 26 stadium concerts.

"The first big act that we ever did was the Rolling Stones. Since that time we've done virtually every major group including super acts like Bruce Springsteen and Pink Floyd at the L.A. Coliseum. We have also been out on tours. We were the national security directors for the Jackson's Victory tour. The eleven guys that went out with the tour made sure that the Jacksons didn't have any problems." Damon has toured with the Beach Boys for a number of years and Pete has done a lot of shows with Van Halen. "In addition, we have provided the security consulting for the last 2 Run DMC tours.

"We maintain a high degree of supervision over our staff. The structure is similar to a military organization with one person running the event. We'll have lieutenants, who go around to deal with the major problems. Every area is carefully monitored. There is a director, whose men go around to take care of each individual area of the venue and report any problems. Everybody is highly monitored. Briefings are held prior to every event to make sure that the security force understands what is required of them. At this time they are given written handouts so should they have any questions — the answers will be right there in front of them.

"Our main responsibilities are making sure that everyone with a ticket gets into the show and back out of the show in a safe and peaceful manner. Some of the problems that we have are a result of people getting excited about the show. Rather than stay in their seats, they want to come down to the front of the stage, which fills up the aisles. Also, there are those who like to try to get back stage without the proper credentials. Sometimes we have to deal with people who might have their judgment or behavior altered by alcohol or drugs."

These problems are dealt with efficiently and professionally.

"We recruit from universities, military installations, civic groups, athletic teams and ROTC units. We look to groups where we can reach a large number of responsible people at the same time. The people who want to work with us are carefully screened. Interviews are conducted to determine who fits our needs. This doesn't mean that you have to be a 6'5", 250 pound football player. There are three specific qualities that we are looking for in a person: honesty, reliability and intelligence. That comes in all size packages, in all colors, and all races. Like the Marines — we're just looking for a few good people."

> *66 **No** matter how great your shows are, or how much the audience loves them, the cost of touring is enormous and a lot of tours don't show any profit at all at the end of the day. Even so, you must have someone along to see that, at the very least, you get what you were promised. 99*

Tony Iommi,
BLACK SABBATH

Tour Accounting

Jeff Krump

To many touring performers, Jeff Krump is just as important as any member of their band. Jeff is the guy who settles up with the promoter after each show and makes sure that the musicians get all the money that they've earned, something that Jeff's done literally thousands of times. The slighest oversight on a major tour could cost the band hundreds of thousands of dollars.

"If over the course of a 100 date tour the accountant can improve even one expense by $100 a show, that's $10,000 by the end of the tour. Many major tours will generate approximately $30-$40 million by the time it's all said and done. That's a tremendous amount of money and most of it is cash at one point or another." Although all that cash doesn't flow directly through the hands of the accountant it still has to be accounted for. As you can see, finding a 1% leakage can save the band $30,000-$40,000. This is very serious money.

That's why tour accountants like Jeff Krump are well paid. "A touring accountant who works for a smaller band probably earns

109

around $750 a week plus per diems. If you're doing a whole lot of heavy duty settlements for a major act there are some accountants out there making $3,000 a week or better. Real good ones are well worth that. It doesn't take much to justify $3,000 a week salary — when there are some bands that might otherwise waste that much during each show."

A tour accountant has to coordinate the money coming in and the expenditures going out. Jeff says it costs a fortune to keep an average arena touring entourage on the road, excluding any pay for the artist himself. "Just the road crew's salary, sound fees, light fees, lasers, pyrotechnics, trucking, buses, hotels, salaries, per diems, all that kind of stuff runs roughly $100,000 a week. There are many tours that cost twice as much and stadium tours can easily cost over $500,000. This is strictly overhead and doesn't count any salaries for the artists. It also doesn't count management or booking agency commissions or other professional fees. Even as the tour is just starting up there is a tremendous amount of money that exchanges hands in order to get things running. The recent Aerosmith tour operated with a road crew of about thirty-five people. In addition, there were five tractor trailers full of equipment, two buses and a private jet. The entourage was made up of about forty people. All of them got paid, all of them had expenses, and they all stayed in hotels."

As the money comes in Jeff's the one who accounts for it to make sure the band is getting all the revenue it's supposed to get. "During and after a show, the promoter and I sit down and determine how much money came in, first by verifying the number of tickets that were printed or available — you count whatever is left over at the end of the night and whatever isn't there was either sold or given away as a comp. There is an accounting procedure used to deduct this and figure out what the gross ticket receipts are. You subtract out any taxes required by the state and you have your net receipts. In the case of Aerosmith, which is one of the top two or three grossing tours on the road (the others being U2 and Pink Floyd) the band could take out anywhere from a minimum maybe of $30,000 a night to well over $150,000 in some big arenas, where you're doing 20,000 people at $20.00 a ticket.

"We also go through all of the expenses at the end of the night. Out of what's left, all the salaries, per diems, hotels and other

110

expenses are distributed to the crew. The rest of the money is sent to the band's business manager in New York City where it is distributed via check to the airlines, trucking companies and various other vendors and entities. All of these expenses and all advance money for the entire road crew is now computerized and is therefore more efficiently taken care of than in the past."

Jeff went to school in Colorado. "There was a lot of music going on in the Boulder/Denver area; it was a real hotbed for club bands. I went to as many rock shows as humanly possible — and never had to pay to see a show. I would go to the building in the afternoon to meet the sound or the light crews, and just hang out. I was really very interested in what they did and was anxious to learn from them. I would do anything I could to be close to the action. The same with the local bands — whether it was moving their equipment, mixing their sound or helping them with their press kits, bios, pictures, whatever was necessary. Although I wasn't sure exactly what I wanted to do — I knew I wanted a career in this business."

Jeff suggests that young people get involved with the music industry in their hometown first. "Get to know who the promoters are, who the radio station people are. Get involved with local bands even if it's helping on a volunteer basis, but just get to know who they are. At the same time, I would strongly suggest that you go to college to work on a degree in business. A college education in the management area is important for several reasons. First of all, it shows other people that you are able to set a goal and stay focused on it. It also demonstrates that for four years you've overcome whatever stumbling blocks and hurdles are thrown in your way. Lastly, you show you can accomplish what you set out to do. My degree in business/marketing was very instrumental in getting me a job with a promoter and eventually led to my becoming a tour accountant. Often times, a person starts out doing one job and winds up doing another, but at all times that person must remain determined to be the best at whatever he or she is doing. The people who are hard working, honest and keep their goals and directions real clear in front of them are the ones that succeed."

Jeff warns, "be careful not to fall into the trap that many people do in this business. Too often people get into a rut of being a runner or a gofer and they don't make that next jump up. I think that at some point you have to decide what it is you want to do. If someone came up to me and said that they wanted to be a tour accountant, I would say how do you know? What do you think a tour accountant does compared to being a sound man or a light man, or a tour or road manager. I mean, what is it exactly that you want to do? Get some experience at any level. Once you find out what everybody does out there you'll be in a better position to know which one of those jobs you want to do.

"I consider myself to be family oriented, so for me, being away from home is a tremendous sacrifice. I think that the touring side of this business is for young people under thirty-five years old. It's probably a good idea for those who want to tour to get the experience before they get married or have kids. Touring places an enormous strain on your family life. It also puts a lot of strain on you personally. There is physical wear and tear from living on the road and a person needs to be conscious of the need to work out, to take vitamins and get sleep when it's available to them. They need to do healthy things and eat properly.

"There is a popular misconception about life on the road. When a major act is touring it's big business and not one big party. A good example is Aerosmith who recently completed a very successful drug and alcohol free tour. They are a bunch of very talented guys, whose ups and downs in their career can be linked directly (I believe) to alcohol and drug abuse. Conversely their success can be attributed to a move in the other direction."

Touring also interferes with Jeff's enjoyment of social fellowship in his church. "My church is quite important to me. We have a very strong bond with the people there and I miss all of that. Sunday mornings are usually spent traveling, just finishing a show or getting ready to do a show. That's difficult for me. I have friends at home that I rarely see. On the road you become a family of thirty-five or forty people, but it lacks the intimacy of your family at home."

Touring does provide moments for Jeff that very few people get to enjoy. "I have a 3 year old son who thinks Steven Tyler is one of his best friends. Funny, he knows all of the Sesame Street characters, but he knows the members of Aerosmith just as well."

*66 **No** matter how tal-
ented a performer may be, it's going to be a lot
harder and slower to reach his or her potential
as a star without a dedicated and imaginative
manager. 99*

Lennie Petze, Executive Vice President
CBS/IMAGINE RECORDS

Artist Management

Gary Kurfirst

---

*Gary Kurfirst started out in the entertainment business by
promoting dances, or what were called "college mixers" in the late
sixties. "We would rent out the old beach clubs on Long Island and
for three dollars or so you could hang out all night, have a free beer,
and listen to a band. The acts got bigger and bigger. Pretty soon, I
was promoting acts at the Island Garden Arena, a 5,000 seat venue
in Hempstead, Long Island. My first show was the Young Rascals,
The Vagrants, and Vanilla Fudge. We went on to the Singer Bowl in
Flushing Meadows Park, which then held about 20,000 people. The
first show that I put in there during the summer of 1967 was, once
again, the Young Rascals. Next on the list was the Village Theater in
New York City, which about a year later became the Fillmore East. I
brought in Jimi Hendrix, The Who, Procol Harum, The Yardbirds, the
Doors, Cream, Canned Heat, Wilson Picket, and Otis Redding. It
was at that time that I got started hanging out with a lot of the
musicians. Although I was still a teenager, they would often ask me*

113

*questions about all types of things, and I found myself advising
them. That eventually lead me into the management field.*

"The first band I ever managed was a local band called the
Vagrants from Forest Hills, Queens (in a later form it was famous as
Mountain). They could have very well been the first Heavy Metal
band in America and the first major touring entity around. Even towns
that ordinarily did not have Rock 'n' Roll shows wanted them to
perform in their local stadiums."

Today, Gary's clients include The Talking Heads, The
Thompson Twins, Big Audio Dynamite, Jane's Addiction, Debbie
Harry, Jean Beauvoir, Jerry Harrison and The Ramones. "Jane's
Addiction haven't sold that many records (100,000) in comparison to
Guns 'n' Roses (about 6,000,000), but they were nominated for a
Grammy as the best new Heavy Metal Band.

"When I first started, this business was like the wild west. There
were no laws, no protocol; whatever happened, happened. You
would show up at a building and had to fight about getting the light
and sound systems set up the way you wanted. Back then, we went
into buildings not knowing what to expect. Today, major touring acts
have their own lights, sound systems and stage sets." Gary recalls an
incident during one of his shows: "One night I had a show at the
Singer Bowl where the seats weren't fastened down. By the end of
the show, it seemed that 3,000 of the 5,000 seats were on the stage.
We bolted down every chair prior to the next show."

Years later, another potentially dangerous situation happened
while one of Gary's acts was performing in Europe. "There was an
incident where the Talking Heads were playing in Italy and the police
decided to disperse the crowd by using tear gas. One of the tear gas
bombs backfired and landed on the stage. The band did two numbers
and had to run off the stage. On that same tour, the band was playing
at a stadium in Greece when the police came in and said they didn't
want us to play in the soccer field because it had just been sodded
and we would ruin it. You don't argue with the police in Greece. We
were forced to play on a makeshift stage about three feet wide. It was
like playing on top of the dugout at Yankee Stadium."

Gary explains that there are all types of managers: "Some are
hands-on managers. Others keep their distance. I believe that
different artists need different kinds of managers. There are some
managers that are great for some artists and wouldn't be good for

another one. It works both ways. My basic objective is to create an atmosphere, a setting in which the artist and his creativity can develop. An artist is an artist. I just want to keep the artist protected from a lot of external pressures that could affect what he's doing. I block for him, like an offensive line works for its quarterback. I'm good at that. Furthermore, I have contacts after all these years, and if somebody needs something done, I'll get it done for them. Occasionally I'll have some ideas that might tremendously alter what the artist is doing. I will discuss them with my artist and let him see if they interest him. It's team work. I believe every artist demands something different from you.

"I negotiate all the contracts for my clients. My lawyer and I work together on every aspect of the negotiation. The way I work is to find the record label that is best for that particular artist. Then I'll structure the deal, and when the main points of the deal are set, my attorney comes in to handle the final details. Some record labels don't understand the artist. Some others are really cool and care about the development of the artist. The main difference between record companies is that some labels only know how to sell records, while other's maintain artistic integrity.

"If I see a band that I like or hear a record that appeals to me, I'm not shy. I will pursue it to see if they have a manager. Or, one of my artists will tell someone that I'm good and refer them to me. That's actually how it happens most of the time. There are also record company referrals, which happen occasionally. I think they respect the fact that I fight for my artists. They let me deal with my artist as I see fit.

"I learned by making a lot of mistakes and grew up along with the business. The touring business has evolved tremendously and now it's tougher to start. I guess it's good to hook up with a couple of college friends who are talented and work your way up that way. Perhaps approach management from another part of the business like a record company, or work for an agency. There's so much to know now. It's not something you learn in school. It could be effective to tie in with someone who knows what they're doing and learn as a co-manager or assistant. Maybe even as their office boy if that's all that's open to you.

"If you're an enterprising person and want to develop your own lifestyle, this is the business for you. I can wear what I want, set my own crazy hours, and speak to whomever I want, when I want. The hours are excruciating. A twenty hour workday is commonplace, but I know I'm the one who decides that I have to work that day. The travelling schedule is unbelievable. I travel all the time. I went from the Bahamas, to Milwaukee, to Oakland, to the Bahamas, to New York, to San Francisco, to London, to France, to New York, to Bangkok, to Tokyo, to Los Angeles, and back to New York in less than the last two months.

"It's a business like any other business. It's hard and you have to be dedicated. You have to have good taste and you must believe in your artists and respect them for their talents. It's truly an art form. One thing that's helped me was that I think I have pretty good taste. Some of my clients may not have been giants commercially, but artistically they were all very well respected. I manage whom I like and believe it or not, I don't manage an artist for money. I manage them because I genuinely like them and want to dedicate 99% of my waking hours making their creative lives work for them."

66 *Here's my Rock 'n' Roll nightmare: We're in a dressing room in Cincinnati, our soundtruck is in Detroit, our drums are in Chicago and it's 9:00 p.m. How's that for sweats?* **99**

Dee Dee Ramone

Entertainment Freight

Paul Lippe

Vital International Freight Service lives up to its name: an important cog in the touring machine that transports major music industry acts all around the world. Paul Lippe is literally the driving force behind the company. "Specifically, we do the international freight forwarding of equipment for bands who are on tour. Our job entails making the necessary transport arrangements as well as customs clearance and anything else associated with a moving company that operates worldwide."

Paul had always worked in international transportation. It was Paul's love of music and his attraction to live entertainment, that made him decide to pursue touring bands. "The freight moving requirements of the music industry were intriguing to me. Plus, I was used to meeting deadlines in other portions of my business. Today, we ship lighting and sound systems, as well as instruments and, at times, very elaborate stage sets." Paul knows this is no easy task: "For the larger shows we're talking about moving thousands of tons

117

of equipment. For an air freight move, show gear can be somewhat unusual in size and there are a number of factors that have to be considered.

"First of all, arrangements have to be made with the airline to reserve space on a particular flight. Often a tour will finish in Los Angeles before moving on to Europe. The band's gear has to be packed up and transported to the airport in a very efficient manner. This is usually done late at night or very early in the morning. With few exceptions, the first show date in Europe is scheduled fairly close to the last show date in the United States. This makes selection of the proper flight critically important. It is necessary to verify the flight several times. Most times, the added phone calls prove to be a needless exercise, but it must be done. Our sole responsibility is getting the equipment to the next venue on time.

"Negotiation is a big part of the business. Obviously, moving hundreds of thousands of pounds of equipment can be a considerable expense. The transport rates can vary anywhere from $1.00 to $2.00 a pound, so there is constant negotiation with both the band's touring management and the airlines. We have to get the band advantageous buy and sell rates. Another important part of our job is to be familiar with the various customs requirements. Customs differ from country to country. Some are stricter than others as far as customs documentation. Most of the equipment moves on a document known as a 'carnet.' Basically, this document is a passport for cargo and contains a long list of equipment. This list may run from 10 to 30 pages and lists detailed descriptions of all the equipment being shipped on the tour. We like to have the equipment information well in advance, so that we may obtain the carnet without any last minute complications. The carnet then has to be presented to customs in the country it's leaving before the merchandise is exported. The carnet is also presented to customs of the destination country. Japanese customs is very strict and will even go as far as to photograph the inside of tour cases, so that they can compare them with the equipment when it's exported from their country. They want to make sure that everything that has come into the country actually leaves the country and isn't sold by the band while it's in their country. Otherwise, the Japanese duty will be required on those items that stay in Japan."

Freight companies have two sources of revenue: "service fees," which are charged in certain cases where unusual services are required, and "commissions" from the airline or the steamship lines similar to a travel agent.

"Most of our time is spent just making arrangements, planning moves and providing any labor that might be required for the physical handling of the cargo. Most often the physical labor is provided by the tour itself, the trucking company or by the carriers. Our role is primarily that of coordination. We've handled the Los Angeles Philharmonic for about 10 years and most recently worked with the new opera company based in Los Angeles. In the past, we have done work for Elton John, Queen, Michael Jackson, Cyndi Lauper, Genesis, and Phil Collins."

When hiring, Paul looks for people who are effective on the phone. "A large part of our work is done over the phone. Therefore, we need people with good basic communication skills. That doesn't necessarily mean having a charming personality, although that frequently will help, but rather the ability to communicate effectively. We need people who are detail oriented. For example, if someone tells you on the phone that they are going to take care of something, you must follow up and verify it, and then verify it again. Nothing can be taken for granted in this business. Applicants must have a lot of endurance, for this is certainly not a 9 to 5 job. We make a considerable effort to find people who have flexible schedules and who realize that the industry requires phone calls at home from time to time. In addition, there are times that arrangements must be made at two in the morning, as well as on weekends and holidays.

"In this part of the business, common sense is of greater importance than formal education. That holds true on two levels. First of all, to my knowledge there aren't any formal courses of study in entertainment logistics available. Secondly, as far as freight forwarding itself is concerned in the United States, there are very few trade associations that provide courses on customs brokerage or freight forwarding. It would be difficult to find a major university that would offer a course of study that would prepare you for this job.

"Most of our employees begin working as messengers, taking documents back and forth between the office and the steamship lines, airlines and customs. The next step is to do clerical type work in the office. Following that the next step up the ladder is to become involved in some of the shipments by learning how to make all the necessary arrangements. There is a lot of documentation that must

119

be completed, such as the carnets, airway bills of lading, ocean bills of lading, U.S. Customs/Export Declarations, and customs entries. It's a gradual process of learning. Our new people slowly, but effectively, learn the ropes.

"The closest call we ever had was on a Diana Ross tour. She had a final show date in London with a very close first show date in Los Angeles. We had all the equipment put on a non-stop aircraft from London to Los Angeles and we very carefully confirmed that everything was on board the flight. We double-checked that the plane had taken off from London and proceeded to make all the necessary arrangements to meet the flight in Los Angeles. As an added precaution, we called the airline to verify the arrival time. It was at that time that we were told that the plane had made an unscheduled stop in Calgary. Every piece of luggage and all the equipment were stuck in Canada. For the next 8 hours we attempted to locate an air freighter that would fly from Calgary to San Francisco by the next morning. After several harrowing hours, we were able to find someone who could handle the job. We had trucks waiting at the airport to drive from San Francisco directly to the Forum in Los Angeles and we made the show. This goes back to not being able to take anything for granted. Here it is a non-stop flight, which 99 times out of 100 would have flown without stopping, and something unforeseeable happened that could have ruined the show. Thankfully, we practice what we preach about thoroughness.

"Not nearly as show threatening, but probably just as important to the artist, was one of our most unusual air freight deliveries. This one involved Michael Jackson. Michael was rehearsing in the New York area and on three consecutive evenings he had Chinese food flown from a specific restaurant in Los Angeles to his New York location."

Paul notes that the level of technology is changing the business radically. "The questions that I must ask myself are: what will be the technology of touring 10 years from now from our standpoint? Will the vast amount of equipment that moves from country to country continue to do so? Will lighting systems become more available in Australia, Japan and Europe? Is it possible that in the year 2000, video with electronically reproduced sound will enable an artist to stay in Los Angeles and do a live show in Berlin?" Paul observes that newer markets for touring are opening up all the time: "I remember 15 years ago the concept of doing a large scale Rock 'n' Roll concert in Zimbabwe was beyond anyone's expectations and now shows are being done in Eastern Europe, all over South America, and throughout Africa."

It's because of the world getting smaller that Paul strongly recommends that "new entrants in the field should learn another language. Most of the time you'll do business in English; however knowing another language is a real advantage. The more knowledgeable you are about other cultures and systems the better off you will be."

> **❝ D**on't let anyone tell *you that Rock 'n' Roll is strictly a man's world. There isn't a single job, even driving the trucks, that isn't open to smart, talented women.* **❞**
>
> **Marianne Faithfull**

Truck Driving

Yvonne Mateer

Driving the equipment for a large tour from city to city may sound routine and easy, but drivers like Yvonne Mateer have learned that it's a lot more complicated and difficult than you might imagine and requires great adaptability and endurance.

It sounds like a bad pun, but Yvonne Mateer became a truck driver by accident. Yvonne began her career with Aztec Staging of Ann Arbor, Michigan. "My first responsibilities were to provide the set-up for the stage and that often meant moving pianos and all kinds of other stage equipment. Occasionally, I would help out by driving short distances, but soon found myself driving all the time. I made my decision to become a full-time driver while on tour with Kiss. The regular driver was too tired to drive and we needed to get to the next venue. So, I got behind the wheel and drove to the show. That was twelve years and about a million miles ago.

"The one thing I learned rather quickly was that there is no such thing as a typical work day. Each day will change a little depending on how far the drive happens to be and the amount of equipment that has to be picked up. Some days I'll have absolutely nothing to do and other days I find myself behind the wheel for 20 hours.

"Prior to a tour going out, my employer (Ego Trips) tells me where and when to pick up the band's equipment. At that time I'm given a venue schedule, places, dates and times that must be met at all times. The most important part of this job is to get where I'm supposed to be on time. That's the bottom line. I don't have to be concerned with unloading the truck because union crews usually have that responsibility. The second most important aspect of the job is to keep good relations with my fellow workers on the crews, in management and on the other trucks.

"Being a female I'm a bit more conscious of my work being scrutinized by others. There are some people who'll watch women more closely because this has traditionally been a man's business. I regard the fact that others are watching me as being a very positive thing for me. It most certainly has made me more determined and I feel that my concentration has improved as a result." Yvonne has been so dependable over the last four years that she is out on the road an average nine or ten months a year. She has transported band equipment for such acts as Aerosmith, Earth, Wind and Fire, George Michael, Anita Baker and Julio Iglesias and many other artists.

"I've worked for Ego Trips for the past four years. They provide fairly diverse tours for me and that helps to keep the job interesting. The best part of my job is having the freedom to move around from city to city. This is a great way to see the country. On the day of a show I have to be at the venue for the load in and the load out. Normally, the rest of my time is free. Most of the big acts work the same venues, so it's allowed me to make acquaintances around the United States. My schedule gives me the time to visit with my friends around the country, which is really nice.

"There have, however, been some frightening moments on the job. One incident in particular stands out in my mind. Years ago, in the days of no power steering and very slow, unreliable trucks, I had a bad accident when I jack-knifed on an icy mountain road. There was a truck directly behind me as we were both climbing a mountain in the early morning hours. I remember it was quite dark because the sun wasn't up yet. As we were going down the other side of the mountain about 35 mph, the truck behind me jack-knifed on an icy patch and stopped just a split second before I did. Had he not jack-knifed, there's no doubt that he would have gone right through my truck. It was pretty miraculous that we both were able to pull out of a near-catastrophe without any injuries and with all the gear still intact. We made the next venue on schedule.

"Another scary moment was meeting my husband while on tour (just kidding). He worked for L.S.D. (Light & Sound Design) on the Julio Iglesias tour. I was driving on that same tour. We had been on the road for a few months before even noticing one another. However, one day we starting talking about church. Well, it turned out that he used to be a missionary years ago. I had always been interested in religion and hadn't met anybody out on the road that went to church. As a result of our conversation we went to church together one day and quickly became friends. A short time later, we began dating each other and about a year after we met we got married.

"I would recommend this job to only those who were young and unmarried. Of course, you have to love to drive. Obviously, you need to learn how to drive a truck, but there are schools that will teach you how to drive the big rigs. Like other jobs, there are pros and cons to driving a truck. This is a great way to go to the places that most people only daydream about. It enables you to move around and have fun for a few years. However, I wouldn't recommend this job as a lifelong career for people who want to get married and have children. I've seen a lot of marriages break up out here. Being away from your spouse for months at a time is not conducive to a good marriage."

Yvonne stresses that driving a truck can be just as rewarding for women as it is for men. "This job takes a person with a lot of endurance, someone who is dependable and has a great deal of self-discipline. The trucks are well equipped and very easy to handle, but it takes skill and not strength to operate these vehicles safely. If you would like to enter this exciting field, don't allow anything to stop you."

Jay Adams

Rick Barretto (Tiffany (r) & Aunt)

Howard Bloom

Leroy Bennett

Amy Polan Clarke

Zeb Cochran

Ron Delsener

Carol Dodds

Bill Elson

Tom Duncan

Leo English

Coy Frisbee

Dan Ferguson

Paula Esposito

Nicholas Gold

Arthur Giegerich

Mike Johnson

Jon Dworkow (& Billy Idol)

Michael Keifer

Pete Kranske and Patty

Joi Huckaby

Franz Harary

Bob Goldstein

Jeff Krump

David McNeil

Robert Morrison (& Groupie)

(Billy Idol &) Dave McCullough

Richard McDonald

Robert Paulsen

Thomas Reedy

Jane Rose

Tim Rozner and Aerosmith

Peter Moshay

Barbara Skydel

Russell Simmons (right) and Lyor Cohen

Scott Sanders

Jim Silvia

George Walden

Lori Somes

Lee Stanley

Torben Smith

Jeremy Thom

Gary Kurfirst

Bill Zysblat

Harry Sandler

Lynn Goldsmith

> **66** **G**etting the music I'm playing out to the audience — the way I want them to hear it — takes real collaboration between me and my sound engineer. **99**
>
> **Jeff Beck**

Sound Engineering
David McCullough

David (Dansir) McCullough is as fine an audio engineer as you'll find in the business. With a career spanning two decades, Dansir has seen tremendous changes in the technology and sophistication of sound equipment. Even for a seasoned pro like himself, it's a constant learning experience.

Dansir recognized early in his career that a good sound person who is flexible is always in demand: "I've tried to diversify myself as much as possible in this business so I don't get type cast and people won't just call me for heavy metal acts. I want them to know that they can call me for any group and that I'll come in and do a good job." Dansir's flexibility has allowed him to work with acts as diverse as Bob Seeger, Billy Idol, John Waite, Pat Benetar, Alice Cooper, Triumph, Van Halen, Aerosmith, Cheap Trick, and Pattie Labelle.

"When I first started out, I didn't make any money at all. But, now I make a comfortable living and live on a 20 acre farm in Northern Michigan with my wife and four children. I went from being a roadie to sound man and that's been my forte, doing sound. I was always the kid who, whenever I heard a radio, always fiddled with the tone control knob. Although my interest was always in the sound of music, I never had any desire to be a musician."

Dansir has come a long way both professionally and personally. "I come from a broken home. My stepfather was very abusive and beat me up a lot. Consequently, I didn't do that well in school and I really didn't have any interest in formal education. My best friend was a girl who happened to be crazy about guys in bands. One time she took me to a show with her. We went to see one of her boyfriends, who was a lead singer of a band called Panic in the Pack. They needed help loading the truck that night, so I just pitched in. My thoughts were, 'Hey, this is a cool thing to do.' There were a lot of women around. It was a good time and nobody hassled me. At 15, I ran away from home and hooked up with a couple of different bands. When I was 17 years old, I had an opportunity to work for Bob Seeger. My pay was around $10.00 a show. I was just a young kid who didn't know anything and did most of the work. My mother had always told me, 'David, no matter what you do in life, do it as best as you possibly can.' I've always followed her advice and it's one of the main reasons that I'm where I am today."

Despite other changes in live entertainment, Dansir's work schedule has pretty much remained the same. By 10:00 a.m. the sound crew is allowed to set up. "The first thing we do is unload the truck and all my gear, which includes the boards and effects (sound boards). The sound board allows me to control the sound that's coming from the stage. Each musical instrument has a microphone or a direct line to my board and I can control everything from out front in the audience. Reverberators add echo, fullness, and delay, which can double vocals with harmonizers and flangers. Flangers make a gurgling type sound that you can put on cymbals or vocals to enhance them. We have many effects that the audience is unaware of, but the engineer can use to produce a sound as close as possible to that on the album. A noise generator, for example, sounds like a jet taking off. A real time analyzer shows you on a graph exactly what the room is lacking or needs, and you can then correct many of these problems with a graphic equalizer. A high tech graphic equalizer can give you every frequency from 20 cycles up to 16,000 hertz, the whole spectrum of sound."

After set-up, the next step is to do a "sound check." Dansir has learned that voices, tones and everyday noises have to be taken into consideration when setting up the room. "I adjust the sound system to the room, even run a couple of CD's and listen to them to see if it needs more treble, mid or more bass. Then, I go back to the graphic and adjust it. Around 4:00, the band will come and make sure that all their sounds on stage are right and everybody is comfortable. The artist will normally play two or three songs, perhaps rehearse a little. That gives me a feel for what it's going to be like that evening. We eat dinner after the sound check and come back to the venue an hour or so before show time. After the concert I go through the motions of taking apart all the equipment that I set up in the morning.

"I'm like an extra musician because I have to understand the music, the personality, and I have to be there with them. Sometimes you have to be a shrink, a babysitter or a pal. You have to learn how to control a drummer who throws sticks at the monitor man. Musicians can be a strange breed and have to be treated with kid gloves. They are the stars. You have to treat them with a little bit of indifference and to find a way to relate to them somehow."

Dansir would recommend this career to anyone, but cautions potential sound engineers that "It's not all a bed of roses. Don't fool yourself into thinking that it's just a good time and wonderful music. Or that it's a joyous trip around the world and everything is so beautiful. Anyone who has that impression is in for quite a shock. It's tough out there and you have to stay on your toes because there is always someone waiting to get your job.

"Today, there are audio engineer trade schools all over the United States. You can learn the technical side of the business, but trade school can't prepare you for an 18 hour work day or what happens on the road: Once you're on the road going to a different city every day, you don't know what time or day it is. After you've paid a lot of money to acquire the knowledge that trade schools will provide, you may find that unless you're street wise, it will be tough to break into the business. The philosophy is that you've 'got to pay your dues' someplace. The hands-on part of the job is the truest test of whether you are going to make it or not. I don't care how educated or well versed you are in school, what counts is if you can make it on the road."

In Dansir's opinion: "You can learn more on the road than in school. Sound and lighting companies frequently hire inexperienced people to work in their shops. They may have you pulling cables, soldering wires, painting cabinets, whatever, for six months to a year before giving you a chance to go on the road. Monsters of Rock was a major production of equipment. There were 360 sound cabinets, two complete sound systems, two entire lighting systems, five stages and a total of 51 trucks. It was so big that virtually 80% of the personnel were rookies. The key positions were filled by veterans, who had to show these kids what to do. The tour was responsible for many new people getting a chance to go on the road with a major act.

"There was some real excitement during the Monsters of Rock at the L.A. Coliseum. Metallica was on stage and were playing like the heavy metal monsters of all time. There were 100,000 people in attendance. There was reserved seating on the floor, but about half way through the second song, twenty to thirty thousand kids from the top rows rushed the stage. I was in the middle of all this at the sound board, 150 feet away from the stage. There was a barricade built out of scaffolding and plywood protecting me and my equipment. It was 15 feet wide, 50 foot long and about two stories high. The crowd started coming down the aisles, chairs were flying like paper and barricades were being snapped in half. The security people just stood there. I thought to myself, there is no way they're going to take me alive. The security lost the floor. Everything got swept up in this mass of people. It looked like a volcano erupting, but instead of lava coming down, it was people. The rest of the day was total chaos. People were climbing all over trying to take over the sound board. In order to protect myelf, I was swinging mike stands and kicking people. I've been in this business a long time and there was no way they were going to intimidate me. So, I just went for it. (Needless to say, they didn't get the board.)"

Dansir stresses the need for self-control. "The lifestyle can catch up to you. Some guys drink too much and become unhealthy. Frequently, they have to pull themselves off the road. There are so many things that can tear you down and remove you from this business. You have to be able to pace yourself and put up with being away from home 8 to 10 months of the year. People outside of the business don't fully realize that it's like being in a circus. You set it up and tear it down, then go to the next town."

Dansir offers the following advice to those determined to work in the business: "You have to use self-control, be consistent, and watch your health. You can't drink or do drugs while you work. Some guys do drugs, that's their problem, but when it starts impairing their performance they're gone. A sound person is just as important as the musicians and they rely on you. If you're drunk or doing drugs then you are not doing your job. If you choose sound as a career you must watch your health, get enough sleep, and eat right. The key in this business is consistency. Once you get to a certain level, you want to stay there. People learn to trust you and know that when they hire you they're going to get a reliable professional to do an outstanding job."

Dansir has a lot of fond memories of working with Ted Nugent. "When touring we didn't have a tour bus or a train or anything, we drove by car to all our gigs. There was the time in Frankfurt, Germany when he blew the transmission in his brand new Mercedes rental car, and we had to get to the airport. There was only my car and his and there were already 4 people in each vehicle. He still had reverse left, so he followed me down the Autobahn doing 60 miles an hour — in reverse."

Another performer Dansir admires is Pat Benatar. "Her tour was a family situation. Her three year old daughter was out on the road with her with a Nanny. Pat's tour was affectionately referred to as the 'White Picket Fence Tour' and I had a great time with her and the gang. I had a very good relationship with them. We went through three monitor guys on it because she couldn't hear herself properly, but I mean that's just one of the things that happens. Not everybody works out."

Dansir sees his job this way: "The musician has all he can handle being a star. People constantly want to talk to them. The artist is constantly hounded to the point that he can't eat lunch or dinner without somebody bothering him. The only job that he should have is to get up every day, to go about his business, walk on stage, have somebody strap a guitar on him and he plays, that's what he's there for. My favorite motto is 'never let the musician think.' That's why we're here. It's not meant to be derogatory in any way. It's just my way of saying, hey, don't worry about it, I have a handle, I have it covered."

> **66 A**nybody *from the outside world who comes backstage is always amazed to see how efficiently and professionally our stage crews work with each other. They may come from all parts of the world and look like they haven't been to bed for a month, but when it's time to work they go at it like a drill team.* **99**

> **Steve Howe**
> **YES, GTR, ASIA**

Lighting Crew Chief

Richard McDonald

"Being a musician wasn't what motivated me to get involved with the Rock 'n' Roll scene. I had always been fascinated by the creativity involved with stage lighting," says Rich McDonald.

In high school, Rich did some AV (audio-visual), but concentrated on the school's theatre production. He also worked at a nearby theatre, not for pay, but for the learning experience. "After high school, I went to an electronics technical college for about a year on a scholarship. While going to school, I handled the lighting for a number of local bands. It was through that involvement in nightclubs that I eventually lost the scholarship. It was due to all the classes I had to miss, not bad grades. But, that was the extent of my formal education.

"When I started to do the lighting gigs with local bands in high school, it was strictly for fun. It wasn't my goal to work in rock, but rather it was theatre work that particularly interested me." However, the jobs that were available for Rich kept him working with club bands. He soon began to get a reputation for the creativity displayed in his shows. Eric Todd (of BML Stage Lighting) had a band playing at a club that Rich was working and they became acquainted with each other's work. Rich began buying supplies from BML and one day when BML was short-handed, Rich helped out for "a few days" that turned into six years.

As a crew chief for BML, a typical day for Rich, on something like the recent Aerosmith tour, begins at 8:00 a.m. "Once the first truck is unloaded, the rigging begins with a small crew. At this point the stage is pretty much covered with steel cables as well as all of the electrical hoists. While this is going on, we set up the dimmer racks, run all of the various sets of power cables and get all of the equipment for the dimmer area organized. At 10:00 a.m. the general labor call begins and the rest of the lighting system is loaded and forked up on to the stage. The majority of the lighting work goes on right up until lunch time. All of the equipment is assembled, cabled, hung, and then safety tested. The safety testing is very important and has to be done very meticulously. A bolt, tool or other item left on the lighting truss when it is raised could fall at some point. A tool falling on someone from 28 feet in the air can be fatal. Once the safety check is done, each lighting fixture is turned on and tested before the whole lighting system goes in the air. About this time things begin to slow down and much of the crew that has been working on lights is moved over to work on sound and scenery."

After the lunch break everyone gets ready for a "focus." Rich explains that the "focus" is when the lighting crew climbs up and adjusts all of the lighting instruments as per the lighting design. The lighting equipment often involves a lot more than lights. "We have electrically controlled special effects, curtain mechanisms, electronic color changers, etc." Once the stage set and band gear are in place, Rich and his crew set up all the floor lights and other stage lighting equipment. Then, they put away their cases and empty rack. "When the opening act arrives we sometimes have to make adjustments because they may have a few additional lights to be plugged in with our stuff, or we may have to keep certain things out of their way and then set them up just before the main act goes on at set change. During the show we make certain changes that coincide with what they are doing out at the controls. For example, we'll have fog cues or we may have to move (electrically) pieces overhead or we may have to repatch something for a particular cue."

Rich has high regard for the skills and talents of his crew: "The lighting crew is very well coordinated and disciplined, so although I'm the crew chief — the team needs very little supervision. We follow a specific order in which to do things, so as not to get in the way of the carpenters, for instance. Our truck is unloaded first in the morning but is loaded last at night. We have to wait for certain portions of the carpenters' work to be done so that we don't block off other parts of the stage. In the long run, this simple procedure will save us time as well. By the time we load out after the show, it's 1 o'clock in the morning. At the end of the week we've probably put in 70-80 hours."

Rich feels that very few jobs on the road can be compared with typical 9-5 jobs in other businesses. "When you're working a normal job," he says, "you can have things happen during the day that you won't expect and it will drive you crazy, but you can still leave at 5 o'clock. When you're working in this business, when that truck pulls up and the equipment is dumped out — you're not finished until everything is back in the truck. If it takes you three days to load the truck, well, that's your job. You don't punch out at 5 o'clock because you worked your eight hours. That goes both ways. Sometimes you can have an easy gig and take off a couple of hours in the afternoon. However, most of the time you have to make a 110% effort.

"I've always found that it's been necessary to make sacrifices such as these while on the road. With the exception of a week off here and there, I'm out for close to a year at a time. This can be from one extended tour or a combination of smaller ones. The point is that you don't get involved in this business for the glamor."

Here's what Rich says to young people interested in a lighting career: "There are many factors that you must take into consideration when deciding if you would like to make stage lighting a career. To me, the biggest thing that I've noticed is that friends change. It seems you can't communicate with people in the same way any more. You develop your own expressions with the people you live with and work with on tour for six months at a time. When you get back home it's as though you're speaking two different languages. Even when you do make that transition it's difficult to keep a relationship. I've lost a couple of girlfriends and a fiancee due to this lifestyle. Even if they wait for you they don't trust you because of the conditions of our jobs. You know, there are females all over the place, dressed to the max and trying to coax us into anything, so they can hang out with us or the band.

"Should you decide to get involved in Rock 'n' Roll, here's some of the better ways to go about getting into stage lighting. While in high school or trade school, take any and all classes that are offered in electronics. This would give you an excellent start. It would be a tremendous advantage for you if were a good troubleshooter, because things constantly break down. Should a problem occur during a show — every second is precious. Lighting companies look for people who can think on their feet.

"At BML we have plenty of people who had no previous experience before working in our shop. They get familiar with the equipment by getting hands-on training. The experienced guys in our shop lead the way for the new employees. You need a willingness to learn, good stamina and a desire to succeed. Stamina is very often an underestimated quality. Once you've gotten sufficient shop experience and know-how, you can go out on the road starting with local 'one nighters.' If you can handle that first difficult year — you'll make it. If you develop a drug or alcohol problem you'll never be able to work a 14 hour day coherently and therefore you can't be counted on. Some people can stay up all night, have a hangover and work a 16-hour day and it doesn't bother them. Somebody else may not be able to get out of bed. As soon as someone can no longer be depended on he's off the tour. You have too much responsibility to get caught up in the nonsense."

> **66** The first night I saw
> automated lighting in action (Genesis 1981), I
> realized that our work had been changed forever.
> Now, several years later, what I consider to be my
> best work has been possible ONLY through this
> technology. **99**
>
> **Allen Branton, Lighting Designer**
> **MICHAEL JACKSON, DAVID BOWIE**

Lighting Technology

David McNeil

When David Allen "Dexter" McNeil was in the 7th grade he began fixing things like guitar amplifiers. "I got involved with the drama club as a high school freshmen in New Jersey. We did all types of plays — musicals, drama, comedy. It was four years of great fun. We also had all sorts of outside entertainment programs where people would come in to rent the stage. Invariably, they would need someone to deal with the lights, which is how I got a lot of my lighting experience.

"My high school was pretty hip. I volunteered to work as a DJ on the school's radio station. From there, I took over as the chief engineer for two years. We did things like remote sports broadcasts of the football team, track meets and that sort of thing." Dexter was such a child prodigy that Rutgers University admitted him while he was still in high school. He finished high school and earned his college degree in engineering at the age of 18. That's when he started doing lights for bar bands.

"A friend of mine was working for a band at a place where I was working as an electronics technician. He told me that he was doing lights, but that they needed somebody to do sound. I didn't know that much about sound, but he assured me that he'd teach me. So, I started going to gigs with him. After he left the band, I decided that I liked doing lights better, so another sound man was hired. The club scene got really tedious for me, and I left the band to pursue more challenging lighting projects.

"Currently I'm a contractual employee with VARI-LITE, a very innovative automated lighting company. VARI-LITE is the trademark for a certain kind of lighting instrument that is completely remote controlled from the lighting console. It can adjust the focus and position and it's got 90 different colors. You can change colors in a tenth of a second just by pushing buttons on the console. It's got seven different global patterns that you can insert in the light beam, again just by pushing a button. Also, just like any other lighting instrument, it goes from zero to full intensity.

"VARI-LITE hired me for my present job to maintain their installation at the Palladium in New York City. In addition, I serve as the house electrical engineer. I'm also the house rigger and video engineer. The best way to describe it is to say that I'm responsible for anything that has wires on it.

"The job is very challenging, especially with the taping of Club MTV, the cable television show. Typically, they shoot 15 episodes of Club MTV in two days. The first day my call starts at 4:30 on Sunday morning, when the club is just closing. The place is definitely an around-the-clock, non-stop environment. At 4:30 in the morning, I greet the guys who just parked the 45 foot tractor trailer on 13th street with cups of coffee in hand. From there I come in the building and the first thing I do is get power to the truck. That will take anywhere from 20 minutes to an hour, depending on how much effort it takes to get the cables out of the truck. A lot depends on the mood or how much sleep the video guys have had. On one particular episode, the truck came from shooting a show in Atlantic City, and the guys hadn't gotten to sleep yet. That meant that the video guys had worked a good 35 consecutive hours.

"We're ready to shoot video by about 12:30 or 1:00 o'clock in the afternoon. They'll shoot 7 half hour shows. Each half hour show takes between an hour to an hour and a half. The following day shooting

135

begins at 10:00 a.m., so I'm usually here at 8:00 o'clock to get the VARI-LITEs out, and to make sure that any problems they had the day before on my end get straightened out. With my other duties, I won't get out of there until midnight. In terms of sacrifices, when you're really busy it doesn't leave any time for personal life. Even though I'm working in town these days and not on the road, I haven't been home for Christmas for five years. This year was the closest I've gotten to going home to see my parents for the holidays. I was able to go home on the 20th of December to have dinner with my family. Of course, I worked Christmas night at the club. You don't usually get holidays off if you're in the entertainment business, because the rest of the world is celebrating and they want to be entertained."

Dexter thinks that young people have a good chance of breaking into the field. "The business is always advancing technologically. There are plenty of opportunities for a good lighting person. You can work nightclubs, videos, conventions, and there are opportunities for you to go out on the road with all types of bands. You definitely need to get a good education in electronics, which will take you two to four years. Computers are a very intregal part of the business. Computer trouble shooting and repair will help you dramatically in dealing with the new generations of equipment that have been coming out over the past couple of years. We utilize computerized lighting consoles and automated lighting instruments and so on. Volunteer to work on a school play, take some technical courses. High school stage experience is excellent. You will not only learn how to use lighting and other stage equipment, but will begin to pick up on the 'lingo' associated with the business. There's no substitute for hands on experience."

> **66** *Touring is hard work. Somebody smart has to come along to see that at the end of the day there's something left over so that all of that work is worth while.* **99**
>
> *Tommy James*

Tour Business Management
Douglas McNeill

The business manager of a tour does a lot of his work after midnight in a different town every night. When most accountants are home watching television, Doug McNeill is just getting ready to set up his office in the back room of some theatre or arena and go to work.

Douglas Daniel McNeill had to use his experience as a professional football player to help him successfully tackle stadium tours for Michael Jackson, Madonna, the Police, Rod Stewart and many other major acts all over the world. Production costs for shows like this begin at $150,000 a week for even some of the smaller acts. With major headliners like Prince the costs are closer to $700,000 a week and for Madonna they may run upwards of a $1,000,000 a week. Doug feels he has devised a system to assure that artists are duly compensated for their work.

In 1971, Doug formed the department of facilities for the City of Richmond, Virginia. As the administrator for the department he

137

supervised five very different facilities, a 13,000 seat multi-purpose arena, an intimate 3700 seat theatre, a 30,000 seat football stadium, a 12,500 seat baseball stadium and a convention facility. Simultaneously, Doug began his own advertising agency specializing in entertainment oriented promotions. It was through his company that he was given the opportunity to become the tour business manager for what turned out to be the 1979 Billboard Tour of the Year — the Outlaws and Molly Hatchet.

"A week after the Outlaw tour I went to work for Journey, which was quickly followed by Styx." At one point during the Styx tour Doug came up with the idea to start a company, which combined tour business management with artist representation. "Some of the acts that I have worked with are the Police, Madonna, Rod Stewart, Motley Crew, U2, Stevie Wonder, Tina Turner, Ozzie Osbourne, Def Leppard, Rainbow, and the Monkees.

"As a company our responsibilities begin with generating a budget for the tour. We assist in the negotiations for buses, lights, sounds, trucks, special effects and things of that nature. After we go through a rehearsal period we'll actually begin accounting, tracking and paying the various tour expenses. These may include per diem salaries, hotel expenses, and ground transportation (taxi or limousines). We also pay for items like fuel for the buses and some production expenses such as lighting and sound."

Doug says that the budget for transportation between gigs depends upon the form of transportation that the tour will use. Is this a bus tour or a plane tour? The cost difference can be very significant. Madonna flew a 727 and the Police had a 19 passenger Viscount airplane, while Motley Crue, Ozzie Osbourne, and John Cougar Mellencamp went from city to city by bus.

Another major budget consideration is the size and type of the venues the band will be playing. Doug has learned that there is much more work involved with a stadium show. "Primarily the labor bills are three or four times bigger than arena shows. Not only do you need more workers to build the stage, but more time to actually complete the work. You must also allow more time for production and technical activity. Naturally, you have a lot more security, ushers, and ticket takers as well."

The focal point of Doug's job is what is called "the settlement" of the show. "We must approve and accept various expenses that the promoter claims to have incurred the night of the show. These expenses include ushers, ticket takers, stagehands, rental fees, box office rates, agencies, advertising expenses, etc. Our obligation is ultimately to account to the artist's representative for all the money that came in that night, where it went and what's left over for the artist."

There are several qualities that Doug says he looks for in the people he recruits. "First of all, it's important to have some type of athletic background. The reason that we like our employees to have an athletic background is that it's been my experience that these people usually have the self-discipline both mentally and physically to complete the task at hand. Secondly, a college education with some accounting background is preferable. Last, but certainly not least, is our desire to hire a person of the highest moral fiber. Someone who is honest and has a lot of integrity.

"There are other factors to take into consideration as well. We don't employ anyone who's ever done drugs, let alone doing them now. The accountant, business manager, and the tour business manager are the people who handle large sums of money and must have complete control of all their faculties at all times. You need both stress tolerance and energy in this business. I find that athletes are accustomed to working under fatigue conditions."

One of the sacrifices that Doug's workers have to make is the constant travelling. In fact, he stresses that you have got to love to travel. "If you don't like to sleep on a bus — forget it. Naturally, these aren't the type of buses that you'd take to Grandma's house on Thanksgiving. These are very plush units costing over $300,000. Still, some people may find it to be claustrophobic. Also, there are different quality tours. You have both a Four Seasons Hotels tour and a Ramada Inns tour. In both cases, it's an opportunity to see the world."

Some days Doug and his staff work 15 hours; other days, he admits they may only work 2 hours. "It's not unusual to spend what's supposed to be a day off travelling to the next city, so you really don't have that day off. Some tours are commercial airline tours where you have to fight metal detectors, skycaps or scheduling hassles. Sometimes you find yourself stuck on a bus for 18 hours.

"If I've been unable to discourage you so far, great. There are some good points and here they are. The best part of the job is that you don't do the same thing every day. You're not stuck in the same office. This industry is a very challenging one. Each new building that you go into is completely different from the last. You'll continually hear great music and meet creative people. You get to see the world. In this business you're rewarded both financially and psychologically when you do a good job. Plus, the fact that you control you're own destiny gives you a strong sense of accomplishment each and every day. I challenge you to find another job that can be as rewarding as this."

*66 **Jodi's very imagina-tive and versatile. We enjoy creating styles together.** 99*

Cyndi Lauper

Makeup

Jodi Morlock

You've seen Jodi Morlock's work prominently displayed throughout the entertainment business, but you've probably never heard her name. Have you seen the videos from Hall & Oates, Samantha Fox, Eric B., or Jazzy Jeff and the Fresh Prince? Did you ever ever see the album covers for Simple Minds, The Romantics, James Brown or Hall & Oates? How about Huey Lewis or Bryan Ferry? Well, that's where you've seen some of Jodi's work. Painters work on canvas, carpenters on wood and Jodi on faces.

She is one of the most respected make-up artists in the business, but she is one of the few in her field who never studied it until she was already considered a professional. "My training was solely on the job. However, I do have an extensive art school background and I guess I have made use of that in doing creative new things with make-up. I suppose you could also say that I've always had a knack for it."

When Jodi was in her early twenties, she shared a studio with a photographer. "We experimented a lot with lighting and make-up

141

during newspaper and magazine photo sessions. My roommate and I did a lot of fashion shots for the SoHo News, which was terrific exposure for me. The work was fun and I got to work with a lot of creative, positive people. I got a lucky break when another photographer friend started to do a lot of magazine and album covers. My first big photo make-up job was a Rolling Stone cover."

Although Jodi modestly credits luck for a lot of her success, it is very evident that she's always on her toes and prepared for new things when opportunity knocks. Her biggest career break occurred while she was visiting her longtime friend, Laura Wills of Screaming Mimi's (a very hip, New York clothing shop). "I was at the store one day and Laura told me that Cyndi Lauper's regular make-up artist was out of town and that she had to shoot a magazine cover. Well, Laura introduced me to Cyndi and we did a major job for Interview, which included the cover and a big spread inside the magazine. For some reason, Cyndi and I just really hit it off and she has kept me extremely busy and happy over the past two years.

"I've worked with Cyndi on concerts, photo shots and even on the set of her film, Vibes. When I'm out on tour with her, we usually head for the stadium about 4:00 p.m. for an 8:00 p.m. performance. Cyndi will go through wardrobe, hair and make-up, taking breaks in between so that she can exercise her voice. Cyndi likes to have two hours or so before a show just to relax and get into it."

She has also done the February, 1989 Details magazine cover photo of Cyndi. Actually, it was quite a prestigious group that collaborated on that cover including photographer Robert Maplethorpe, hair stylist Justin Ware and Jodi, all of whom had worked together before on other projects for Cyndi.

Make-up work for videos is interesting, according to Jodi, "but videos are extremely hard work compared to photo sessions. Video work, like film, requires long, tedious hours and a lot of touching up. A make-up artist must be there every second. When you are working with a photographer, it's usually an eight hour day and it's over. However, a film or video shoot can go on for nearly twenty-four hours.

"You'll use different types of make-up for the various jobs you do. For film you need to use heavier make-up, so that it will last longer. You'll spend a lot of time 'between takes' doing touch up. You build it up slowly and then take it down a little bit and then add more, and again take it down. At a certain point you will take it down with a

142

sponge to keep it from getting too cakey. The technique sounds easy, but actually it takes a lot of practice and skill to do it properly."

Jodi stresses the importance of being versatile. "To increase your chances of breaking into the business, you need to know how to do both hair and make-up. It's not until you get to the top or have been working for a number of years that you can afford to do just one or the other. When you're starting out, you should be grateful to get any job. To get a license to do hair, in most places, you have to go to school. Most beauty schools may teach you a little about basic make-up, but you really have to learn it on your own. If you want to learn special effects make-up, horror faces, aging effects, that's a different story. There are several excellent schools for that. I went to Bob Kelly. He taught us how to put on beards, scars, bruises, and how to work with latex. His classes, and others like them, teach you the basic skills you need to get into the union.

"After completing your schooling you should read through fashion magazines to find well-known salons. If you're going to work in New York, the salons you will see mentioned in the magazine would be good ones to contact because most of the better salons will have their own make-up department. Apply for a job working at the make-up counter. This will provide a chance for you to get some much needed experience. You can learn from the other make-up people working there. Most people are willing to teach you if you show a sincere desire to learn. Also, you will get to meet other artists, photographers and models who buy their make-up from the salon. It's likely that someone will know of someone who is doing some photo tests or needs a helper or even a volunteer. It's a possible source of leads for work on other projects.

"Becoming some experienced professional's assistant may be the most practical and desirable way to get into the business. Don't be shy about offering your help to make-up artists you meet in salons or about asking for recommendations at modeling agencies. As an assistant you will help the artist with the basics, like maybe putting on the foundation and the powders." Still, another approach Jodi suggests is to contact cosmetics companies. "They normally provide in-house training on make-up before sending their employees out to stores.

"Everything you learn anywhere will be valuable to you if you have an opportunity to do bands or concert performance. If you can work in a department store doing make-up, then you should be able to work on performers too. Be confident that if you have the eye to do makeup, you'll be able to use it in all types of applications, Rock 'n' Roll, film, theater or whatever you choose. Just keep in mind that the important thing is experience — the more you learn the more valuable you are. To become successful takes a combination of things: personality, ability, creativity and good taste. Every make-up artist has his own particular style. Develop a style that distinguishes you from the others."

Jodi suggests that to move up in the world of make-up you need to put together a portfolio of your work. Based on her own experience Jodi proposes that a safe and somewhat inexpensive way to get faces you've done is to find photographers who are doing test shots and won't mind having a volunteer make-up person. Be careful, Jodi warns, about photographers who have a reputation for taking advantage of young people. "The safest bet would be to approach reputable modeling agencies, who know both models and photographers. They probably have new models who are also trying to build up a book and would like your help. An agency will usually want to see a few of the photographs you have of your work. If they like what they see, perhaps they'll tell you of other models or photographers who are testing. All of this mutual cooperation will not only build up a book for you, but, who knows, it may be building relationships that can work together in the future."

Once you get a good book together, Jodi feels, you'll find that getting jobs will become easier. Jodi cautions prospective make-up artists: "This a very tough business, you must keep a positive attitude throughout many disappointments. It's very important for young people to be aggressive. Pursue any size job as though it was the most important job in the world. Slowly work your way up by starting out with small jobs. Becoming well known is exactly like doing make-up, it's a step by step procedure. Whatever the size of the job, you must be professional at all times. Just hang in there and eventually you will get all the work you want."

66 **T**he production man-
ager of a tour has awesome responsibilities. It's
like hovering in a helicopter over the whole tour,
making sure everything and everybody works the
way it should, gets there on time, starts on time,
looks good, finishes on time and gets to the next
city without any problems. *99*

Jim Koplik
CROSS COUNTRY CONCERTS

Production Management
Robert Morrison

He's been on the road for stretches as long as two years at a time. He's wanted by a lot of people from coast to coast. A brief description of someone on the FBI's most wanted list? No, it's the work experience of production manager Robert (Mo) Morrison.

"You have to expect and accept it — it's a whole way of life. Sometimes there are breaks between legs of the tour, like the Michael Jackson tour when we took off a month between Australia and the States for Christmas." Even if you're not actually on the road, you're still working crazy hours. "I was a site coordinator for the July 4 Liberty Weekend Show in 1986. I worked on that project for four or five months. I lived at home with the exception of the last two weeks before the show. However, my work hours were 8 in the morning until 11 at night. Do you consider that being home or on the road? It's a life style to which you (and your family, if you have a spouse and children) have to become accustomed."

The job of the production manager entails doing a little bit of everything for a touring artist. He is responsible for helping the artist

145

with the complete design of the show. That includes both the rehearsal and the actual running of the show from city to city. The job often includes putting out bids (long before the tour) to the vendors for the sound, lights, transportation, lasers, staging and whatever else that particular show requires. "You must get the best possible bid for your client. Money is always the bottom line, but there are other considerations as well. The lowest bid is not necessarily the best bid. The craftsmanship of the scenic shop, along with other aesthetic and creative details often determines who is going to be your support team on tour. This is no easy task as you're dealing with lighting, sound, trucking, busses, travel agents, and so forth. The preference of people higher up on the ladder, such as the artist, manager, lawyer and booking agent must also be taken into account. The production manager also oversees much of the travel arrangements, union calls in each town, security, dealings with the local promoter and even the catering service. In effect, he's a juggler of all different crafts and trades."

When Mo was in college he began learning his trade by working on stage crews. "I really started to think about working in show business when I was a kid. I learned to play the drums and actually became a very proficient chart reader. I studied quite seriously from the age of ten until I was around twenty years old. While attending school I was always getting sideline gigs and constantly looking for that eternal rock band that just never happened for me. I thought that I could play great, but here I was playing weddings and bar mitzvahs — when all I really wanted to play was Rock 'n' Roll. I sidetracked a little in college and got into lighting design. I was still drumming but it was starting to fade out with the pressures of college and all. In any event, I was no longer willing to practice eight hours a day. After ten years of frustration I decided to start working stage crew in Rock 'n' Roll. I began by unloading trucks, helping set up shows, making 35 bucks a show and most importantly, having a great time."

About a month before graduating from Sarah Lawrence College (outside of New York City), Mo was offered a job as the production manager for one of the top promoters in the country, John Scher. Mo worked for him from 1974 to 1982 getting (what he calls) his PhD in production. "It's a building block. You just keep going and things will develop for you." There seems to be only one accredited school for those who want to become a production manager and that's the

146

college of hard knocks. Here is an abbreviated listing of some of Mo's curriculum: hundreds of high school and college bands, Blue Oyster Cult, six years with the Grateful Dead, the Simon and Garfunkel World Tour of '83, the Rolling Stones, Site Coordinator for the David Bowie Serious Moonlight Tour, production manager for the J. Geils Tour, Cyndi Lauper, Tour Manager for Raquel Welch and the Michael Jackson (Bad) Tour.

Mo says that working in the entertainment business isn't for everyone: "Without question there are a lot of great moments out touring, but there are many negatives as well. Life on the road can be tough. Probably the most difficult part of being out a long time for a majority of people is that you miss virtually every holiday. Mo recalls a time when he missed nine consecutive Christmas Days and New Year's Eves because he was out on a tour. "Now, I'm finding that a Christmas break is becoming the one holiday most artists seem to respect. This is probably out of their own desire to have that holiday off." Still, he says, "you must ask yourself, am I willing to give up seeing my family or friends on holidays?"

What's the reason many people want to go out on tour? For Mo, originally it was the closeness to Rock superstars and the excitement that surrounded the whole scene. "The recording stars, Rock 'n' Roll music and all the good times were most important to me. Now, fun is only a minor part of it. Yeah, I had a lot of great times, but now that I work with bigger acts it's so much more serious and professional. However, even in the old days I always tried to keep everything in its proper perspective. I still try to have fun, but let me tell you this is very hard, very strenuous and mentally taxing work. I've seen a lot of people crumble under and quit. They go home, or just out on a drug binge and you never hear from them again. Believe me, it's a very stressful and anxiety-ridden occupation. If someone is telling you differently, he's probably not doing his job very well."

147

> **66 Whenever we go out on stage we must be able to count on the fact that those three or four truckloads of equipment, instruments and supplies have been unloaded, assembled, plugged in, tuned and ready. Unless that happens, showbusiness tradition or not, the show can't 'go on'. 99**
>
> **Chris Frantz**
> **TALKING HEADS**

Stage Equipment Technician
Peter Moshay

Peter Moshay is generally known as a drum technician, but he's actually a technician for the entire band. "I usually work on the whole stage performance doing technical repair of electronic equipment, programming keyboards and drum machine sequencers."

Before getting into touring with major acts, Peter worked at music stores around the Valley in Granada Hills, CA. What fascinated Peter more than anything else was all the new technology available in musical equipment. "I started to buy drum machines and Simmonds Electronic equipment to enhance my own performance as a drummer in a band. Since I was owning and selling equipment at the same time, I became somewhat of an authority. People whom I had sold to in the industry knew that I kept up with the operation, usage, innovations and maintenance of the gear.

"A lot of professional musicians don't really know how to program equipment, so they hire others to perform those services. I was

148

constantly getting calls to go over and show people how to set up and use their new equipment. For the most part, I would help them out with the gear that they just rented or purchased. Often, I would get calls to rush over to a studio or help a band prepare their gear for a tour. I had gotten so many offers to go out on the road that I thought 'what the heck, I'll try it.'

"The first band I worked for was Quiet Riot, setting up a live system for their tours. They were the first group that I knew of that used a lot of electronics on the road (especially the drummer). At the same time I was also putting together a live system for Barry Manilow. He asked me to go out on the road with him because I understood his electronic system and he was having trouble finding people with the technical knowledge to maintain and program his equipment. At that time, there weren't many guys hip to the new equipment and technology. The popularity of technically advanced gear increased dramatically and it seemed that it helped artists find new ways to express their creativity. This kept me extremely busy touring, consulting and even spending considerable time in the studio working on records."

Among dozens of other acts, Peter has worked with are the Cars, Journey, Kenny Loggins, and Hall & Oates. "I love being around music in general, but I particularly like working with Hall & Oates. I don't have a favorite band; I love them all equally. Just give me good music and I'm happy. There isn't anything that I don't like about this business. To me, every night is like Saturday night. You're around people who are always excited and having a good time. Being around music all the time is a constant high and to be a part of something that I've always admired is a thrill beyond compare. It would be difficult to explain the feeling of being on stage with the artists and helping create the sound that the audience loves."

A typical day on the road for Peter starts with a lobby call about 10:00 in the morning, to meet with other crew members and go over to the gig. "Once you arrive at the venue, you begin to unload all of your equipment. This usually takes an hour or so and then you do routine maintenance on the gear. This includes repairing cables, fixing gear, and stringing guitars. After lunch, you get everything set up for a 3 PM crew sound check. This is where the sound crew goes over all of the equipment to make sure it works properly. We sometimes even jam a little for the house sound guy, so that he can tune the room a bit. Then the band comes in and performs their own sound check, playing a couple of songs. After they finish, we clean up the stage area. Generally, I tidy up the stage and do a quick sound check. If there was something that the artist didn't like, I'll correct it at that time. Finally, we have dinner and get ready to do the show. Immediately following the show is the load out. I'm responsible for loading the band's equipment, which usually takes an hour and a half."

Here's Peter's advice to candidates for a career like his: "Education is the key to getting into this area of the industry. The phrase, 'knowledge is power' is very true. Learn computer programming because this is a very technically oriented field. Although you don't necessarily have to be a musician to succeed, you must become familiar with various instruments. Be seriously dedicated to what you are doing. Distinguish yourself from others by obtaining more knowledge than anybody else out there. You have to have something to offer people. The best choice appears to be technical expertise. I've worked steadily for years, but I'm always looking for innovative methods of programming. Now, I go to music stores looking for the latest equipment."

> **66 O**ne of the funniest
> sketches I ever saw on 'Saturday Night Live' had
> John Belushi playing a security guard at the back
> door of St. Patrick's Cathedral while the Pope was
> visiting New York. The priests and nuns that John
> wouldn't let in backstage obviously didn't call
> Dave Otto to get their laminated passes. **99**
>
> **Dan Zanes**
> **DEL FUEGOS**

Entertainment Graphics

David Otto

In 1979, Dave Otto revolutionized backstage security simply by redesigning backstage passes. Today's passes with various shapes and color codes can be attributed to Dave Otto's innovation.

Boston was touring the country with a hot album with an even hotter cover design and did a show in Cincinnati. Dave recalls vividly: "Their album cover design was a very flashy upside down guitar which resembled a space ship. When they arrived to do their concert, we convinced them to allow us to print their passes, the first four color pass that had ever been done." The band loved the creativity displayed by Dave and were doubly pleased to find that it didn't cost them any more than the standard one color pass. On the back of the pass Dave had put his company name and phone number. "As Boston went from city to city we found that business was suddenly going through the roof." When touring people and artists from other bands saw Boston's backstage pass (which was at the time the state of the art) they began calling Dave for their own tours. Since that time he's done work for The Who, Springsteen, Bob Dylan, Santana, Joan Jett, Robert Palmer, Phil Collins, Prince, and Michael Jackson, U2, Sting, Pink Floyd and hundreds of others. Every pass on the cover of this book was produced by Dave Otto.

The printing field gradually picked up new technological awareness. More thought was given to the tour's security problems. Major tours attracted major counterfeiters and difficult backstage security. Because the big bands were going out with major sponsorships, Dave had to come up with even more elaborate passes. For a huge Rolling Stones tour that included many outdoor dates, Dave devised tickets and passes with bright foils on them. "We put special foil on the back that was virtually impossible to duplicate." This just about eliminated any possibility of someone sitting outside of the Silver Dome or the Orange Bowl and printing thousands of tickets every day. The Stones didn't have to worry about counterfeits throughout their whole international tour.

Counterfeiting, a big concern back then, is just as big a problem today.

There was an emergency in the summer of 1988 when one of the groups using Otto's passes had their bus broken into. The only thing that was stolen was the box of backstage passes. The band was going to play in another city only two days later. The ticket system had to be completely revised. "We produced four color process passes and shipped them out to them in time for the next show." Instances like this made Dave see the need to put together complete packages for the touring artist. Items like anti-counterfeit tickets, backstage passes, luggage tags and dressing room signs. "What we saw was that when we provided all the necessary items for a tour, the band and the management people were less concerned about delivery and security problems. One place doing all the design work under one roof and printing all of the backstage passes provides an additional means of security. It's also essential that the printing company design the art work. It adds an extra dimension of safety when only the printing company knows what security features are going into a certain pass."

Another innovation that is credited to Otto is the use of fluorescent inks on passes. Years ago, when bands toured they used a generic pass that would allow people to follow the band and get into venues all around the country. To eliminate that problem Dave devised a coding system. "We initiated different passes for before the show, after the show, photographer, and press. The crew had its own 'all access' laminated passes to the backstage and dressing room areas distinguishable from the other passes, all of which had different shapes and color codes. People soon stopped trying to get back in the next day. In addition, our new system of using fluorescent inks made the different kinds of passes easily recognizible by the security guards at the various venues."

Otto has a large work force employing commercial artists, strippers, cameramen, press people, bindery people and papercutters. "All of our pressmen must be experienced because our presses are difficult to run without a working knowledge of the equipment. We do have co-op programs. People come in and work a few hours a day, which enables them to learn in a commercial environment while still attending school. High school counselors may have some names of companies that participate in similar co-op programs. If not, young people should take the initiative and make those calls themselves. Most high schools have shop classes that can teach you the basics. There are trade schools that offer very informative classes. A more sophisticated education can be obtained at schools like The Rochester School of Technology, one of the finest printing colleges in America."

Dave speaks enthusiastically of the future of printing. "What makes the printing industry so exciting is that even in a recession year people need printing. Especially in the entertainment business. Also, it's not the same work day in and day out. One day you are maybe printing a six color pass with hot stamped foils for Michael Jackson and the next day you may be running letterheads. There is a new challenge every day. You can earn a good living. Pressmen can do well and good artists make good money. Printing also provides the opportunity for you to utilize your creativity."

66 **R**igging *is quite academic. There are two ways to do it, perfectly and safely, or not at all. If it's one of my shows, no artist or crew member ever hits a stage until it's the former. The latter is not an option.* **99**

George Sewitt, Tour Consultant
BILLY IDOL

Rigging

Robert Paulson

While attending San Jose State College, Robert ("Rocky") Paulson was offered a job working for a lighting rental company. One of his co-workers was a member of the IATSE (International Alliance of Theatrical and Stage Employees). This friend informed Rocky that none of the organization's members would climb the steel in the ceiling at the Cow Palace and that if it didn't scare him, the job would be his for the asking. "I did the rigging there for about a year and a half before applying for membership. Shortly after being accepted I was offered a job with NBC touring as a rigger with the Disney On Parade shows."

What exactly is rigging? Rigging is the process of suspending loads, speakers, lights and other show elements from the ceilings of buildings. The physical skills required are quite similar to those of steel workers and even mountain climbers. The physical attributes are only one component; a working knowledge of cables, ropes, hoists, and other rigging devices is absolutely necessary. It's

154

mandatory that the rigger understands what effect the loads he or she is suspending will have on the structure from which it is to be suspended, how it will take the weight. The number one priority of the rigger is to ensure that the show is hung safely while maintaining the integrity of the show design.

Although the rigger must achieve the effects that the designers and producers have in their heads, he really answers to no one. The rigger is charged with the responsibility of hanging the show safely and efficiently. When it comes to the safety of the performers and the audience the rigger must not submit to pressure from anyone. He must do whatever he deems necessary to hang the load safely regardless of time or other constraints. He must firmly stand on his convictions even if it gets to the point of placing his job on the line. One accident, however "small" can cause serious injury to someone or extensive damage to the equipment.

The average rigger understands his responsibilities and knows that there is no place for drugs around the workplace. Drugs (including alcohol) ran rampant through Rock 'n' Roll years ago. However, today the leaders in this industry realize the negative effect they had on the business.

Rigging requires a lot of team work. If one person on a rigging crew is inexperienced or not a team player, it can drastically slow down a job. With each rigging team being so small it's fair to say that each rigger has a major effect on the show.

"My job with NBC ended in the mid 70's. At that time Rock 'n' Roll tours were becoming more elaborate. More acts were hanging large PA's and elaborate lighting systems as that technique was becoming increasingly popular. The industry had very few experienced riggers to suspend those heavier loads from the ceilings of arenas throughout the country, so those of us that had done the Disney On Parade shows were able to 'jump to the head of the class' because of our previous experience."

Rigging has become a very competitive field. The pay is quite good and there is a large amount of responsibility, therefore many people already in the business seem to gravitate towards rigging. The most recent entrants into the field tend to be those with some sort of background in computers. The emphasis lately has been to use computers to control electric hoists and winches. This, however, requires that the riggers be knowledgeable in electronics as well as their own field of rigging. "I hope that we will see the new breed of riggers armed with an even greater expertise in this area.

"This business has provided me with a wealth of experiences and challenges. Throughout my career I've worked on a variety of shows and projects. They range from 'Disney On Parade' and NBC's production of 'Peter Pan,' to Pink Floyd's 'Animal' and 'Wall' tours. Today, I do mainly industrial type shows for major corporations such as IBM and AT&T. In addition, I've gotten to work on a few feature film projects like 'Poltergeist' and 'Staying Alive.'"

Rigging has allowed Rocky to have a career that is "very stimulating and seldom boring because you never know what is around the corner. For the same reasons that it is stimulating, it has a negative effect on my personal life with my wife as we're unable to plan vacations or other things in advance."

As in any profession, in order to achieve a high level of success you must often make sacrifices. According to Rocky: "Many times you have to sacrifice short-term benefits to achieve more important lifetime goals.

"The only place I know to start in this business is at the bottom. Only the Universities with major sports arenas can afford you the opportunity to do rigging as a student. Therefore, it's best to seek out a college that has theatre courses available to you. There are a large number of schools that have facilities that attract major touring acts.

"Probably the best entry into the business would be to get a job with the IATSE in a local that has a major arena. Once you have the job, be better than anyone around you. If you are punctual, conscientious, and can get along with people — you will start to climb in the industry. As elementary as it seems, attitude is often more important than knowledge."

156

> **❝The way you look,
> your style, your clothes, are all just another way
> of communicating. It should tell the truth about
> you, the same as your music and your words. ❞**
>
> *Jean Beauvoir*

Wardrobe Design

Lynn Pickwell

Dressing a star and taking care of the wardrobe of a major tour is what Lynn Pickwell has done for Bruce Springsteen, Whitney Houston and many others. It takes skill. Those battered jeans and torn T-shirts may not be as "casual" as you think. It's all a part of how the show looks to the audience and a lot of hard work goes into making it look easy.

Bruce Springsteen didn't buy his Tunnel of Love wardrobe off the rack at Bloomingdale's. The clothing was designed by Lynn Pickwell. "It was a big risk to switch him out of the standard jeans and torn vest to a more romantic look. That involved many conversations to decide how we were going to handle that without alienating his large following. Yet, he was at an age, a time when the material in the album was much softer than he had ever done before. We felt there should be a change of look. There was a lot of strategic planning that went into those changes. If you got the chance to see the Tunnel of Love tour, you probably noticed that by the time he was doing

157

Rosalita and all the old standbys the new clothes were gone and he had stripped down to the black T-shirt and denim jeans. It was a $6 Hanes, and when the audience left, it would leave with the memory of that wet black T-shirt."

Lynn started out as a fashion writer, even though she went to school to study fashion design. "At a party in Los Angeles, I told a director friend of mine that I would like to get into wardrobe. About two weeks later he called me up and told me that he had a video coming up for a group on Atlantic Records; they had no money, but, if I would work for free, the wardrobe job was mine. I agreed to do it.

"The song from that video went right up the charts and the artist ended up getting a tour out of it. I went on the road for the first time.

"It was at that point that my college background began to pay off for me. Here was this image-creating business that I had completely overlooked. Although it was something of a fluke that I ended up on the road, it soon became a way of life. I began doing heavy metal videos — Grim Reaper, Anthrax — you know, a lot of leather, studs, really outrageous things.

"After that I started getting called by bigger and bigger groups. Once you get yourself onto a circuit where you do name people, then you consistently stay busy. Last year I did videos for Stevie Wonder, Whitney Houston, Bryan Adams, and Springsteen. I was then hired to do The Tunnel of Love Tour for the E Street Band, including the horn section that he added and, of course, all of Bruce's clothes.

"Whitney Houston's video for 'So Emotional' has gotten a tremendous amount of work for me. I think it was the first time that people really liked the way Whitney looked. My position there with Whitney was really in conflict with the director, as he wanted her in jeans and a very short, short, denim skirt and a jeans jacket. I felt that Whitney needed a wardrobe that would keep her looking Rock 'n' Roll, but would let the public see a little touch of her class. Therefore, we went with an olive green leather jacket, a very good color for her skin tone, and everyone loved it. Whitney had backed me from the beginning by telling the director, 'I like Bon Jovi but I don't want to be Bon Jovi.' It's been especially gratifying to see Whitney wear my outfits when she accepts so many of her awards."

Lynn thinks that to make it in this business it is essential to have the ability to interpret a director's vision and a good "sense of fabrication." The person who "really understands how different fabrics work when constructed has a real advantage." Sometimes a certain fabric is going to alter the look of a garment completely. A particular skirt won't wear or look well in one fabric, but in a different fabric, because of its puckering and its texturing, it gives someone a flattering look even though it fits like a glove.

She suggests that young people look deeper than just learning how to design, sketch, or sew. "Dressing a musician for a video or a celebrity for his or her public image is completely different, because now you're getting into how they are perceived by the public. You need to understand people's skin tone, hair coloring, body shapes, silhouettes. You need to be able to change button treatments, zippers, and collar treatments. You must think about the way light hits clothing. You don't want things reflecting and glaring while you're shooting it. I still take classes at UCLA; I'm amazed that six years ago, I had nowhere near the amount of knowledge that I have today. Yet, there's still so much more that I am eager to know. Now that I'm also working behind the camera, it makes me ten times more aware of what goes on with wardrobe, and what works and what doesn't.

"As far as educational requirements, I would suggest a liberal arts or fine arts program within a university. Then, perhaps, a one year program would get you an associate degree, which is like a tech degree at a fashion design school. A fashion institute is good, but you miss the value of the well-rounded education that you can get in a university or state college. It's my belief that having a comprehension of other subjects such as history and English is important. One of the biggest assets that I got from college has been my knowledge of historical periods, because it gives me a reference point for everything I do.

"Should you decide to get into the business, be aware of the amount of hours you'll be required to work. All year long we work a minimum of 12 to 16 hour days. I work non-stop, including weekends and most holidays. Although I would be working anyway, I benefit from working weekends because it's much cheaper to rent equipment for the weekend than for a weekday.

"I have two assistants at all times on almost every project. One of them sets up appointments for me and stays on the phone virtually all day to keep the job moving. The other is out in the market running with me. I also have a couple of people I bring in on bigger jobs to make hats or craft capes, coats — whatever. Sometimes we have had to dye clothes throughout the night, as well.

"A great place for any high school or college student to start out would be with a production company. People who work under department heads such as costume designers, art directors or production designers, are called 'PA's' (production assistants). They're important positions. Go out and find production companies and let them know that you're willing to be a PA. They may give you as little as $50 a day, depending upon the production. More than likely you'll work a minimum of 12 hours a day. You may even put in 27 or 28 hours straight for that money, because you're really there to support the crew. When I say support the crew, that means in every facet of production.

"There's so much that has to be done all the time, constant setups, breakdowns, cleanups, making sure that things are packed right, making sure nothing is forgotten. You know, sometimes I'm on a set where I'm three miles away from the clothes and things have to go back and forth five or six times. When that's the situation, my assistants may have to run back and forth for the clothing instead of me. Other people may be back at the office painting, or sewing something. I have been out on baseball fields with a sewing machine with an assistant and one of the grips had to run an extension cord to a high school a mile away so we could get power to sew. There are many times like that when we simply have to improvise to deal with last minute problems. So, assistants are very valuable people. If you work for good department heads, you won't feel like you're abused, but for quite a while you have to give long, long hours for very little money. Some people have the nature for it, while others don't. Those who do will continually be asked to come back.

"Financially, it's difficult in the beginning stages. However, the money is very good when you've established your name and get on the circuit. It's safe to say that you'll then be working all the time. Of course, there are rewards in this business other than monetary ones. For me, it was going out on the Tunnel of Love Tour. I just had such a wonderful time being out on the road with Bruce. It was a gift I gave myself because I hadn't taken a vacation in years, and it was one of the best Rock 'n' Roll tours ever. In general, I find musicians to be some of the most wonderful people to be around. They're just very spiritual, very much at peace. It's great to be around such creative people."

160

Stage Management

Thomas Reedy

As a teenager, Thomas (Rocko) Reedy worked in music stores around Chicago repairing guitars. He also played bass guitar in different bar bands, but Rocko says, "I knew that if you want to make it big, you had go to one of the coasts. I wasn't ready to leave Chicago (at that time) because all my family and friends were there. Performing was a lot of fun, but unless you are willing to make sacrifices there's not a big future in playing clubs.

"I happened to do some guitar repair work for one of the members of Styx. He really liked the job and asked me if I would like to go on the road as a guitar tech. This was an offer that I couldn't refuse. I toured with Styx for seven years. Although I was hired on as a guitar tech the job developed into much more. Styx was a successful band, but we didn't have a production manager. We simply switched roles with each other. Each person took a turn at being responsibile for different jobs. I took care of the stage for the set; a couple of other guys handled the lights; there was a lighting crew chief, a sound crew chief and that's the way it went throughout the tour. This enabled me to develop skills in all different areas of production.

"After Styx, I toured with Survivor. They, like myself, were based out of Chicago. I was out on the road with them when they were having quite a bit of success with Eye of the Tiger. Their subsequent album, Vital Signs, made them headliners for the first time. The band was doing 5,000-6,000 seats in arenas around the country. About fifteen minutes before a show in Tampa, Florida, the bass player had to be rushed to the hospital for an emergency appendectomy. The arena was packed, all the gear was set up, the support act was in the middle of their set, and at this point everybody was freaking out (especially the promoter). I said, wait a minute. I've been listening to this stuff for two years, I play the bass, no problem, dude. So, I played bass on that gig and it worked out well enough that I finished the last month of the tour playing bass as well as being the production manager!"

After Survivor, Rocko worked with Robin Trower, the Kinks, Aerosmith and a lot of other major acts as a stage manager (They never asked him to play bass).

When Rocko is touring, his first duty of the day is to meet the crew chief or union steward at the venue. "I usually bring one of riggers from our crew along and introduce ourselves. We schedule the time for the first call of the morning, which is usually 8:00 a.m. All the details have previously been worked out on paper prior to the performance, but we still have to make sure that everything is going to happen as planned. We usually know in advance how many union stage hands and house riggers will have to be there. Also, we'll note any structural changes that must be made.

"After the load in, the crew starts to set up. Normally, work begins by rigging the 'points' (the places on the ceiling from which you are going to hang things). At this time, I'm already working with the steward and our crew to unload all the gear from the first truck. The lights are brought in and some of the stage hands begin prepping the lighting equipment before it goes up in the air, assembling it in place. The sound crew truck comes in and once again more of our crew will work with them. Then both the sound and lights are hung above the stage. In the case of a band like Aerosmith, we would bring in additional stagehands at about 10:00 to work with the sound people.

162

This way everything runs smoothly. I must have the set and the band's gear put together. If we're in a situation where we are tight on time, the work doesn't even stop for lunch and work continues while we eat. After the sound check and the show itself, the whole process is done in reverse, at twice the speed.

Rocko doesn't know of any reputable roadie or stage manager schools to suggest. Instead he urges young hopefuls to get into theater production. "I find some of the best people that I've worked with are those with a theater background. Working with any type of touring Rock 'n' Roll production can be the most lucrative, but there are other types of useful touring experiences, like the circus, theater or even the Ice Capades. They use very similar production techniques to the ones we use on the road. So, for kids starting out, I would say get involved in high school theater or school sponsored concerts. (When I was in high school, we called them concerts because nobody danced.) Also, working at a local club can open a few doors. Just about every band on the road now started out as a bar band." Learning the ropes, to Rocko, means: "Start at the bottom, make mistakes and learn by them. No matter how bad things seem to get use your own intelligence and learn from your experiences. It won't be as difficult for you the next time you do it.

"During my first 50 shows or so, whenever I would go out in front of a crowd of people, I flipped out over the fact that this was the big time. 'I'm here, and now it's not so cool anymore because I'm scared to death.' After getting over my rookie jitters and was on the road a while, reality finally set in. This is a very serious business. It is a lot of work, but the thing that you have to do is become involved and enjoy the job of making it all seem like magic. We are the people behind the scenes. We don't get a lot of credit. However, the pay is good and we get a lot of satisfaction from a job well done. I love the business that I'm in and that makes it a lot easier to get up at 8:00 in the morning after finishing a load out or arguing with stage hands till 4:30 a.m.

"The best attribute you can have on the road is a good sense of humor. When you get to the gig you must check your ego at the door. They are the two most important things that I've learned. I can think back to a lot of mistakes that I've made, blowing up and expressing my opinion or not being willing to change it. Sometimes I allowed my opinion to be changed just because I didn't want to be 'unpopular.' Everyone is going to have a different attitude, but you have to learn to

163

watch what you say and the way you present it. Never forget that you must achieve the final goal of getting the show done. I hate to say it, but the show must go on. I try not to have a lot of interaction with the bands. I think that it's important to maintain an employee-employer relationship in any business, particularly this one. I don't want to be their best friend. I make it a point to introduce myself, but I find that if you do a good job, the band will remember you. A good job will shine through further than anything else. I feel very lucky to have a job that I love. I look forward to going to work every day. I don't think most people outside of this business can say that."

66 **W**hen you're a per-
*former, it's not easy to think about much more than
your latest song, your next show, your overdue
album and that sort of thing. But soon you learn,
sometimes the hard way, that you, or someone you
trust, like Jane, really must stay on top of a lot
of other things. That's what I think a manager is
supposed to be. 99*

Keith Richards

Artist Management

Jane Rose

*Jane Rose was a child psychology major working towards a
master's degree and "had absolutely nothing to do with music"
when she was in college. To Jane and her friends the entertainment
business certainly didn't look as if it might ever be her choice of
career. But here she is, managing Keith Richards.*

How did that happen? According to Jane: "A friend of mine
worked for a promoter (Howard Stein) in New York City. I found it
fascinating that people were actually making a living this way. I was
living in Woodstock then, but I made it a habit to visit the city at least
two days a week, just to see them in action. At first, it was strictly to go
in to have lunch and watch them work. Occasionally, I helped answer
the phones, which was quite fun. The energy in the office was so
exhilarating that I decided to move back to New York. I really didn't
want to be a teacher anyway, but everyone said, what else can a girl
do when she finishes college. Well, now I knew.

"The promoter was starting to do very well and I began to know
everyone on the phone who was important to him. He offered me a

job and I ended up being his right arm. He expanded his promotions to five states and because I primarily dealt with all the various agencies that furnished talent, got to know a lot of the agents. After a couple of years, Peter Rudge offered me a job as Vice President of Sir Productions. Peter managed Lynyrd Skynyrd and the Who and was the tour manager for the Rolling Stones. Although I had acquired a working knowledge of contracts and promotions, I had never met a musician in my entire life. I had seen plenty of performers backstage at the Academy of Music or Madison Square Garden, but had never been introduced to an artist. My baptism under fire occurred a week after starting my new job. I went on the road with Lynyrd Skynyrd. It was the first time that I worked the 'settlement' on behalf of a band. The idea of a woman working for them was very amusing to the band. They treated me like a little sister. I took my responsibilities quite seriously. It was exciting to see them grow as a band and I really cared about them personally.

"After the Skynyrd tour ended, I worked in the office. At that time the Rolling Stones were in Germany doing an album. Because Rudge was continually running here and there, I began speaking with Mick Jagger quite frequently. Eventually, we got to know each other through our phone conversations. I finally met him in the office when the Stones were preparing for their 1975 tour. Apparently, the band felt comfortable with me and I became their liaison, their connection to the company that managed them. I was still working with Skynyrd, but enjoyed less and less working for a 'management company.' I liked the idea of representing one band and felt a need to be consistent with that whole concept. Besides, Skynyrd was getting very big and the situation was becoming political. Jagger told me that the band needed their own office. We all discussed me making a move and it was done very amicably. With that, I started working for Mick and eventually the Stones.

"I was constantly learning about the business. Peter had taught me a lot about touring, dealing with record companies and much more. My education in touring was extensive because I had worked on both sides of the fence. I felt that I had a lot to offer to the band. This was a golden opportunity to do what I had always wanted to do — represent one entity and be loyal to one band. It didn't matter to me if it was renting a house for them, finding out about a movie deal, making phone calls, getting a cup of coffee or putting a concert together. They had my complete loyalty. I just made sure that whatever it was, I did it right.

"Although my responsibilities were to the entire band, my day to day activities revolved around Mick. My involvement with Keith accelerated when he got into trouble in 1977. Mick and everyone around the band were very concerned about Keith's health and well being. Mick and Keith were very close. Keith wanted to clean up and get himself together and chose the method of treatment for himself. Mick and I found a place for him, where we could visit and follow through with him. We wanted to help him to get well. It's funny, I had always been terrified of Keith. His whole image scared me. He looked like walking death when I first met him. I wasn't a Rock 'n' Roller and his reputation was frightening to me. However, when I was introduced to him, he was so lovely and polite! I was shocked that he was so sweet, obviously a very misunderstood person.

"I helped Keith organize his benefit concert for the blind and also started getting attached to Keith's legal situation. My duty at that time was to be supportive in every aspect of his life. He needed lots of attention. I believed he would recover and felt that he needed others to believe in him as well. Many so-called experts thought he wouldn't make it. You know, 'once a junkie, always a junkie.' But, I didn't believe that at all and neither did Keith.

"After the 1981 tour, in an effort to establish his own identity outside the Stones' organization, Mick wanted to have his own office. During the previous three years my day to day contact was with both Mick and Keith, which often became awkward because they have a strange relationship. They are both very volatile and eventually they agreed that it would be better to have separate offices.

"Above all, Keith trusted me. My decision was made — I was with Keith." Jane sees herself and Keith as "very much alike" in the way they approach things: "He is a very ethical person, straightforward, and I'm the same way. We're not afraid to speak our mind and neither of us lie. You tell the truth and that's it. There's nothing else to remember. Basically, we get along because we're both fighters. There is a great deal of mutual respect between us. He believed in me to the point that he asked me to represent him.

"Money has never been my motivation. Quality is. Perhaps it's some type of maternal instinct, but I want Keith to have everything that he deserves. Maybe it's not the same for all women, but I was probably raised to be a wife, you know, to enhance the environment, to make everything around me bigger and better. In the music industry, the artist is the king and that's the bottom line. As a manager, I've always thought of myself as the number two person. I am not responsible for Keith Richards' success, Keith Richards is responsible for it. I do the things that I really believe will get him what he wants, help him achieve and give him the necessary support for him to come through. My job is to make what he wants happen."

Keith's solo career began with the movie Jumping Jack Flash. Jane recalls: "He was very nervous about producing that song for Aretha Franklin because it was his first venture outside of the Stones." Jane was the associate producer of the hit movie, Hail Hail Rock 'n' Roll, which proved to be a wonderful transition to a different part of Keith's career. Keith produced the soundtrack LP and was the musical director, getting the arrangements of the songs, setting up rehearsals, and mixing the sound track. He liked it, and did it so well that it is now an important part of his musical activities.

Jane believes that there are a lot of opportunities for women in the 1990's. "Women have proven themselves in this business and are now more readily accepted by the industry establishment. Sometimes you have to let things go in one ear and out the other. As a way of testing you, people will take shots at you. You must have a strong sense of who you are. That is the only way a woman can survive and succeed in this exciting business."

Another key to success in this or any other career, Jane believes, is education. "The more you know, the more you can draw upon. Degrees are not important, education is important. I think that women should get in this business because they understand what it is to nurture and what it is to believe in something. If you want something, go for it. The most important question you can ask yourself is why am I interested in an entertainment career. The answer should be that you love it and really care about the quality of the music."

Jane's suggestion for would-be managers: "I would try to get in the door by taking any job in a related field. Get in an environment where you can learn. It may be answering the phones in an agency or record company. Take pride in doing tasks that may seem menial to others. Do a good job at whatever you're asked to do. The more you're willing to do the more people will depend on you and the more responsibility they will give you. When you have built up that respect all around you, maybe that will be the right time to start thinking about becoming a manager."

> **66 When you've had a good time somewhere, it's even better if you can take something home as a souvenir. Merchandise isn't just to make money, but to add to the feeling that you're at 'an event'. 99**
>
> **Chip Rachlin, Manager**
> **PHOEBE SNOW, ACE FREHLEY**

Tour Merchandise

Alvin Ross

Do you ever look at the Billboard charts to see how your favorite group's latest album is doing? Would you be interested in betting on the future success of some unknown act that appears out of nowhere and stays on the charts for a few weeks before fading out? Yes? Then maybe tour merchandising is for you.

In a way betting on new bands is a lot of what Al Ross and Larry Johnson of Nice Man Merchandising do for a living. Nice Man is involved in tour merchandising of artists and marketing them into retail outlets.

"We kind of watch the charts. Larry and I sit down and follow the charts, to look for the bands that we think are going to make it. It's not difficult to know what a big act is doing because all of the companies are going to go after the superstar acts. We think the secret of the business is trying to follow the young acts, the smaller acts, the baby bands, and try to sign them early to a long term deal, where it pays for us to invest some money in the band's career and hope that the band will make it later on.

170

"In essence what we often do is call the manager or whoever is representing the artist to ask if the XYZ band is getting ready to do a tour. If so, we tell them that we would like to bid for the merchandising rights. If they are interested, they will respond by sending us all the upcoming plans for the band. This will usually include information such as when the album or single is going to be released, the management staff, the band's agent, what label they're on and if they have a tour already booked. If they are scheduled to tour they will send us the entire itinerary, which includes the dates, venues and the capacities. Based on that information we would go back and put together an offer to try and secure those rights. At that point you're either in the same ball park with them or you're not. If your offer is pretty much the same as everybody else's then you kind of hope that the relationship you have built with the band or the reputation you've built up in the industry might lead to getting to the act over your competitors."

Al got his start in the music business doing public relations. From there he got involved in managing bands, first with the Raspberries and then as a partner managing Kiss. It was that relationship with Kiss that led him into merchandising. "I saw what a successful merchandising business could do and I always liked working on the creative side with acts anyway." Among the 50 or so acts for which Nice Man has created and for whom they have sold merchandise are David Lee Roth, REM, Amy Grant, Stryper, Bryan Ferry, Rod Stewart and Cyndi Lauper.

"Once we book an act for merchandising we sit down with the manager (and in some cases the artist) and prepare for the entire tour. Bryan Ferry was very much involved in the development of the designs for his tour merchandise. We present to both the manager and artist what we believe to be the kind of T-shirt we can offer on the tour. Perhaps the two most important considerations are the quality and price of the garment to be sold.

"When the cost and quality of the merchandise is decided on, we then go out and produce all of the items. Everything is subject to the band's approval. We load up a truck with enough merchandise for the first two or three weeks of the tour, or until we can get a feeling of what's going to happen out there, and we hit the road. We just follow the band around from venue to venue. There are certain bands where the road crew will work with us and do their own vending. They set up stands, display boards and do their own selling. However, there are many buildings that have what they call in-house vendors where we just count the merchandise and give it to them. We still supervise things, but they do all the selling and settle with us or the band at the end of the night.

"The biggest problem that we have is that some of the buildings charge as much 40% off the top for the right to sell, and that's excluding any sales tax you have to put on top of that. Therefore, although the building takes no risk at all, it gets more money than the act does. Many venues are making more money than the artist whose merchandise is being sold.

"Bootlegging also presents a problem, but not every band is really subject to bootlegging. Primarily the big acts who play the larger venues are bothered by it. With those bands you really work with the manager and the building. Often we'll go out and get a federal injunction (a court order) that allows us to confiscate any bogus goods we find being sold. We simply give the proper papers to the security force working for us, local marshalls or a private security firm, and they enforce the law. In most cases the cost to do that is normally split between the artist and the merchandising company.

"A merchandising company offers employment in several different areas. There is a production director who coordinates all the artwork and heads up all the production in the company. He or she oversees the complete production of the books being printed and the shirts being made. Nice Man has a national tour manager to whom all of the men on the road have to report. The mail order department that fills the orders which are generated through advertisments is a major operation. The biggest part of the support staff, however, is the office staff — clerks, secretaries, assistants, etc."

The most visible employees are the road crew. Al picks them carefully. "I find some guys want to go on the road for the wrong reasons — that is, for the glamour. They see it's Rock 'n' Roll and think that's great — we're going to go out there and we'll party every night. Well, we're the wrong end of the business to do that because what really happens is that a guy gets in his truck, checks his merchandise in the late afternoon and at about 2:00 o'clock in the morning he checks it out. Then he'll probably drive 500 to 600 miles to get to the next city. Perhaps he'll get three or four hours of sleep before he's got to go check the stuff in again and go through the same routine. Normally, the good touring acts will work an average of four and a half days a week. Even though a guy has a couple of days off, technically he's rarely off at all because he has to spend that time driving to the next show or finding a place to sleep for a few hours. So if you're looking for glamour, this isn't the place. If a person works hard he can make a very decent living and get the opportunity to travel all over the country. But, that's it!

"If we do a Rod Stewart tour in America we may also get to handle the merchandise for that tour for the rest of the world. He'll go to Japan, Australia, Europe or wherever. This presents an opportunity for someone to see the world at someone else's expense. A background in accounting is helpful because there are so many numbers to deal with. Obviously, we're looking for guys who are not only honest, but who are responsible, serious and of course, not involved in drugs. These qualifications are an absolute necessity because the road man is responsible for a truck and merchandise worth probably $200,000 to $300,000. This is one reason why our lead guys are paid so well. A lead guy in our business, who has proven himself, can earn anywhere from $50,000 to $75,000 a year.

"A road guy coming in without any experience isn't going to make a lot of money initially. However, if he is not afraid to work hard and is attentive, that situation will change somewhat rapidly. In essence when a guy is out on the road he represents what our company stands for. We are not out there with him all the time. He's the one who deals (on our behalf) with the tour manager or band on a day-to-day basis. Our road guys must be congenial and have to have enough diplomacy to put up with a lot of nonsense. I should also mention that he may need the ability to get by without a lot of sleep.

"It can be very political on the road. It's not your place to take anybody's side. You're a guy who's there to do a job, to perform a service. If you're the type of person who gets homesick, this is not a job for you. We have three guys on the road right now who haven't been home more than two weeks in the past eight months. It's great for a single guy but extremely tough for a guy who's married.

"When we advertise or go to schools for our staff, we search for people who are diligent and who will commit to being with us for a while. A guy on the road gets paid a salary, a per diem, and in addition to that we pick up his hotel bill so when most of the road guys come home — they can live on their per diems alone. Each person who's

173

put in a couple of good, tough years ends up making serious money. They've earned the right to get to that point."

Nice Man is a company that's still on its way up. "Our growth in the past couple of years has been dramatic. I believe that we're a terrific place for young people to work if they're interested in making merchandising a career."

66 *A great promoter's rep is essential to every band's production manager, because when we walk into the building everything has to be right. If we have an emergency, he has to be able to connect immediately with anything from doctors to generators. Who else would know where to get sushi delivered at 3 a.m. in Terre Haute?* **99**

Jake Berry, Production Manager
AC/DC, METALLICA, MOTLEY CRUE

Promoter's Representative
Tim Rozner

Many local promoters have a top staff member who is the local "Production Manager," the counterpart of the head of production that many touring artists carry with them on the road. These two experienced professionals then have to work together to produce the best show they can. Tim Rozner is a great production manager.

Tim Rozner has produced live concerts, videos, and has been the site coordinator for films. All his projects have something in common; they are high pressure and require creativity. As the production manager for Fey Concerts, a very busy promotion company operating mainly west of the Mississippi, Tim's responsibilities are considerable.

"I'll start out getting all the necessary details from the promoter, including show time, the location of the venue, what time the doors will open, the expected size of the crowd, and whether it's reserved seating or general admission. Also, I have to find out if the band will require any special kind of security, staging, sound, lights, labor, and other additional equipment. I see that all those things get done and are ready for the show on a timely basis and in a cost effective manner on budget. Basically, the job of the production manager for a promoter is to maintain the highest industry standards, while using all his local relationships, knowledge and experience to keep costs under control and to maximize both the promoter's and the band's profits."

Tim's interest in the entertainment field goes way back. "My parents always encouraged my four brothers and me to play instruments. I always loved music, but electronics interested me even more. Shows like In Concert, Midnight Special and the earlier versions of those programs fascinated me. To see the connection between music and electronics, especially lighting and special effects, from the technical side fueled my desire to learn more about it."

In high school, Tim enrolled in every radio, theater and television program that was available. "I progressed from having a radio show as a freshman to doing multimedia shows in my sophomore year. I was producing a 32-projector show and one of my teachers was directing it. We co-wrote the program, which eventually evolved into a 48-projector multimedia show using film clips and slide projectors manually synchronized with music. These shows became very popular with my classmates.

"The whole school would attend the assemblies to see the presentation. It gave me my first real opportunity to feel like a producer and the thrill of controlling a major production in front of a large number of people. We even 'attacked their senses' with lighting effects, smoke bombs, flash pots and live performances. I experimented my first year with the school itself as an audience and tried out shows based on contemporary music synched with action.

"The highlight of my production experience in high school occurred during my junior year when we did a show based on the Beatles. It was very well received, but later that same year, 'A Way With Words' and 'Beatlemania' came out. We really did a lot of speculating about whether our high school show on tour in Illinois had actually inspired some of the ideas that they used in those professional shows. To produce our version, we searched for six months to dig up every photo, film clip, and news article that you could possibly think of and put it together as a 90 minute show, all

176

synched with Beatle music, using 48 projectors. I'd like to think I did it first.

"Toward the end of my senior year, a friend of mine began to buy vintage guitars at various pawn shops in downtown Chicago. He was the only guy I knew who could get backstage passes, even during sold-out concerts. When you're in high school and can get allowed backstage consistently, it's very impressive. I followed his lead and began to buy guitars myself. I would go to the Chicago Auditorium Theater or to the Amphitheater and sell them to rock stars. Thanks to my persistence and my knowledge of the guitars I was selling, I was able to get into shows. The more I got backstage to see the stars, the more fascinating the technical side of things became. The entire behind-the-scenes working of the lighting, sound, and the pressure back there, along with the immediacy of the show-must-go-on attitude really made me want to get involved.

"I enrolled at Columbia College because they offered courses in music production. After a year, I decided go to the (then) party school of the world, Southern Illinois University, to enter their theatre arts program. In the interim, I produced shows at a youth organization called the Corral. You could join for a small fee and see bands like Styx, The Ides of March, the American Breed, and a lot of Chicago based bands. In fact, Survivor played there before getting big. However, the Corral was becoming less popular and a friend of mine, Rocco Reedy, and I decided to do something about it. We let the members know that we would try anything to save the club. The father of one of the club's members represented a number of artists. Scott Cameron, who managed blues greats Willie Dixon, Muddy Waters and many others, wanted to help the organization by bringing Muddy in for a show. Everything went smoothly. Scott told me that he was very impressed with the job I had done and promised to be in touch with me some day.

"True to his word, I got the promised call from Scott Cameron between semesters. He asked me if I would be interested in touring with Muddy Waters. Of course, I said, 'Yes.' At 19 years old, I found myself doing my first European tour. This was a wonderful experience, a great opportunity to work with a very organized company. They were small, but right in the mainstream of the industry. Working with Muddy focused me and directed my emphasis on what is important in this business. It also reminded me of my upbringing, that is, my parents' sense of values, their advice to do the best I can on any assignment and their attention to small detail. My association with Muddy made me realize that the small jazz and blues clubs are just as important and can be just as thrilling as the 75,000 seat arenas, like the U2 shows in Giant Stadium.

"I worked with Muddy for about four years. One of the things that will live with me forever, and is often missing in this world, is loyalty. He taught me all about it. It's something that you can't buy, a sense of loyalty. Muddy had a terrible illness and I could't let him think that because he was sick I might leave him. I stayed with Muddy through a year of his illness and neither of us worked at all. It was important to make him feel that I had confidence in his recovery, that he would get better and that we would be doing shows again. I really got close to starvation while trying to give mental support to a friend. I felt real close to him. He was a great influence in my life. After a year, Muddy recovered sufficiently enough to do a couple more shows. As a matter of fact, the last show we did was on Eric Clapton's birthday. Muddy, myself, Muddy's wife and Muddy's manager flew down to Hollywood, Florida. It was the last show of Eric Clapton's tour and Clapton's manager flew us down as a surprise. Eric had given up alcohol and was doing great business. Muddy was perhaps Eric's greatest single influence in the music business and that was the last performance that Muddy ever gave.

"I was an ironworker for about a year and a half. It was an ungodly amount of money per hour, but it meant I had to go up and risk my life every day. Also, it was hard for me to go to work for other artists directly after Muddy's death. Eventually, however, I was able to do some projects here and there on other shows.

"The Chicagofest was always a very big attraction. In fact, it may have been the best outdoor, all encompassing music festival in the world. Everyone, who's anyone has played there, but a political conflict in town made the festival lose its city subsidy and that almost cancelled the festivities. However, it managed to survive without city sponsorship. I thought that the best thing that I could do would be to work on that festival. It was the first year that it wasn't city-sponsored. We held it at Soldier's Field and I was the overall production coordinator. We advanced, coordinated and produced 200 acts in the time frame of one month. It was an amazingly complicated undertaking for such a short amount of time.

178

"People directed me to Jimmy Lewis, who had been touted as one of the better on-site producers in the business. I had seen Jimmy at every Chicago Fest, but had never before gotten to know him. He turned out to be really helpful, particularly because he told me of a production manager position available at Redrocks in Denver. Redrock is an outdoor amphitheater located in the foothills outside of Denver. It is a naturally perfect acoustic outdoor amphitheater built out of a rock formation that is millions of years old. I applied for and got the job as the production manager for the biggest Denver promoter, Fey Concerts, and immediately began producing shows at Redrock. I also did some one-off projects, that is, projects where I acted as an independent contractor on my own.

"Through all these projects, I've managed to build very good relationships with many different groups, such as U2. In fact, I had the pleasure of working with that band on Rattle and Hum, producing the concert for the actual film shoots in Denver, Colorado, and Tempe, Arizona. Another very special relationship I have is with Aerosmith. The band has always been one of my favorites. I did my first air guitar riffs listening to their records. So it was a big thrill to do the last ten shows of their Done With Mirrors tour. The band at that time was not doing good business. Late one night, I got a call from Aerosmith, informing me they needed a production manager and that they were in a difficult situation. They only had five days to start the next leg of the tour, which also happened to be the most crucial part of the entire tour. Always having a great capacity for flying by the seat of my pants and accomplishing things at the last minute, I accepted the challenge and we completed the tour with some pretty good success."

Tim notes through years of experience that "different acts attract different types of audiences. Sting, for example, has a very sensitive audience, a very hip kind of crowd. When he was with the Police, they were a young, energetic Rock 'n' Roll Band with an audience that was pretty much the same as Def Leppard has today — lots of pretty girls and young Rock 'n' Rollers. Today, Sting has well-dressed people of all ages that come out to hear him play. They're very into both the music and the message. It's an interesting crowd. You can really see the difference compared to the audience for other groups. When you get an AC/DC crowd, you'll have what we call 'road warriors.' I just finished a tour with Aerosmith and Guns and Roses. They attract the AC/DC type audience."

It would be difficult to work with so many great artists without having some fabulous memories. "To me, the 1987-88 Aerosmith 'Permanent Vacation Tour' was the equivalent, if not greater than, the 1988 Dodgers World Series win. Nobody thought they could do it. They were given no chance to win their battle and in the process, they came through trial after trial, with a grand slam in the 9th inning. They maintained their standards throughout the tour by fighting a very courageous battle. This fight was difficult for them because they had been totally consumed by the fast lane of Rock 'n' Roll, the fast cars, huge houses, big money, and the whole experience. Therefore, I believe that they had a further way to come than most people. For them to build on their audience, to maintain both their physical and mental cleanliness over a very grueling year of touring (including a successful Japanese leg) was a major accomplishment.

"The band's problem had been every kind of 'substance abuse' you can think of, anything and everything. This was something that had been not only part of their physical life, but it was part of their mental life. They made no secret of it. In fact, their image was the guys who always were messed up on stage. You could expect anything from an Aerosmith show. But when they decided to clean themselves up and do that tour, they and the rest of the world learned that they are still one of the premiere Rock 'n' Roll bands in the world. We're all very proud of them for what they've accomplished. I think they're proud of it too."

Tim advises, "The Rock 'n' Roll industry isn't for everyone. The best advice I can offer to anyone who's interested in the technical side of Rock 'n' Roll, is to get as much schooling as you can. Year after year this business becomes more competitive and more high tech. Individuals with a greater amount of technical knowledge will go further in the business than those less skilled. Another thing is to keep an open mind. It's funny how fast you're out of high school, then college and all of a sudden find yourself out in the real world. Rock 'n' Roll can move on and leave you behind, so start your career while you're in high school if that's the work you want to do. Stay involved by participating in college or working with club bands. Be prepared to start as the lowest man on the totem pole. Nobody, and I mean nobody, in this side of the business has ever been an overnight sensation. I got my big break because I was prepared when I got that phone call. I was ready because I had worked hard through high school and college to gain the necessary knowledge.

"This is unlike any other business. It is also big business and it's big dollars. It's not what a lot of people think. This is not a business where you get tons of chicks, where you sit around and people throw money at you or let you ride in limos everywhere. All that sometimes happens, but it's only a rare by-product of the business. The business aspect is first and foremost in every single person's mind. To a performer, his music is the most important thing. But, I can assure you that the reason his music is going to be heard is because record company executives, touring companies and promoters think this person is a viable business commodity. You have to be one too if you want to be part of it. Do yourself a favor and remember that this is a business. Be a well rounded individual. Get practical experience wherever possible. Above all, take your formal and practical education seriously. Do your best at whatever job level you're performing. Prove yourself by starting from the bottom and working your way up."

*66 **S**ome promoters go from hall to hall, putting on their concerts in many different places with different seating capacities. But sometimes the venue itself does it's own shows on its own stage. When that's the way they decide to do it, the venue needs someone in charge, a professional promoter of its own, to make it work. 99*

Jane Geraghty
PREMIER TALENT AGENCY

Facility Management

Scott Sanders

Scott Sanders started working with a local promoter in Tampa, Florida, when he was fifteen years old. "My first job was putting flyers on windshields in college parking lots to promote concerts."

While attending college in Florida, Scott promoted some shows on campus and even managed a band. "They were working clubs, but I got an idea that we should try to get a gig at Disney World because it paid more money and provided better exposure." At the same time, Scott was a DJ at Y95 in Tampa. "I started off just playing Casey Kasem's American Top 40 records and not saying a word. One day the jock didn't show up for work after my shift and I went on the air scared to death, but I did it. This brief experience helped me get a radio job at college. The summer before my senior year I went to Los Angeles for a fraternity convention and to see some record company people about future employment opportunities. I got lucky! United Artists Records actually hired me as their college promotion rep, to try to get records played on the radio station in Gainesville and to deal with the retail outlets there. They paid me a healthy $50 a week plus $50 in expenses and I felt like I was really in business. I worked for them throughout my senior year.

"When it came time to graduate, I sent my résumé to Bob Jani, who I heard was the head of entertainment for Disneyland. I had no idea that Bob was about to leave Disney to go to New York in an attempt to save Radio City Music Hall. Fortunately, he had taken my résumé with him. He made his presentation to the Rockefeller Group and was hired as President and Executive Producer of Radio City Music Hall Productions. He called me during the spring break of my senior year and asked me to come to New York for an interview. I was very excited. I had never been to New York in my life, but I said okay, great. He flew me up and we went to dinner. We spoke about employment at both Disney and the Music Hall. At the end of dinner, he informed me that I could have a job at either place. Before giving him my decision, I finished my spring semester and interviewed at several other places. But I came to the conclusion that I would take the job at Radio City. At first, I didn't want to come to New York; it intimidated me a lot. Even after I accepted the job, I thought I would stay here a year, maybe two. It's been nine years and that thought hasn't crossed my mind since.

"We used to rent the Music Hall out to other promoters at first, because it was very difficult for me to get talent to produce our own concerts. Many agents didn't want to sell us their popular acts because of their previous relationships with other New York promoters. So, I recommended that we just make a rule that we would promote every date in the building ourselves. Our first show was Diana Ross in October of 1979, which proved to be a huge success and sent us on our way. We now have over 50% of the Manhattan concert market, grossing anywhere from $14 to $18 million per year. We have even branched out to promoting venues like Roseland and we've also done shows at both Carnegie Hall and the Joyce Theater. Our sellout rate is about 95%. It's a true success story in the sense that we started out with a zero percentage share of the market and now we have over a 50% share. This clearly shows that if you believe in yourself and work hard you can do anything you want."

"People used to think of Radio City as a middle of the road theater and we wanted to demonstrate that we could promote anything here. We have worked with artists from the Grateful Dead to Liberace and from Iron Maiden to Richard Pryor. We've had Robert Palmer and INXS bringing the house down on several occasions. Of course, Radio City has long been known as the home of the Rockettes and we have managed to keep them as an important part of our production activities."

In Scott's opinion, "One of the best ways to get into the business is to start at the college level. Frequently, colleges have concert committees that need volunteers. The shows are generally produced with student body funds, or sometimes the school has a budget for promoting shows. Try to get involved in that area, so that you can start dealing with some of the booking agencies that represent touring bands. Most agencies have a particular agent who is responsible for staying tuned into colleges and clubs. A lot of these acts may be just catching on and this would be the ideal time to get to know them.

"I believe a college degree is very beneficial. First of all, it shows that someone was able to have the self-discipline to go into a challenging situation and complete four years of what may be considered very demanding, boring or impractical work. A person who gets a degree in marketing, advertising, public relations, music, theater or whatever it is, clearly demonstrates he or she is able to take on a challenge and succeed with it. Show that you are able to achieve a goal you've set for yourself. I think that it makes for a more well rounded, valuable person.

"Much too often, high school or college students either don't work at all while they're in school or work at the local fast food chain. Working in a variety of unrelated jobs may help you pay your rent or fraternity or sorority dues, but may not be the right answer. Certainly, that kind of work doesn't begin to build a résumé that looks attractive to an entertainment employer. If I get a résumé from someone who worked on the college concert board, for another promoter, a radio station or even a public relations firm, it looks like they're building a solid foundation for the future. Even though people frequently volunteer their time to concert boards for no pay, it still looks good on a résumé. When I get a résumé from someone who as a teenager started to build for his or her future in the music business, I'll seriously consider them for employment.

"To get a job in New York or Los Angeles with a major promoter is extremely difficult because there are only a limited number of promoters in each of those cities. That's not to dissuade anyone from trying, however. Frequently, promoters have heavy concert schedules in the summer and need part-time help. This is a good way to get your foot in the door. If you have a credible background, it would be a good idea to let a potential employer know in some way, shape or form, how you might be able to help them. Call them on the phone or write letters. Try to come up with some unique way to get their attention. Send a bouquet of balloons with your résumé in it. People tend not to like overly pushy people, but there is a fine line between trying to be too much of a lady or gentleman and being aggressive. In this business you are not going to succeed unless you're aggressive.

"New entrants in the promotion field start out as secretaries. That may not be what you want to do, but it's a good way to break into the field. Although you're coming out of school with a Master's degree, you have to be prepared to make $250 a week, or even less, as a secretary or clerk. You have to look at these entry level jobs as 'dues' to pay. Some people come out of college and think maybe they've already paid their dues. They'll tell themselves, 'I've labored through four years of college with a 3.5 average and I'm ready to start at the top.' Well, that's a long way from how it really is.

Scott explains how "deals" are put together: "An agent calls me and says Iron Maiden is going out on tour and that they want to play New York. Naturally, we would love them to play at Radio City. We estimate what we think the ticket budget will be; that is, we get their production rider, figure how much the stage hands are going to cost, catering, limousines, advertising, ushers, teamsters, ASCAP, BMI license fees, insurance, security and a number of other expenses. We have to figure out how much we can gross from selling the tickets. Let's say that we gross $100,000 and the expenses are $40,000. We now have $60,000 left. The $60,000 gets divided between the band and the promoter. We'll make an offer to the agent of perhaps $40,000 and a percentage. These days, the average promoter profit is about 15% of the net after expenses, so that the average band gets 85%. In a simplistic way, this is how deals are done. Taking into consideration that you're making yourself liable for at least $80,000 by guaranteeing $40,000 to the band and $40,000 in expenses, it's a very big gamble to make what may turn out to be only $9,000 at best. You had better know what you're doing.

"Once the deal is made, the process begins by first putting the building on hold for the scheduled date, getting ad mats and promotional pictures from the record company or the artist management and producing a radio spot. You then must implement all of the advertising and marketing, order the tickets to be printed, and contact the ticket agency who will be selling the tickets. The promoter's production manager will contact the artist's production representative to find out what the show is, how many trucks they are bringing in and when they want to load in. Then you order the stage hands and teamsters. As soon as you can, you start selling tickets. You also have to set up catering for the artist and get limousines to pick the band up at the airport. You coordinate with the building personnel, the security, and the ushers. It's a lot of preparation and anticipation."

A special treat for the staff is sneaking visiting artists backstage so they can watch the show without being noticed by the audience. "We've had Prince, Mick Jagger, and Boy George backstage. One time, Michael Jackson came to see Kool and the Gang dressed in a trench coat, a hat and a fake beard. When you get those kind of calls, it's your job to get them into the special backstage areas and make them comfortable. The funny part is that after all those problems and all that hard work, at the end of a great night, even when the evening has only made your company $9,000, you feel exhilarated and rewarded. You've made an important artist and an equally important audience very happy and everything's gone well. That's a great feeling and it's what makes you want to get up the next morning and do it again."

*66**T**he road manager carries an awesome degree of responsibility with a band on tour. As the management team's point man on the road, his role is demandingly multi-faceted. At once he is therapist, parent, confidante to the band. He bears ultimate responsibility for moving the equivalent of a million-dollar business and its personnel from one city to another every day. In essence, the road manager is an extension of me on the road.* 99

Tim Collins, Personal Manager
AEROSMITH

Road Management

Harry Sandler

"The Road Manager of a tour is right up there at the top of the chain of command, working just under the artist's own manager. He's sees to it that everything about the tour lives up to the expectations of both the manager and the artist. Few people make it up to that level of command. Each of them has a special story. Harry Sandler has made it to that point and here is how it happened."

Whatever John Cougar Mellencamp wants, Harry Sandler makes sure he gets it. It's his job. As Mellencamp's road manager and management assistant, Sandler is somehow involved in virtually every concert, album, movie, music video, and personal appearance that affects that Indiana singer. Harry goes as far as handling even the most minor details concerning the hotels that Mellencamp stays in while on tour.

Sandler has been a management associate in Mellencamp's organization for a few years now, but his climb to the top was not a short one. A high school dropout who moved with his family from Atlantic City to New York in the early 1960's, Sandler did what many other music-crazed youths did at the time: He hung out in Greenwich Village, got hooked on Bob Dylan and befriended guys in local bands.

In 1965, he moved to Philadelphia, where he got his first break carrying the gear and doing sound for a local band. At the time, he says, "No one knew that you could make money in the music business. I thought I was just having fun, trying to figure out what I was going to do." Returning to New York, he worked at the legendary Fillmore East, where he earned as little as $20.00 a night. But he rubbed elbows with stars and the stars-to-be, such as Whoopi Goldberg (who worked backstage in those days).

The 70's held different cards for Sandler. He decided, for vague reasons, that he wanted out of the music business. So he abruptly switched vocations and became a photographer. It worked for several years, but he tired of that as well and he jumped back into the music business, working as a sound mixer for a bar band in New Jersey. That, too, was short-lived for Sandler quickly hooked up with a British touring band that needed him to set up the stage, mix the monitors and even drive the equipment truck from gig to gig. This job was followed by similar ones for soul-singer Teddy Pendergrass and vocalist, Ellen Shipley.

By 1980, Bruce Springsteen was a household name. Sandler had been lucky enough to meet the person who held the key to the next three years of his future. He joined Springsteen's inner circle as the road manager for the E-Street Band.

Being a road manager for a Rock 'n' Roll star may sound like a dream come true, but certain sacrifices must be made. One of the major considerations is financial in nature. "Don't think you're going to start out making $500 a week. If you're interested, take what you can get and build on it."

Despite Springsteen's stardom and obvious financial success, Sandler made relatively little money considering his responsibilities. "I got paid $450 a week," he says, adding that road managers for other artists made anywhere from $800 to $2,500 a week. "But," he adds, "I would have worked for nothing to show that I could do the job."

Sandler's credits as a tour manager also include tours for Billy Joel and Stevie Nicks as well as participation in the Woodstock and US festivals.

"Sometimes I literally have to be at two places at the same time, like when Stevie Nicks was playing LA the same day I was working the US Festival as Production Manager. After 20 hours at the festival I had to be shuttled by limo to Stevie's show and work another whole night non-stop."

According to Sandler, road management duties can range from finding a hotel for the band down to the details of their dressing rooms. "There are hundreds of definitions of road manager," he says. "I talk to the production people for the promoter in each town, to make sure that the backstage accommodations, the dressing rooms, are right for the band, and I make sure that everybody else working on the tour is doing his job.

"There's a woman on the road who does the tickets and passes. I make sure she understands what's going on. I deal with the guy who runs the production part of the tour to make sure that the building is in shape." Becoming a tour manager does not just happen overnight. Persistence and personality are key factors to landing a job. Getting a foot in the door means working as an assistant taking care of dressing rooms, doing tickets and passes, or being a runner for a promoter. "It's a relationship/personality business. How you get along with people will dictate how far you get," he says. He advises meeting as many people as possible. Sandler tells of a 19-year-old guy who wants to be in the music business so badly that he is willing to trade his cushy bank job for one that requires checking a record store's inventory and its album display. "He was bugging us for months about getting a job. This guy will end up working in the music business because he shows that he is serious," says Sandler.

When Mellencamp isn't touring, Sandler's typical day begins around 10 a.m., at the offices of Champion Entertainment in Manhattan. "I deal with all the correspondence, you know, people who want John to do a lot of different things and save the world. I work with John on personal things and whatever is going on down the road. It's just like a regular job."

Sandler says that one thing bands don't tolerate is an employee who takes drugs. "Even a band that takes drugs themselves, don't want to come off stage and see someone who's supposed to be taking care of them as high as they are. Eventually, you'll be out of there. It's funny. You'd think it would be just the opposite, but it's not. This is a business. A real, big business."

189

> **66** *Tours just don't happen, stages just don't set themselves up and buses and lights and sound don't operate their own controls. Every production needs a manager of all the different crews and sections that have to work together. There aren't many people around with that kind of broad experience and authority. A woman with those qualifications, particularly one who can earn the total respect of her fellow professionals is even rarer. It's certainly a role model that young women can look up to.* **99**
>
> *Tina Weymouth*
> *TALKING HEADS, TOM-TOM CLUB*

Production Coordinator
Deborah Sandvik

Deborah Sandvik never dreamed that three years of touring as production manager for "Sesame Street Live" would lead her straight to Pink Floyd.

"I was a week away from going back to join up with Sesame Street for my fourth year. In fact, I had already started packing my office when I got a call from Morris Lyda. I had met Morris years before when I was working at Illinois State and he was in town with Genesis. He told me that he had joined up with Pink Floyd for a year and was looking for somebody to work with him. I had no idea how big the tour would be. All I knew was that they were going to be out for a year. After careful consideration I called the Sesame Street people in Minneapolis and told them I had been offered what I thought was a great opportunity. They assured me that I wasn't putting them on the spot and they agreed that it was a wonderful opportunity that shouldn't be passed up."

190

Deborah packed her gear and arrived in Toronto. "I went directly to an airplane hanger in the Toronto Airport where Pink Floyd was rehearsing. It was nearly empty. However, when I walked into the production office, there were computers from one end of the room to the other. My immediate thoughts were that this was going to be a very well organized project. Less than two hours after I had landed, we were already hard at work putting the show together."

As the production coordinator for the "Momentary Lapse of Reason Tour" Deborah worked extensively with the crew. Among her job responsibilities were getting the proper foreign visas for everyone, making all the necessary reservations at quality hotels worldwide, arranging transportation from one city to the next, ensuring that the entourage was paid their per diem (living allowance) each week and seeing to it that everyone was where he was supposed to be at designated times. To accomplish this vast undertaking required daily communications with all the crew members informing them what time load in would be, lunch would be served and all the important information that anyone would need on the road. Of all her duties, there's little question that Deborah's most important contribution to the tour was being at the core of communication central.

To find out how Deborah reached this exciting position, we must delve into her background. After graduating from Illinois State University with a Bachelor's degree in Recreation and Park Administration, Deborah soon found that she was overqualified for entry level positions for all the jobs she really wanted. But, she was offered a graduate assistantship at Illinois State in the area of "student activities." The job was working with the university's concert committee.

"I.S.U. always had wonderful shows and a full schedule each year, which made it very exciting to be involved with the committee." Among the performers who played there were Genesis, Phil Collins, AC/DC, Triumph, James Taylor, Robert Palmer, Prince, Rick James and the Pointer Sisters. "After my second show I was bitten by the showbiz bug and knew that this was what I wanted to do. I thrived on the level of energy that I saw all around me. It wasn't only in the entertainers, but also in the crew who were involved in setting up and tearing down each show. It may sound boring, but I loved going through all the contracts. What started out as a temporary position wound up as a full time job. When my boss left to go to another university, I was offered her job."

Shortly afterwards the auditorium manager left and Deborah was appointed the acting manager. "My job entailed managing the auditorium, doing all the booking and setting up all the shows for the performing arts series. About the same time that I was offered the permanent management position, I received a call from a company in Minneapolis called Vee Corporation, which had the Sesame Street Shows, the Muppet Babies and the Muppets on Tour. They wanted to know if I would be interested in coming up for and interview and I figured it might not be a bad idea to check out another option before I was committed to staying in Illinois and went to see them. During the course of the interview, I had already decided that I liked the company. When they offered me a job as the company manager of one of their touring productions — I accepted."

"For three years prior to joining up with Pink Floyd, I worked with Sesame Street. The greatest benefit of working those tours, which consisted of nine months on the road touring North America, was that it afforded me the opportunity to check out what it was like to live on the road. Also, it taught me how to manage a group of people who had to travel together for extended periods of time. The major difference between that and having a job in a stationary position, was that you never really escape from the people you work with. It's not like going home at night, closing the door and knowing that you are not going to see the people you work with during the day. When you're on the road, you constantly see them in restaurants, bars or even the local movie theatre. You never really lose contact with them, which can make it quite difficult at times. But, if you have a group that gets along very well, it's much easier to deal with that part of touring."

Touring can be very draining. "Normally, we would travel overnight from the previous city and arrive in town at 3 or 4 in the morning. I was responsible for getting the crew checked into the hotel. I would generally throw my bags in the room and catch a couple of hours sleep before going to load in. Some of the guys would go from the previous night's show directly to the load in. Due to the tightness of the schedule, they sometimes were unable to check in at the hotel and had to begin setting up equipment for the next show without any sleep. Around 5 a.m. the crew would unload 16 trucks. The rigging and quad sound system would be in place a short time later. The crew would begin building the stage and setting up the lighting to get ready to do a show.

"I had to get the production office all set up. The communication area was very crucial to the show. We utilized walkie talkies to make sure everyone was capable of being reached at all times. The office equipment was next to be set up. We used a FAX machine extensively in order to receive information for the show or the next leg of the tour. All the computers had to be in place and on line as well. It was quite a bit of work. The crew would start bringing in questions or problems for the day, ticket requests, and passes for their girlfriends or family. It was easier to get things done early in the morning before the phones began ringing off the hook. Around mid-day the backline guys would come in and put the band equipment on stage while the rest of the crew took their lunch break. The sound check would take place shortly after lunch.

"At production meetings we would identify any problem areas for the crew members and tell them what the game plan was going to be for the loadout. Morris Lyda approached the show as if he was the coach and the crew were the players. Our show worked so well because the communication was always there, and everybody knew what was expected of him.

"Morris is a real pro who's been around for a number of years and is very well respected in the industry. His effectiveness at managing people was the main reason that the tour was so successful. In fact, given the enormous size of the Pink Floyd tour, there's no question in my mind that he is the only person who could have pulled off that job. It was pretty special to me to be involved in the show with him. I learned a lot from Morris and Robbie Williams (the production manager). Robbie was more the administrator and the two of them worked very well together.

"Playing in foreign countries was somewhat problematic. The language and currency difference was one thing, but working in different time zones presented a communication problem with the people back in the States. The daily activities had to be shifted so that phone calls were made at certain times to coordinate with business hours in the U.S."

A potential tragedy was narrowly avoided when Pink Floyd played Rome. "As they're known to do overseas, the promoter oversold the date. The venue had electronic gates where you insert your ticket and it registers the number. You pull it out and the gate opens to allow you entrance. Once the appointed ticket capacity was hit the gates automatically locked. But, there were still at least twenty-five hundred people waiting outside to get into the show. The band was on stage and completely unaware that any of this was happening. The crew was advised by the local authorities at that point that we might have to evacuate, that is, hop on the bus and make a run for it. The crowd outside the gates were beginning to get nasty. Suddenly, we found ourselves surrounded. It was unclear whether it was military personnel or just the police, but whoever it was, they were heavily armed officers. We had no idea what was going to happen. The next thing we knew, we got word over the radio that the authorities were hurling tear gas. The smoke was hitting our people at the mix position and making it so they couldn't see what they were doing. The sound techs couldn't even see the controls and our lighting designer wasn't even able to see the stage.

"The crowd then turned on our sound crew out in the mix area because we had smoke machines set up behind them, and the crowd thought that it was our smoke that was affecting them. We had to send out people from backstage not only to provide first aid but to give them some kind of protection as well. Before long even the people on stage started getting hit with the fumes. The only thing that we could do was to squeeze lemons into water and dip rags into it to absorb the fumes and kind of neutralize the effect of the tear gas.

"Some less dangerous, but interesting things also happened on that tour. For example, David Gilmour had a problem with one of his nails. It was being worn from strumming his guitar. It was very irritating to him because he was also wearing off layers of his skin. I got him started on a regimen of coating his nail with krazy glue, which seemed to have alleviated the problem. However, one night before a show, the wardrobe person came running into my office and asked me how to get krazy glue off someone's hand. Apparently, some glue had dripped out from the side of the tube and glued David's fingers together. We were lucky to be able to make a solution of nail polish remover and acetone and remove the glue and David did the show."

For people who are looking to break into the business, Deborah cites as the two most important keys to success, contacts and experience. "Probably the best way to get experience would be to run errands for crew people. Even if it means driving the van carrying the crew back and forth between the hotel and the venue. I've seen people do just about anything to gain experience and to make their contacts in the industry.

"A college education will provide the skills that are necessary to get ahead. This is especially true if you work on any type of concert committee or stage crew. More important than anything else is to establish relationships and to maintain them. You never know when you might meet up with them. I had no idea that Morris and I would ever cross paths again after having worked together on the Genesis show. It just goes to show that you should never discount any contacts that you make in the business. It never hurts either, to send an occasional résumé or to make an occasional phone call just to check in and say, 'Hi.'"

Concert Promotion

John Scher

John Scher of Monarch Entertainment believes that his phenomenal success as one of the biggest promoters in the country is due to one basic rule: "Play the acts when they're young. Give them an opportunity to play for you when they first start happening and put them on shows as opening acts. More often than not, when they're bigger, they'll stay with you.

"Promoters need to thoroughly understand the acts they plan to play. Just putting tickets on sale without knowing how to promote that particular band to the public can be disaster." John Scher makes it his business to know "which are the hip record stores, in what malls the kids hang out, what radio stations play what band's music. In other words you have to really know everything about your market. Knowing how to use the retail outlets, radio, MTV and newspapers is absolutely essential for a successful promotion. You can't just approach it with the idea of selling concert tickets. You've also got to think how will this help the artist, his manager or agent in the overall marketing of the act's career. A good relationship with the media and with your public can help bring along that artist's career, particularly in the early stages, and make them all your loyal friends while you're helping to increase their appeal to the ticket-buying public.

"To be a successful promoter, fundamentally, you need good ideas, eyes and ears for talent and a competent, hardworking staff." John assigns assistants to scout the music scene. For example, somebody on staff loves heavy metal; another loves new age music and reports on that; then there's the blues, jazz, and Rock 'n' Roll. Each person on the staff is expected to stay on top of his or her genre. "We have staff and booking meetings at least 3 days a week where we exchange ideas."

John also operates the Ritz in New York City. "Having a venue like the Ritz gives us a phenomenal opportunity to present all kinds of music. It's amazing that in early 1988, Guns and Roses played the Ritz and by the end of the same year they were selling out stadiums around the world. One way to discover artists early on is to look for certain key indicators. For example, in the new music genre you listen to WDRE in New York, a station that is likely to play a record or an artist earlier than others. On a straight ahead pop rock level, WDHA in Dover, New Jersey, is likely to pick-up on a new artist before, say, WNEW or K-Rock. We like to keep good relationships with those program directors, music directors and jocks. They turn you on to bands. You watch the early progress of these bands and if you're in the position to hear a buzz, no matter how little it is, before it really gets brought to the mainstream, you better be ready to react. Often you can surprise a manager or an agent by calling up and saying, hey, I just heard your new band, the XYZ, and boy they're great.

"Sometimes you pick up a good buzz from record stores. Jackson Music in Red Bank, New Jersey, or Cheap Thrills in New Brunswick, New Jersey, are two good indicator stores for us. What we hear from those locations can make us call a manager or agent and say, we're interested in your band, let's find the right show in New York." For all of you future promoters, John advises that you "stay ahead of the game by reading the trades and the tip sheets. However, you must also have grass roots relationships."

When John was attending Long Island University in New York, he realized that northern and central New Jersey was a huge market all by itself. "This doesn't apply strictly to Rock 'n' Roll, but virtually everything. It's a market of close to 8 million people and has the second highest per capita income in the country. In addition, people who live in North Jersey really don't like going to New York. Northern and central New Jersey was a market looking for some focus. There are huge numbers of colleges: Rutgers, Seton Hall, Princeton, Farleigh Dickinson, and a whole stream of New Jersey state colleges, Patterson State, Montclair State, Newark State, it goes on and on."

In order to to test that market, John ran a series of shows in South Mountain Arena and another in Upsala College in East Orange featuring Sly and the Family Stone, Emerson Lake and Palmer, Mountain and the Byrds. "Once our theory proved to be successful, we opened the Capital Theater in Passaic, New Jersey, in the early 70's and started doing 40 or 45 shows a year there and another 20 or so in Asbury Park during the summer." Some of the opening acts that John booked early in their careers at the Capital were Bon Jovi, John Cougar, Metallica and Bruce Springsteen. He also did shows at Roosevelt Stadium, a venue that seats 30,000 people in Jersey City, then in the Rutgers Athletic Center and eventually at the Meadowlands. Monarch has slowly expanded its operations to Buffalo, Albany, Binghamton, and Ithaca. John admits, "It's a little harder in upstate New York because you don't have the radio stations that can really help you promote."

Monarch has promoted acts where the necessary guarantees to the artist have ranged from $250 to hundreds of thousands of dollars. "You must be realistic in business. A brand new band that has a real big buzz happening may get $2,000 to $5,000 a show. A band below that level, in the itsy bitsy stages of getting somewhere, will not get a gig that pays more than $200 to $500. Keep in mind, if you're paying the artist $2,500, you probably have at least another $10,000 in costs and that's $12,500. If the tickets are, say, $12.50, you have to sell a thousand of them to break even. Very often an act that you paid $2,500 isn't going to draw a thousand people. Maybe they'll draw 600 people. So, you know, you can do the arithmetic yourself and see what the loss is. Once you have them booked, you can go back to all those radio, record store or record company people that turned you on to that band and try to get more support and promotion from them.

"In the early stages, opening acts are not very risky. You're not on a limb for a lot of money. It's that next step, when people start to become club headliners and get anywhere from $2,500 to $10,000 a show, when it becomes a crap shoot. Arena headliners command huge guarantees. You have to ask yourself very important questions. How much money is at risk if the show doesn't do well? How much can you make if it sells out? When you think you have the answers you make your decision — and you never forget that it will take four or five winning shows to make up for one loser.

"Every day is a challenge. The money can be enormous when you're right and the risks are tremendous when you're wrong. The stress factor is great. Because the business is so competitive, you have to make sure that you and your company are on top of things at all times and that you don't miss a trick somewhere along the line. The next most important concern is that you maintain the best possible relationship with the act. To do our job effectively we have 36 full time people and a couple of hundred part time workers."

John's advice to newcomers: "The best way to get into the promotion area of the business is first, go to college. Get on a college concert committee and/or work at a college radio station. You'll develop valuable skills doing that type of work. Although those places might operate on a smaller scale than we do, they use the same fundamental principles in promoting shows. You will learn about putting together promotions and, indeed, at this level, you can be even more creative because you often have lesser known acts to deal with. Also, through the concert commitee you'll meet a lot of agents that you can contact after graduation. Working at a college radio station can be beneficial as well. It will keep you on top of the latest trends in music and help you to develop a good ear.

"There are often entry level positions at companies like mine and at others all over the country. We don't hire a lot of new people other than secretaries, but are always looking for highly qualified people. Another course of action is applying for an entrance level position at a record company. This is an excellent way to get to know promoters in your area. Also, don't overlook the many different kinds of regional theatres. They can provide terrific on-the-job training."

> **❝A**rtists on tour must
> have people responsible for who is and isn't al-
> lowed to get close to us. Sometimes it's a matter of
> safety. Other times it's just to allow us to have some
> privacy and peace of mind while on a hectic tour-
> ing schedule. Nobody does the job better than Jim
> Silvia. **❞**

Rob Halford
JUDAS PRIEST

Tour Security

Jim Silvia

It was the tragic and senseless murder of John Lennon that brought Jim Silvia into the entertainment business. Jim was contacted by an attorney in New York City who knew of his extensive law enforcement background and asked Jim to handle tour security for a client of the law firm. At that time, there were many managers who had expressed similar concerns for their band's safety and Jim Silvia had a new career.

Jim's first tour was in 1981 with Judas Priest and he has since worked with the band on seven other tours. Some of the other bands Jim has worked with include Journey, David Bowie and Iron Maiden.

Security people like Jim Silvia simply afford stars personal protection. "It's not so much that they need protection from people 'out to get' them. Rather, they want the freedom to move about without being bothered by a multitude of people. This can be a problem at hotels where people show up in the middle of the night and expect to find a party going on. To be realistic, if there were a party every night, a band would never get through a week of a six month tour."

The typical day of a security manager begins early in the morning, the time for meetings with the security people provided by the local promoter. The purpose is to sit down and specify what measures are necessary to ensure the safety of both the band and the spectators. The protection of the equipment must also be discussed as well as what precautions should be taken to secure the entrances to the building.

Jim: "One time when I was out with Journey, there was a guy in West Virginia who had gotten into town two or three days before we did and happened to be staying at the same hotel. Normally, when we arrive at a hotel, I make it a point to find the security person on duty, to let him know who I am and how he may best assist me. When I contacted this particular security person, he mentioned to me that a guy staying at the hotel had been hanging around the desk asking a lot of questions about the band. The next day one of the other security people told me that a maid thought she had seen bullets in his room. When I found that he had left the door to his room wide open (ahem), I went in and did indeed find some bullets. After getting a description of the guy, I went down to the show. We managed to find him hanging around the back door, waiting for the band to show up. We took him inside and discovered he did have a gun with him. He was then turned over to the police. Three days later I was informed that this guy was wanted for five murders in two states, along with kidnapping and a couple of other serious charges.

"The more typical problems that you encounter at concerts depend upon the group playing and the people who come to listen. There have been occasions when people have brought in fireworks that have resulted in a couple of teenagers losing their eyesight. Some idiot in the back decides that he wants to get in with the group somehow and so he starts throwing fireworks into a hall that has 15,000 people in it. You just can't do that. As a result of such incidents I began to do body searches, although they are prohibited by some state laws around the country.

"The people who have paid their money to see the show should be able to sit down and enjoy it just as much as anybody else. They shouldn't be subjected to fireworks, knives, guns, bottles or anything else being thrown by a drunken or drugged out punk. I would say that less than 1% of the people who come to the shows are the troublemakers. Everybody else is there to enjoy themselves and have a good time. Unfortunately, it's the 1% that gets into the newspapers. Therefore, anything that can harm anyone else is taken away. If it's something that's legal, we'll give them receipts and they can pick it up at the end of the concert. Otherwise, it's contraband that gets thrown into a barrel and hauled off into the garbage.

"Often people may try to sneak in cameras or tape recorders — they won't harm anyone, but do infringe on the band's rights. However, the biggest problem by far is beer bottles. Bottles are the worst things in the world to bring to a concert, even if they're not thrown. What do you do with an empty bottle? You're going to put it on the floor. Three things can happen: (1) someone is going to slip on it, (2) it's going to break or (3) it becomes a missile. In any case the likelihood is that someone's going to get hurt. The intention of the security crew isn't to keep people from having fun. Instead, it's to provide a safe environment in which the crowd can enjoy the concert."

Jim suggests that one way to get involved in the business is to find out what company in your area provides security for the bands that come in to play your particular city. "When you go to a concert, speak with some of the people working it and ask them how they got hired. If you're given an opportunity to work a security detail, it will probably be doing crowd control or backstage security. You may be stuck outside in Duluth, Minnesota, during a January snowstorm watching equipment. Maybe you'll find yourself watching trucks for eight or ten shows in the pouring rain. Everybody has to start at the bottom. There's a learning process through this, like there is in anything else. You don't just walk in and say I'd like to do security and expect to get a cushy assignment. The fact that you know karate or can hit people real hard doesn't entitle you to preferential treatment.

"Before you decide to get into the business, there are several things to take into consideration. If you have a home life when you go out on the road, it's likely you won't have the same home life when you return. That's a sad fact of life. You've got to make a lot of sacrifices. When you leave home for extended periods of time, you really lose touch with your family and friends. If you're married and have kids, it can really get to you. Some people get extremely homesick while on the road and find that they just can't take it.

202

"On the positive side, every day is different even though you are basically doing the same thing. You're always on the move, constantly travelling and meeting a lot of new people. As far as the money is concerned, you're paid very well for what you do. The better you do it, the better you get paid. If you want to do it for a year and get out, you'll never last. You don't get into something like this for a year because you want to travel or you want to be with a band. Bands look at you as an employee. Even though you become friendly with them, you're never their friend, their buddy, their pal. They have their thing to do, and you have yours. It's a very professional organization that has to have clear cut definitions as to who does what and when. That's just the way it is. If you think that you can handle the responsibilities along with the hardships, then you may find security a very rewarding career."

*66 The manager plans
your tour, sends you to places where you're hot,
and takes care of all your business so all the artist
has to do is perform. He makes your look, style
and image so that wherever you go in the world,
they already know who you are. The manager runs
the music business just like a supermarket—he
makes sure all the commodities for sale are in the
right place at the right time. 99*

**Darryl McDaniels
DMC OF RUN-DMC**

Artist Management
Russell Simmons

*All those who think that it's all been done and that every form of
music has been discovered ought to meet Russell Simmons.*

As a sophomore at City College in New York he first produced
Rap shows with such artists as Curtis Blow, Grandmaster Flash and
DJ Hollywood. "They were the first rap artists. They hadn't even
made any records. We would play college parties and get a terrific
response from both black and white students. It was impossible at
that time to get a record deal, or set up a concert tour, but a friend of
mine and I went into a studio and recorded Curtis Blow. We had the
record on the shelf for ages. Then the Sugar Hill Gang's first record
came out. That was the opening — the very first commercially
accepted rap recording. The record companies started scrambling
for talent. The promoters wanted shows from them and rappers
started to get 'deals.' That's when we signed Curtis Blow to an
exclusive deal with Polygram. For a long time, I felt that I was the only
person who understood what rappers were doing creatively. They

must have felt the same way, because I became the manager for most of the top acts."

Here's a spectacular list of the rappers that Russell manages: LL Cool J., Run DMC, Eric B & Rakim, EPMD, Public Enemy, Jazzy Jeff and the Fresh Prince, Whodini and Roxanne. "I give them direction and creative input and I expend a lot of energy trying to encourage saleable material from them. I try to emphasize the importance of concentrating on the things that are real and that people can relate to, people of all ages and backgrounds. I want them to record music that will be around for a long time." Russell also encourages them to get out on the road and make sure their audience can see them in person as much as possible.

"If you want to get into artist management, the first thing you should do is find a unsigned band that you really believe in. Look for someone who has his own unique qualities, something that will distinguish him from others. Spend time with your artist. From the outside you may see things that might make him better. When the time comes to get the group a deal, you just bang on people's doors. You keep on banging until you can get them the kind of break they need. At that point, find a powerful and experienced music attorney, who can assist you in obtaining the best possible contract for your client.

"I'm not a historian, but I do know how to interpret and learn from what I see. I don't know a lot about the blues and jazz, but I do know that they are art forms that have lasted for decades. It's my belief that when people are properly educated about rap, it too will last. That's one of my most important goals, to have my acts playing Las Vegas twenty years from now. I recently attended a panel discussion that was presented by Senior Vice Presidents of black music marketing from record companies. Someone stood up and stated that the problem is that there's not enough talent out there. That's nonsense. It just takes a little effort to go out and find the talent, figure out a way to present them and come up with a style, an image for them. In my opinion, you can't dress every new artist in some shiny purple suit and make him break dance. It just won't work. Every artist is different and should be encouraged to display his own personal style.

"Rap is primarily teenage music. It just keeps getting more creative and more popular. That's why the artists that started it are still around. Maybe you don't realize it, but rap has been around for about

10 years and the same people who were making records then are still making records now. Sure, a few faded from the scene, but they simply didn't grow up and develop with their audience. The original artists are now getting older and and you may notice that they are changing what they sing about. That's as it should be. When they were sixteen, they were singing that you can't live without radio. Now, that they're in their twenties they're singing about more important things. That's part of the process.

"Rap is a generational music. It's in the stage that Rock 'n' Roll was in, in the fifties. Early Rock 'n' Roll was special. But people don't necessarily want to hear the same old thing that they heard when they were kids. So it's changed; many of the artists have grown up and developed along with them. This same thing applies to rap. Don't forget, rap was supposed to be a fad and it wasn't supposed to last. My brother Run has been with us for 6 years. Their last album, which was considered a flop, sold 1.5 million copies. Maybe it's hard to believe, Run DMC has been with us for 7 years and Curtis Blow is working on his tenth album."

Russell's philosophy for success is plain and simple: "Opportunity is not just sitting there waiting for you. You have got to open your own doors. Your dream can be a reality if you want it badly enough. I see managers come and go. With some of the newer entrants, you can see the enthusiam and feel the energy. That's what it takes to make it. If you use your energy positively, it will eventually pay off for you. At all times you must maintain your level of integrity. Only one group out of the 106 people I've managed since 1979 has left our company. The best and most important thing in this business is honesty. Like many other industries, there are some unsavory managers. The fact that Def Jam and Rush have grown so dramatically over the last ten years is the best proof I can offer of what can happen if artists are treated fairly and dealt with honestly. The interest of the artist is always in the forefront of all our business dealings."

> **❝ A** *word to would-be suitors: Whispering 'sweet nothings' in Barbara's ear doesn't work nearly as well as gentle murmurs of 'gross potentials'.* **❞**
>
> **Brian Lane, Manager**
> **YES, ASIA, 3, GTR, IT BITES**

Booking Agency

Barbara Skydel

The Beatles may have sung "Hard Day's Night" but super agent Barbara Skydel lived it back in 1969, after a Led Zeppelin concert in San Bernadino, California. The concert was a birthday gift from a doctor to his son, who wanted to be a promoter. In the end, the Doctor's inexperience became a learning experience for Skydel and a test of her ability as a road manager. "I was counting dollar bills and small change," says Skydel, recalling the nightmare. "I was in a little room. It must have been 115 degrees. It was a six hour settlement and we got our money in crumpled dollar bills and sweaty five dollar bills, but we did get paid."

Skydel has come a long way since then. Her ambition and persistence, not to mention style, musical taste and intelligence, are a few of the traits that have made her a shining star in the music business. She's now the Executive Vice-President of Premier Talent, a New York-based booking agency for musical talent. Their clients include Jon Bon Jovi, U2, Bruce Springsteen, Van Halen,

Whitesnake and Suzanne Vega. Skydel entered the talent business as a secretary in a theatrical agency after graduating from college. She then went on to work as an assistant to famed pianist Peter Nero. Among other things, she made his travel arrangements. "I had meetings with airline companies about his accompianist's bass fiddle. He didn't want the bass to go into cargo, so I had to meet with VIPs of every single airline to make sure that they would keep one empty seat for the bass. They used to tell the stewardesses that the bass was on a diet and didn't want to be served any lunch."

After a series of other jobs, Skydel finally landed at Premier Talent as an assistant to executive Frank Barsalona. "Frank recognized that I had a lot of potential and energy. We shared an office and I listened in on every one of his phone conversations and every meeting that he had. I worked 18 hours a day," says Skydel. She'd be in the office at 10 a.m. after being out until 4 a.m. scouting clubs for new acts. "It was very exciting and I loved it." After a year of this grueling pace, Barsalona promoted her to a full-fledged agent.

One of her biggest challenges was to book two unknown acts into an already-filled weekend festival in South Florida. Her aggressiveness and self-confidence paid off: "I knew that the show was booked up solid and I realized that I was asking the promoter to take two unknown acts, but I told him that he would thank me the day after the festival. The two bands I finally was able to sell him were King Crimson and Grand Funk Railroad." Then Skydel really had to muster up some courage. " I said, 'Look, I'm new and I can't afford to have any screwing up so you've got to pay me all the money in front.' He almost fainted, but then he started to laugh. He said. 'Are you crazy? Nobody has gotten all the money up front.'" But Skydel did. Her acts were the only ones whose money was paid in full before the date.

Mother Nature played a nasty trick on the festival, pouring buckets of rain down the entire weekend. Unruly fans burned the bleachers and the promoter lost a fortune. Skydel's earlier courage paid off. Her two groups were the hits of the festival, making front page news, and Skydel wound up being the only agent whose bands got paid in full.

Three years later, she became a vice president of Premier and a few years after that, moved up to her current position of Executive Vice President. Her instinct in finding good, new talent has continued to pay off handsomely. She recalls seeing Suzanne Vega the first time the vocalist played with a band. "She wasn't an obvious artist you would sign. I thought she was incredibly talented and someone who would certainly have a long career. She has already gone far beyond what anybody could have anticipated and we're very proud to have played a part in it."

Sometimes it's just a question of timing, like the time Skydel signed Jon Bon Jovi after he and his band "opened" for another band at the Meadowlands in New Jersey. Jon was just finishing up his first album and still didn't even have a manager. Knowing only what she saw on stage that night, Skydel asked for an introduction. Soon, Jon and his band joined the ranks of Premier and became Barbara's good friends.

Barbara describes Premier's basic function as booking engagements for its artists and negotiating their contracts for concerts, movies, television or records. Tours are usually booked in conjunction with record releases, but not everyone is suited to play Madison Square Garden. "You decide where you think it would be best for particular artists to play, whether they should headline a night-club, a showcase club, or be a support act (opening for a headliner) on a tour." An important aspect is to establish a good relationship with various promoters, the ones who ultimately decide whether or not the group plays their venues.

Although the music business can be glamorous, Barbara echos the view of many other professionals in her business: "Young people who are attracted by the notion of meeting high profile rock stars are not what the agency executives look for. Chances are best for someone who is enthusiastic, willing to work hard, go the extra mile, have good basic skills like typing and shorthand, and are really willing to learn the business from the ground up.

"The unfortunate thing is that you can't come off the street and say, I want to be an agent, because this is a job you can't learn in school. There is no degree in this. It's more difficult because it's more undefined. You have to learn many new things and you can't do it except from the bottom of an office which provides an opportunity to learn." Although Skydel has certainly made a name for herself in the music industry, the reality is that there are few top female executives in booking agencies. "I do think it's harder for women but I hope that young women will see from my example that it's not impossible. I think it depends upon the woman and how determined she is to succeed. It's my hope that there will be many more women doing these jobs in the years to come."

*__66__ __W__e have an obliga-
tion to the fans that have chosen to spend their
time and their money to be with us. We must fill
that time and the space between them and us with
magical sights and sounds.__ 99__*

__Jon Anderson__
__YES__

Scenery Manufacturing

Torbin Smith

Every show needs some kind of stage setting or scenery. The men and women who build it are skilled, creative and proud of their work. Torbin Smith is one of the best.

Here's one way to get into the business. Torbin (Torp) Smith grew up in the USA, but married a Danish girl that he met in school, and moved to Denmark. One day he was sitting on a park bench in Copenhagen when some Americans, who were there as members of the Rolling Stones road crew, approached him hoping that he spoke English. One thing led to another and Torp asked if there was a chance for a gig and they put him in touch with (production manager) Chip Monck. "Chip asked me if I could operate a super trooper spotlight. Fortunately, I had used that particular piece of equipment extensively when working for my college theatre department." That was it. Torp was hired to work for the Rolling Stones on their 1970 World Tour all because he was sitting on that park bench!

That was a million to one shot, but it happened to the right guy. Torp had been building scenery in the USA since he was 16 years old. He had volunteered to be an apprentice in summer stock theatre in exchange for a chance to appear in some shows. "I would help out in the scene shop and they gave me some bit parts — that's pretty much how it happened. I was hesitant at first but then I really got into it. That was my senior year in high school.

"It seems that I had always wanted to build scenery, and that's pretty much been my passion ever since I was a kid. It's hard to explain, but I really love the temporary aspect of building scenery — you just build it and it goes away. That holds some sort of strange philosophical thing for me."

Torp's company builds scenery primarily for the Rock 'n' Roll touring industry, but they also build displays for trade shows and scenery for television commercials, and other productions. "The skills that you develop can be used in any type of scenery building environment whether it's theater or any number of commercial venues. It's all applicable. In addition, we do lot of straight scenery, which means that it's riser platform levels that are decorated in one fashion or another to give a certain look. However, we may be best known for our mechanical work.

"We recently designed a special set for Stevie Wonder to place the stage in the center of the arena for greater seating capacity. We built a 44-ft. square stage to play in the round. It contained a 40-ft. turntable and on top of that was an 18-ft. turntable where Stevie had all his gear set up. The two turntables would revolve in the same direction or opposite directions. That way Stevie would be presented to the audience on all sides. For David Bowie, the set was built by a number of different companies because there was so little time to build it. The part that we did was called the spiderhead. The spiderhead contained an elevator which David would get in and he would rise up to the top and do a number up there. We've also done work for Run DMC, Night Ranger, Aerosmith, Neil Young, Ozzie Osbourne, Sheena Easton, Pat Benatar, Julian Lennon and for the Farm Aid and Amnesty International Concerts."

One of his favorite creations was an 8 ft. mechanical spider for Ronnie Dio. "It looked like a road warrior spider that came down from the overhead lighting grid and landed on stage, walked around and reared up on its hind legs to blast the audience with light. It was a pretty fantastic looking design."

Torp suggests for anybody who wants to try to get into the business, "Theater school is an excellent place to acquire all of the skills that you need to build scenery. Although the kind of scenery that we build for Rock 'n' Roll is different from theatrical scenery, it still gets you accustomed to production schedules. The development of skills of all types is extremely important. The guy who has the most all around skills is the guy that's going to have the easiest time getting the gig. Over the past ten years touring has become a major industry and it's being treated as the big business that it truly is. It is a place that requires professionals and the people who have specialized skills are in great demand throughout the industry."

Torp believes staying in school is essential. "Getting a lot of formal education would be your best bet. Courses in electronics, engineering, design and art, mechanical drawing and computers would prove to be most beneficial. There is a phenomenal amount of communication that happens by computer, therefore an aptitude for computers could very well provide your entrance into the business. Lighting systems are now computer controlled as are scenery movement and rigging systems. Naturally, as the industry continues to become more sophisticated — the more computer knowledge a person has can mean the difference between getting or not getting a gig.

"If you're not a college graduate it doesn't mean that you won't make it in the business; it just makes your goal a little more difficult to achieve. Not everyone that we hire has a college education. In fact, some of our most valuable people are those who have learned specific skills in high school or trade schools — such as electronics, welding, carpentry, or drafting."

Torp has some warnings to give about the business in general and working for him in particular: "If people show up for work drunk, they go home. And they stay home. There's no denying that drugs are out there. Unfortunately, they're everywhere in our world. You could be working at Chrysler and it's there. However, I personally don't feel that it helps anyone's performance and I certainly don't want anybody who is working for me around machinery to be under the influence of either drugs or alcohol.

"Furthermore, lazy people don't last in this business. When you're talking about the millions and millions of dollars that are generated by the top acts in this business, nobody is going to wait around for the guy who doesn't make it on time. If you're not there on time — you're out. Nobody's going to babysit you. You must have a real dedication to thoroughness. Not only do you have to do things right, you've got to do them on time. That is what's expected of you. The rest is up to you."

> **66** *A really positive story in a national magazine or on television can bridge the enormous gap between artists and their potential fans and, especially while you're first trying to make it up the ladder, bring those fans in the door to see you.* **99**
>
> **Katy Valk, Publicity**
> **MCA RECORDS**

Publicity

Lori Somes

Good PR's like Lori Somes don't like to talk about themselves. They'd rather tell you all about their clients' careers than their own. But, we were able to persuade Lori to tell us a little about her personal experiences as a guide and inspiration to young people, especially young women, who have a longing to enter the field of communications. This is a rare look at Lori's career.

Lori Somes provides a good example of what a bright, well-rounded woman with determination can accomplish. By serving her clients faithfully she has risen from a temp in secretarial pool to a Vice President and partner in the new public relations firm INPRESS, Inc. Lori originally pursued drama studies, but not to become an actress. She wanted to learn how to be part of a TV-magazine format like 60 Minutes. "The fact that I had absolutely no training in journalism or media didn't matter to me. I was too busy struggling just to pass the typing test for a temporary secretarial company, to give that any consideration. My thoughts were that if I could get even a temporary job with any TV station my foot would be in the door. As fate would have it, I succeeded in getting interviewed by a number of news bureaus, but I never passed their typing tests. It seemed like every time I took a typing test, my fingers quit on me. I made lots of excuses and pulled a lot of tricks to make them let me take the test over again. I'd pretend that I'd lost my contact lens, had the flu, sprained my wrist, anything.

"All I wanted to do was to work for 60 Minutes. The closest I got was working as a temp for CBS. They were pleased with my work and I was overjoyed to be offered my dream job, a secretarial position at 60 Minutes. But, they backed down because the temp agency that placed me had a contract with CBS that prohibited CBS from hiring any temporary employees (like me) unless they bought out the agency's contract. That was that and I was crushed. I had come so close!

"But my temp job paid off for real after I worked three days at Columbia Records. Someone there thought I might be useful in the publicity department and transferred me there for a week's trial. This time Columbia decided that they wanted me enough to buy out my contract and I signed on full time. However, deep down I still longed to work in television. What I really wanted to be was a television news producer.

"Nine months later, Columbia Records cut its budgets and decreed that the last people hired would be the first to leave. That was me. But all was still not lost. Through a referral, I went to work back at CBS Nightly News for Walter Cronkite, on a television job I'd have sold my soul for a year earlier. The strange thing is that I now took the job with some hesitation. Amazingly, I missed the music industry. Music had become extremely important to me and while at Columbia Records I saw its impact on our culture as well as the power it possesses as a communication medium. Hearing Peter Gabriel singing Biko on an Amnesty International tour is a precious moment that simply touches the soul. You don't know whether to laugh or cry. It possesses you and in such an emotional moment powerful changes can take place.

"When I learned about a secretarial position that had opened up at Epic Records (part of the CBS records group) I went for it. After only one year there — during which I learned a tremendous amount about management — my title was Manager of the Publicity

Department of CBS Records International. It was a great title and an exciting job. I found myself dealing with the press and other media all over Europe, England, Asia and Australia on behalf of CBS' recording stars. I worked that international market for more than 4 years before I developed a real longing to try my new publicity skills in the American music scene. However, I realized that I needed to learn a lot about the US market and had to renew my US contacts to work effectively here. I thought (rightly) that I might be able to learn the most in the least amount of time by going to work for a publicity firm that was really active in the music world here in the USA. Howard Bloom's organization certainly filled the bill. They offered me the opportunity to relearn the business from the US side. It was a little like starting over, but I felt lucky to be allowed to try. It was also luck that only three months into the job I was assigned to work with a new band that was just then exploding into the music scene and adding the word "rap" to everybody's vocabulary — Run-DMC.

"Run-DMC presented a special challenge. They had hit it so big, so quickly, that it was like a runaway horse. The trick was to keep enough control over their exposure to be sure that the media understood the origins of rap and the band's positive messages. The guys were briefed on the questions that they might be asked by interviewers, but they were really very bright and naturally likeable.

"However, I did have one experience with Run-DMC that tested all my skills. It was in Long Beach, California, when their concert was interrupted by gangs, and 52 people were injured. The 'riot' made national news and it was make or break time for Run-DMC, a very serious PR problem. The right story had to emerge or Run-DMC's career might be seriously impaired. I had a week and a half to work on it, calling everyone from Dan Rather to local anchor persons to talk about Run-DMC. Rap is such an important part of black culture, but white America had to learn that rap music doesn't incite people to violence. The truth was that LA gangs that had nothing to do with the music had simply decided to have a free-for-all and break up the concert. Rap, the music born in the inner city, is truly music for everybody without any inherent violence. Fortunately, the press acted responsibly by writing about the real cause for the disturbance and the incident was soon out of the public eye.

"While working on the Run-DMC crisis, I was also preparing to lead a number of press people on a junket to Budapest to see the heavy metal band, Scorpions, play behind the Iron Curtain. I was lucky to be a part of it. It was an absolutely wonderful experience and it provided some very much needed relief from the tense Run-DMC ordeal."

Lori was later assigned to work with The Talking Heads. "When you work with the Talking Heads there is a lot of pressure. They are considered to be one of America's best bands and you have to be ready for that. They are very particular about their press coverage. They are, in many ways, very protective of their privacy and artistic integrity. The challenge is to choose the right press coverage. Their interviews have real impact because they're exclusive and rarely given. This is important and thoughtful work."

Even though Lori and her partners now run their own P.R. agency, INPRESS, Inc., Lori has not forgotten how it was to start from 'square one': "Over the years I've discovered a lot of ways for young people to get a foot in the PR door. First of all, I highly recommend that high school students take advantage of internships. There are a lot of places in New York and other big cities that offer internships. Among them, shows like David Letterman, some network news programs and even small entertainment companies. Be prepared to do grunt work. As an intern don't expect to be invited to discuss cover stories with the Editor-in-Chief of Rolling Stone. Also, don't expect to be paid very much, if at all. In addition to internships, journalism or writing courses are an excellent idea. On the other hand, so-called media or communications courses might be interesting, but are not likely to deal with the technical side of the business and probably won't have a lot to do with preparing you for the real world. Typing is something you'll do continually, so it doesn't hurt to take a class. Also, so many of our communications are handled electronically that a working knowledge of computers could be a real advantage.

"My own intern recently helped me work on a Run-DMC press conference at East Side High School in Paterson, New Jersey. We had to pull it together in three days. There was a tremendous amount of work involved and she got a thrill from being involved in this successful project. It was particularly gratifying for both of us to see the results, the clippings, the day after the press conference. There was an enormous amount of print exposure as well as coverage on Entertainment Tonight and MTV.

"You have got to be prepared to lick some stamps and do a lot of xeroxing. The pay is low, so low that it must be a major consideration.

If you're living by the skin of your teeth, life can be difficult. But if you are determined to break in, you've got to be willing to take a job for reasons that have little to do with monetary benefits — provided that job looks as if it will later present opportunities that will make up for the low pay. Working in Rock 'n' Roll can keep you young. It also can take a lot out of you. It takes a lot of work and a long time to learn the 'ins and outs' of public relations.

"Like most jobs, the more you are willing to put into it, the more you will get out of it. One of the best ways a woman can get into the business is by being a secretary in the promotion, marketing or publicity departments of a record company. An entry level job with a management company, concert promoter or even with a booking agent could also be an excellent entry into the business. Working at a record store isn't going to do it. You may hear a lot of music, but it's almost certainly not going to lead you to a job in public relations. It's not, as some think, demeaning to be a secretary. It's a way to learn the game, to let you be part of major projects and once in a while you may even pick up some secrets of success from some of the people you work with. Sometimes the right break is a matter of luck, but putting yourself in the right place at the right time can give luck a little help. When that opportunity comes your way, be sure you're watching for it and that you make the most of it."

> **66 C**oming from a merchandising background, I see the band's merchandiser as a direct link between them and their fans. I rely on merchandise not only for income, but for the band's image as well. Because of the great sums of money being handled by the merchandiser, he or she has got to be someone in whom I have utmost confidence. **99**

> **Richard Sanders, Manager**
> **WHITE LION**

Tour Merchandise

Lee Stanley

How many T-shirts have you bought outside after seeing your favorite band in concert? Did you ever wonder who the people are who are collecting the money rather than spending it? Lee Stanley has been working in the merchandising area of Rock 'n' Roll for 10 years. Currently he is a tour representative for a merchandising company. That means that inventory is shipped to Lee at different locations and he takes the merchandise from concert to concert during a tour and is in charge of selling it at each show.

Here's the way Lee describes his work as a merchandiser: "Before the show starts, we issue shirts to the selling booths. After the show, we count all the merchandise and subtract the returns from our beginning inventory. That tells us, for example, how many shirts we've sold at X amount of dollars and how much cash we should have on hand, when the figures check out right. Before we leave we have to calculate and pay local taxes and the percentage the building takes. The rest of the money is our 'gross profit' and goes back to the company that I work for and they split it with the band based on whatever deal they made."

Lee's association with the Rock 'n' Roll business began in North Carolina with a local band called Triple Tree. "I started out doing lights and sound on stage. I had six five-gallon cans with floodlights in them and an eight-channel custom mixing board with A7 cabinets with monitors. I kind of fell into the business because of a friend who was a guitar player. He had a band that was just starting out and they had nobody else on the stage crew. He explained to me that there was very little money to be made, but I'd find it very exciting. So, I decided to give it a try. After about 2 years in North Carolina with that particular local band, I was offered my first job with a touring band called Blackfoot. Things didn't quite work out with the band, but through a contact that I had made along the way, I got a job with Winterland (one of America's leading merchandisers). Since then I've been out with Rick Derringer, Edgar Winter, Johnny Winter, Tina Turner, Run DMC, the Beastie Boys, Chicago, Kiss and a lot of heavy metal bands. It seems that the heavier the music, the more T-shirts we sell.

"Merchandising is very big business and there are a lot of opportunities. The best way to get into it would be to first go to an arena or coliseum because they hire vendors at their rock shows. When a group comes into town, you will eventually meet the people who are doing the tour and you can tell them what you would like to do. Just give them your name and phone number and tell them if there is need for anybody to help out to give you a call. Don't forget to get the company's name and phone number. I would start calling the merchandising companies and inform them of your desire to start out in the business. Let them know why you would be good at it and how you can help them.

"There are really very few courses that would benefit you at an entry level with the exception of math. However, to move up in a company, it's helpful if you have a little business experience behind you. If you're going to college, take business administration as well as some accounting classes. The business is very competitive and this additional education may give you an edge.

"Most jobs have difficult times and this is no exception. For most people being away from home for extended periods of time is rough. It's a different story in my case because I never had a family life. I grew up in an orphanage and have always considered myself to be a

221

survivor. Until I got married, the road always held a great deal of interest for me. Still there are other disadvantages. There is a lot of driving involved and a lot of long days. On this job you spend an average 15 to 18 hours a day.

"When you start out in the business you have to expect that you will be the low man on the totem pole. So you get all of what they call the 'dog jobs.' If you're with a lighting company, you may be the person who climbs up into the rafters. In the merchandising area with a major tour like a Springsteen, there may be five merchandise people out there, each with his own job to do. Someone more experienced may take care of the money or the inventory, and you may be the one who's stuck doing all the physical labor like driving and unloading the truck.

"Everybody has heard stories about the use of drugs in the music industry, but the last couple of years I have seen a big difference in the drug scene. There's a very positive attitude on the road now. A number of tours are going out now with restrictions. If you're going to work on this tour, don't do drugs. If you do and you get caught, that's it. Aerosmith just had an extremely successful 'drug free' tour.

"I've seen drugs ruin careers. At times people let drugs take control of them. When they get to that point, they lose the perspective of what they're out there to do in the first place. Keep in mind that this is a business and not a big party, like it was during the early days of Rock 'n' Roll.

"If you're ready to work hard, earn a good living, travel the country and build a career in the merchandising business, we would like to have you join us."

> **"Set designers have made themselves a very important cog in the present day touring industry and are now an integral part of all pre-production work. Designers today are not just producing sets and interesting visual concepts, they are producing sets that integrate and travel as part of touring systems, working to simple parameters like truck sizes and load-in restrictions. A set designer with production values is an asset to any organisation. Unfortunately a designer without this knowledge is about as much use as a chocolate kettle."**
>
> **Steve Iredale, Production Manager**
> **U2**

Scenic/Staging Design

Jeremy Thom

Somebody has to sit down with a pencil and paper and plan what the stage should look like for a particular performance. The key person who is responsible for this is the scenic designer. Jeremy Thom is one of the best and here's how he became famous and successful at it.

Jeremy Thom briefly attended Dramatic Arts School to study acting, but it didn't last. "I was there for a moment or two, dropped out and got a part in a west end show, which folded before the dress rehearsal." It was then that he realized that he probably wasn't going to be able to feed himself as an actor and started to look into alternatives. The most promising seemed to be stage design. "I had worked on several theatre projects for a lighting supply and design company during school holidays. Luckily, when my acting career abruptly ended, they needed additional staff. I started as storeman in the lighting stores, but quickly moved upstairs to the design department because they saw that I had some talent for technical

223

drawings and lighting plots. Before long I was working for the chairman, doing all of the design for the theatres. Eventually, I assisted not only on theatre shows but on the opera and ballet as well."

A short time later, Jeremy heard about an opening at a lighting company that specialized in supplying lighting equipment to rock bands. "This provided an excellent way for me to learn about what seemed to me to be the most colorful aspect of the business, so I accepted. My first tour was with the Osmond Brothers (not exactly hard rockers), but a Deep Purple tour followed immediately."

Most of the large bands coming to Europe and virtually all of the European bands who toured Europe utilized the services of Jeremy's employer. That gave Jeremy the opportunity to work for David Bowie, The Who, The Stones and many of the major acts in the business. However, his first love in the business remained the designing of sets. "Though it was great working on lighting with the best bands in the world, I knew I wouldn't be happy unless I got back into set design." In 1975, Jeremy and a partner formed Plumbline Designs, the first company specializing exclusively in the design of touring stage sets for the music industry.

Jeremy finds it difficult to describe the unique thrill he feels upon seeing an idea be scribbled on a blank piece of paper transformed into a magnificent working set. By interacting with the artist and/or his production manager, a fine set designer like Jeremy can convey to the audience precisely the image that the band requires. That interaction is at the heart of the creative process for Jeremy. "I tend to work very closely with whomever it is that's making the artistic decision about the set design." Every detail of the upcoming tour is discussed: where they are going, what venues they'll be playing, the bands line-up and whether they want the set to be based on their latest album cover or to create a new image. "Then I go off by myself and produce the initial sketches to send back to the artists. I repeat this a number of times."

An integral part of the design is resolving how to erect and pack the components of the set. When packed into truck-dollies it must be able to fit snugly into standard trucks, Japanese trucks (world tours), air freight pallets or sea containers. In addition, the set must be able to be put together without tools (nuts and bolts are easily lost) in the shortest amount of time possible. The designer must also try to make it so it can be assembled by the fewest possible stage hands, mostly by making its weight manageable. A combination of all these factors can effectively reduce the cost of using the set on tour by thousands of dollars per week.

These techniques of set design didn't come to Jeremy overnight. "It's taken me years of trial and error to come up with a design approach that works in most applications. Untold hours at the drawing board have gone into conceiving designs that look good and, most importantly, work well on the road." To become a good designer, Jeremy believes you need to spend years touring, "so you get to know everything you possibly can about everybody else's gig. You need to know about lights, sound, how the equipment can and can not be used, and you need a basic understanding of how a tour is set up and managed. You must also learn how a stage or production manager can help you. These are absolute necessities to be able to design sets that look good and function well. Getting the ideal combination is not a matter of luck, it's a matter of skill and experience. The best way to begin to obtain all this knowledge is to serve an apprenticeship."

The stage sets for indoor and outdoor shows each present different design challenges. Jeremy considers U2's 1987 outdoor set as one of his most interesting projects to date. "One thing that intrigued me about the set design was that it had never been done before. They were doing an open air set using their new 80 foot span roof with two sets of large PA drapes (huge curtains that hide the vast bank of speakers) on either side, both designed in different styles. These drapes could be changed between the support band's and U2's set to give the stage a different look for each band. PA drapes (especially large ones) usually must be kept fairly tight to avoid tearing against the scaffold support system. The problem we had to overcome was that in order to raise and lower a drape, it had to be slackened or bunched up without tearing. I am proud to say that our design worked well, exactly as we planned it."

Jeremy encountered another technical problem on a David Bowie tour in 1987. The entire stage had been built by others to look like the giant 'Glass Spider' that David wanted, but little consideration had been paid to how that stage design would go on the road. "I was asked to resolve the problem posed by the spider body which comprised the roof area of the stage. Essentially, it was a 40 foot diameter bubble standing about 15 feet high. The whole unit needed to be affixed to a standard rental roof, suspended 30 feet above the ground and full of lighting equipment." Jeremy's solution was to design an inflatable body, a huge balloon that could be hung from the roof and be suspended fifteen feet over David's head. The trouble was, however, that with any outdoor breeze, the shape of the balloon made it behave like an enormous kite, capable of possibly flying the whole roof away with it. "I couldn't change the shape to solve this problem because it was part of someone else's design, so we had to find another way to anchor it down." Jeremy enlisted the help of engineers and computers in Germany and fabricators in England to design a special anchor for the spider. In fact, they actually built two spiders, so they could be leap-frogged between venues to more shows to be played each week. The Spider, when deflated, required only 6 feet of truck space and could be put together by the regular stage crew without any specialist crews. It is often the solving of a practical problem like this that provides me with the biggest challenge and the greatest interest."

Asked about his favorite designs, Jeremy picks a few examples of sets he built for Ozzie Osbourne. One was a gothic castle with three arched windows almost 30 feet high, with walls in between them. "Ivy actually 'grew' up the walls imperceptibly, slowly, during the show. At the end of the concert people realized that something was different — the castle was covered with ivy. A nice little effect that I liked a lot."

At another point in Ozzie's show the stage was hidden from view by a large curtain that was painted to look like the stones of an enormous castle wall. "At the desired moment the entire curtain disappeared in a flash. This was achieved by rigging the curtain (which covered three sides of the stage) from a series of interlinked Kabuki pipes. This releases the top of the curtain so that the weight of the fabric drops it to the stage floor. It happens so quickly that if you blink your eyes you'll miss it. In case someone didn't blink naturally, we fired off very bright flashes at the back of the stage."

A third set for Ozzie that pleased both Jeremy and the audience was a reflector table full of food (including a boar's head) that was wheeled on stage. While Ozzie was singing the first verse of a song, an executioner grabbed him from behind. There was a very dramatic drum roll as Ozzie was lifted on the table and his head was "chopped off." The executioner picked up "Ozzie's head," put it on a plate at the opposite end of the table and the "head" then sang the next verse. "That was only a fundamental Victorian magic trick — just adapted to Rock 'n' Roll."

To young people, Jeremy has this advice: "If this sounds like something that you would like to do — get started now. Get involved in your school's theater department, high school or college. Take every available course in lighting, mechanical drawing, engineering and design. Formal education is important, but practical experience is equally important. If there is a local ballet or some other performing company in your area, make every effort to work for them, even if it's as an unpaid volunteer. Any of this experience might be critical for your future success. Apply as an assistant at a company that does staging or stage design. It's in your best interest to learn from the creative forces in the industry wherever you can find them. Hook up with any venue, no matter how small, to improve your skills.

"Finally, if you're near a major metropolitan area, go to the local arena and offer to unload trucks or whatever work it takes to meet the road crew. Eventually, if they see that you're determined to make it in the business, and not afraid to work hard, you may get offered a touring job. If you can make this happen, you will probably have some opportunity to meet and speak with established set designers and maybe they will let you work with them. It's a matter of sticking with it and staying optimistic about your chances of becoming the next great set designer."

66 **W**hen you manage several artists, it is absolutely essential to be able to count on first rate touring staff. You can't do it all yourself and your artist deserves the best possible stage show. An experienced production company that can handle all of the technical details of the tour leaves you free to dedicate your time to the artist. *99*

Lyor Cohen, Co-Manager
RUN-DMC/JAZZY JEFF AND THE FRESH PRINCE/LL COOL J.

Lighting & Tour Production
Don Tretsky

Don Tretsky is the Operations Manager and Production Coordinator for BML Concert and Lighting Productions. That's a lot like being the overall foreman in a very complicated factory.

As operations and production manager for his company Don can't think of anything he doesn't do. "When a client calls us about doing a show in a given venue and I have gotten all the details from the promoter or the band's lighting designer, I coordinate everything with the venue and with our crews. The objective is to work out a functional design and a reasonable production. Sometimes I'm asked to come up with the actual design for a show and other times the band's designer calls the shots and I work along with him. If the artist doesn't have a production coordinator, then I'll even handle that for them. I try to get all the necessary information that our production people will need to make everything run smoothly. This even requires me to oversee the construction shop to some degree. For the most part, however, I'm doing less of the nitty gritty these days and dealing a lot more with the promoters, production people and artists."

Don gets very busy on the day just before the show: "I make sure that the proper equipment is loaded on the truck, that the crew has their 'float' money, accommodations are arranged and their work plans set. If I've worked that particular venue before, I'll try to tell them what to look out for and give them whatever helpful hints I can. But my biggest concern that day is to see that we have to get to the venue on time to set up. I'm like a father telling his kids not to forget to bring this or that, don't be late, etc. If the guys are late, they know that we will often dock their pay. Lateness can cost a ton of money when it's a union call, in a large venue. Guys who are late don't last very long. Fortunately that kind of thing doesn't happen often because most of our guys are very responsible."

Don has worked with many acts like, just to name a few, the Beastie Boys, The Alarm, Willie Nelson, John Waite, Aerosmith, Roger Daltry, Run DMC, Cheap Trick and Billy Idol. He started in this business handling the lighting for local bands along the Jersey Shore and in Manhattan. "I had done some lighting in high school, but pursued other interests until a band called 'Groceries' asked me to work with them. From there I began to meet people in the industry, including the people I work for now. It was perfect for me because I lived in the area and always was going over their place to buy equipment anyway. I started doing shows for them on a part-time basis, one nighters or a couple weeks here and there. The job of overseeing the shop and coordinating our road crews was often full of frustrations and problems, but somebody had to do it."

Many lighting problems can get solved on the phone, or by getting help from a local contractor or another lighting company. In some cases, they can be corrected by delivering a new part via Federal Express or air freight. "Once every so often the problem is sticky enough that we have to fly out an electronics tech."

Like Don, most of his crew started with local club bands or college concert committees. "Usually we hire people through recommendations, but we don't hire on a regular basis. We'll go for months without needing extra help and then get into a real pinch. When this happens, we'll usually call our part-time people first. But once in a while a guy will just walk in looking for a job at the right moment and get the gig. One unusual thing about us is that we have a 'co-op program' where local high school kids come in after school hours to work in the electronics shop. It's an excellent way for

229

someone to get experience. One of these students has been with us for three years. We had about two or three of them helping out when an Aerosmith tour put a heavy load on us this past summer and the kids were so good I hope they come back again.

"Our shop employs about 20 full time employees and as many as 30 part-time people depending on how many tours they're working on. Most of the part-timers have worked with us somewhere before in the business and know what it's like to get a show out. When hiring we look for people who have some lighting experience in clubs or theatre. However, if we need to get a tour out we'll give someone with only a basic knowledge of electricity or good mechanical skills a chance to work. During extremely busy times we'll hire people specifically for loading and unloading gear. Even these part-timers better 'be there' when we need to meet a deadline."

Don says there's an unwritten rule in the touring industry that once you've taken on a job you're going to see it through no matter what it takes. "We had a situation right before one Christmas where Cheap Trick decided at the last minute to take one of our systems on the road. Three days sounded like it would be impossible to put together a lighting system. Everyone in the shop really came through, working 12-14 hour days and we even made it home for Christmas dinner. Our terrific staff always seems to pull through. In fact, I'm proud to say that we've never had a show go out late.

"For those who would like to get into the lighting business. The first thing you need is an open mind. You have to be adaptable to changes that are constantly thrown at you. Unless you're flexible enough to 'go with the flow' you're not going to make it in the entertainment business. Artists are notorious for changing their minds at the last moment and you have to be able to deal with that without losing your cool. They're the boss. You must have a talent for chilling out no matter how frustrated you get. The last thing you want is to let the client see you lose your cool. A low threshold of frustration can adversely affect your professional ambitions if you're not careful."

Don's advice to the young and ambitious is to take advantage of educational opportunities: "It's an excellent idea to take some kind of Theater Arts classes in high school. There are also electronics classes that may give you the opportunity to work plays and productions going on in the school itself. When I was in high school, there was a Theater Arts Club and we always set up for the local bands in the high school auditorium. This was a terrific learning experience for me. Computer classes would also be a big help because of all of the new computerized equipment that's around now; our lighting consoles are becoming more computerized every day and require skilled operators and programmers."

Don's other suggestions are: "Be willing to work really long hours. Make sure you love music or you won't be able to do any of these jobs day in and day out. It's got to be more than a job. It's that extra involvement in the music that keeps you working all night long to finish the job. Once I drove all night from Boston to Westpoint, maybe 200 miles away, in a snowstorm. I reached Westpoint at 6:00 in the morning, caught 3 hours sleep in the truck, and started all over again at 9:00 that same morning. When the show that night was so good and the audience was so happy, it was worth it."

66 Considering all the
*times and places my bands have played, the money
we've laid out to buy insurance might have seemed
to be an extravagance...until we needed it. Then it
felt like a bargain.* **99**

> **Darren Jordan, Tour Manager**
> **RUN DMC**

Entertainment Insurance

George Walden

Being an insurance agent doesn't sound like a very glamorous job, but some of them know more about Rock 'n' Roll than a lot of performers. Seeing that a tour is "covered" against every possible kind of accident or "risk" takes both imagination and years of experience.

George Walden represents Albert G. Ruben & Co., an insurance firm that has been in business close to 30 years. In addition to providing concert promoters with insurance against most of the risks of touring, the company writes policies for approximately 80 percent of all the major motion pictures that are shot and virtually every major recording act. In fact, they're the largest operation of its kind in the world. "We specialize in providing insurance to the entertainment business and that includes all facets of insurance. Of course, there are the standard policies like workmen's comp, liability, homeowner's and automobile coverage and life insurance. But, most people don't realize that there are other more creative types of insurance available, such as policies that ensure against nonappearance of the act during a live event. Should the band not show up for any reason, whether it be death, sickness or injury. A policy like that can reimburse the financial backers for their cost and expenses.

"We can also develop a new product. One incident that will stand out in my mind changed the concert promoting business all around the country. It was the disaster in the 1970's when 11 kids were trampled to death in Cincinnati before a Who show. Fortunately the band's lawyer had seen to it that they were heavily insured, but as a result of that incident, coverage became much harder to obtain, the premiums skyrocketed and festival seating (open field, no reserved seats) was no longer permitted. Insurance carriers were insisting that the doors to the event be opened hours before the performance, no longer the traditional half hour before showtime. Security also had to be tightened and reserved seating became mandatory. This particular coverage costs each ticket holder anywhere from 20-40 cents a ticket. If there are 18,000 people at 30 cents a ticket the cost per show amounts to around $5,000 per concert. It's a major expense."

As a young man, George had absolutely no interest in working in the insurance business. "My father was a risk manager for Warner Communications and he insisted that I interview for a position with Albert Ruben (they insured Warner). I was planning to go back to school to get my Master's degree and become a whiz kid at IBM or Xerox. But to please my father, I went to talk with a representative of this entertainment insurance giant. I warned my father not to expect much from my interview. My interview turned out to be with the Chairman of the company and his assistant. For some reason (truly unknown to me), they called me back and offered me a job. To their surprise I told them I wasn't interested in their job. Like a lot of other people, I had a pre-conceived notion about the insurance business. Actually, I didn't understand it. Primarily because I didn't have a job and needed one, I thought it over and accepted their offer. I figured that school was still six months away and if I didn't like it, I could always move on. Well, it now happens to be 12 years later and I can't imagine a better business to be in."

In George's opinion, prospective employees should have at least a high school education. "A college degree is not a necessity. To work in the insurance business you must get a broker's license, which requires going to school for a specified amount of hours and then passing a state test. Perhaps the most difficult part of the test is the language portion, for the lingo in this business is a little different from what most people are accustomed to." He admits that "passing the test enables you to sell insurance, but, taking a broker's test and passing a broker's exam doesn't make you a broker. You need to be aggressive, have an ability to write, be able to speak well and communicate effectively with people. To be cordial is one thing, but that's only the surface. You need to know what you are talking about. This means fully understanding the insurance policies that you are selling, and the contract that you're asking people to sign. Most importantly, you must speak to your clients in a language that they can comprehend. Don't speak to them in insurance terms if you can do it in plain old English. Demonstrating a mastery of insurance terms isn't going to help your client, in fact, they're going to look at you like you are crazy."

George hates being referred to as an insurance salesman. "I would say that you are a professional. To call this job insurance sales, is doing a disservice to the business. If somebody is looking for a 9-5 job, don't come into this business. I don't work 9-5. Being in New York, I'm dealing with California when most New Yorkers are sitting in front of the TV. I also do business from my home and people work Saturdays and Sundays in the office. This is not unique to the insurance business, any business is demanding. You must put in the time to fully understand the business if you hope to get some place. Should you want to make a lot of money and to be something, there are no shortcuts. Success to most people means being well off financially and having people call you, because they respect you. Well, that's going to take a lot of work. You must ask yourself is it worth that commitment? Or, do you only want to work 9-5 and make $15,000 a year? My suggestion is, do whatever makes you happy."

For anyone coming into the insurance business with no experience and wanting to start at the ground level, George suggests taking a job as a receptionist or clerical person in an insurance office. "It may be a thankless job, but will provide a real education in the insurance business at a grass roots level. Besides, looking on the bright side, there's no place to go but Up!"

❝I *enjoy working with Justin a lot. Like Jodi (Cyndi's makeup artist) he's very imaginative and versatile and it's exciting to create styles with him.* **❞**

Cyndi Lauper

Hairdressing

Justin Ware

There's much more to styling hair for famous performers than learning finger waves and pin curls. It takes a great deal of skill to design an original, flattering hair style and keep an artist's "look" fresh and natural.

Justin Ware has been helping entertainers look their best for close to 18 years. Ten of those years were spent as the art director for Vidal Sassoon. "My training started at Robert Fiance beauty school and continued through a training program at Sassoon. The program took me through successive stages beginning with 'Jr. stylist,' then 'stylist,' followed by 'director' and ultimately 'Art Director.'" When Justin made it to the position of Sassoon's Art Director, his job included a great deal of travel to international shows. These took him all over the USA and to London, Japan, Madrid, and many other European locations.

"My clientele at Sassoon consists primarily of actors and musicians. As in any salon, one person will recommend you to a

235

friend and eventually you build up your own large client list. The clients I have worked with are particularly exciting. They allow me to display my own creativeness as they are showing theirs. It's a stimulating way to work."

Many well-known entertainers began going to Justin long before they became famous. Today they remain loyal friends. His very talented clientele sounds like Who's Who: Oscar winning actress Diane Wiest, who has been with Justin since before her days in Othello. Singers like Joan Jett and Debbie Harry rely on him to give them their distinctive look. The album covers of bands like the Thompson Twins, Danger Danger, Modern English, and Jimmy Page have displayed Justin's work. Nick and Julie Rhoads both counted on Justin to help them look their best on their wedding day. But, perhaps Justin's most widely imitated look was the one he jointly created with Cyndi Lauper.

"I met Cyndi long before she was popular. In fact, it was even before she was in Blue Angel. One day we were talking and she said, 'I want my own look.' We collaborated on the direction that she was headed and came up with a color. She displayed her new 'look' in a Sasoon hair show in Philadelphia. This was right before I put the checkerboard in her hair. 'Girls Just Want to Have Fun' was just getting popular and we were getting ready to do 'Time After Time.' That's when it all started to become an international phenomenon. There hasn't been anyone in the last twenty years who is more readily associated with a unique look than Cyndi Lauper."

When Justin is working on a motion picture he tries to look through the eyes of a camera: "Each camera is different. A motion picture camera tends to make the actor's hair look very tight and dense. If you were to look at that same person with just the human eye, you would see something completely different. Therefore, you must work with the camera. For magazine work, it's yet another approach. Visually, we don't see what the camera sees. It takes a great deal of cooperation from the cameraman, lighting people, myself and many others to get a good photograph for a magazine. It really takes a joint effort and everybody has to work together."

Today, Justin works at MIWA's, an exclusive salon in midtown Manhattan. Aside from working with a private clientele, he does commercials, magazines, videos films and other events that require his expertise. One of his more unusual assignments was the highly televised 1984 Olympics. "Prior to particular events, I would design a look for a participant that was in character with their event. It had to be functional with their sport. It was really a very gratifying challenge. When a member of the French women's fencing team won a medal she rushed back to thank me and present me with a commemorative medal from her country. She told me that I had given her an edge psychologically knowing that she looked her best in front of millions of people. I know she was speaking the truth: the better you feel about how you appear outwardly, the easier it is to reach for the best that's inside yourself.

"I usually try to color a performer's hair two days before any appearance, performance, photo session or video. The day of the event, I'll basically be styling her hair and perhaps add some temporary colors depending on what she's wearing. I love working with artists who allow me to be creative. Of course, the artist has the final say on the feeling and look that she wants to express. You just start from there and add your own talent and artistic ability to achieve that goal.

"I work with each individual differently. You're dealing with people on a very personal level. Skill is one thing, but sensitivity and communication are equally important. The person you're working with must be comfortable with you. Not only do you have physical contact with them, but you also are instrumental in maximizing their self confidence and feeling of well being."

Justin has the following advice for those seeking a career as a hair stylist: "Someone coming out of high school and hoping to get into the business must first get a license. Depending on your state's regulations, you may put in approximately 1200 hours in a beauty school, take a blood test and submit an application. Afterwards your license must be renewed every two years. A number of beauty schools can provide excellent training. Wilford Academy and Robert Fiance come to mind immediately. As a matter of fact I took Cyndi to both places to help her get prepared for the part she played (a beautician) in Vibes. Also, Vidal Sassoon has excellent training facilities where you work as an assistant for a two year period before you become a stylist. At that point you build up a clientele, set your goals and decide if you want to work in the theater, video, movies or live entertainment.

"A good hair stylist gets to know the feelings of the person he's working with, the mood and direction they are going. The job is mental as much as it is mechanical. You can have all the technical skills in the world, but if you can't communicate with your client, you're in for a lot of problems. Becoming successful in this business, or most others for that matter, takes a lot of work and dedication. Many people are doing it just for a job. If you have a higher motivation you can far succeed the others. The true professional does it because he or she really loves what they do. Nine out of ten times those who love what they're doing become very artistic and very creative in their job and enjoy a great deal of recognition, success and prestige."

> **66** **B**efore becoming a business manager there was no better tour accountant than Bill Z. In those days the Rolling Stones were a seven piece band — five performed, I played the telephone and Bill Z. wailed on the calculator. **99**
>
> *Peter Rudge, Manager (1973-78)*
> *THE ROLLING STONES*

Business Management
William Zysblat

William Zysblat and a partner head up the ZRO Organization, a firm specializing in business management, accounting and auditing services for entertainers. In addition, they provide on-the-road business services for Rock 'n' Roll tours.

After graduating from college, William Zysblat (his friends call him Bill Z) went to work for a big Wall Street accounting firm called Hurdman and Cranston. As luck would have it, their European partners were the auditors for the Rolling Stones. In 1975, the Rolling Stones did an American tour and H & C were asked to audit it. When the accountant on the road ran into some difficulties, Bill was asked to take his place.

"It was the first entertainment anything I'd done. The Stones were playing Madison Square Garden and I was at a desk in my office working on a rather boring project, when someone tapped me on the shoulder and handed me an itinerary. I was told to pack my bags and expect to be back in two months. That night was the band's last show at the Garden, and the next day I was on a plane to Philadelphia with Mick and the rest of the guys."

The tour accountant handles every financial aspect of a tour. This includes paying wages on the road, reimbursing expenses that people incur on behalf of the tour and paying per diems. The per diem is the daily allowance that every employee gets to pay for his food, laundry, telephone and so forth. Even though the bulk of the time spent by a tour accountant is on the mundane things like petty cash, checking out of hotels, or just giving money to the band to keep them going, the tour accountant's primary responsibility is to "settle" the show. That means sitting down with the promoter after each show and going through the contract in detail, working out how much the act has made that night. The quality of a tour accountant is potentially the difference between anywhere from 5 to 15% of the income of the tour.

"The first time I went out," Bill recalls, "I probably overlooked a lot of things including the bill for advertising ten different shows that were coming to the building that probably got charged in full to each of those ten shows as opposed to one-tenth for each band. We probably paid for the police barricades which had been sold to every act since 1962. Depending on the size of the show, there are 50 to 200 areas in which a promoter will interact with an accountant during a settlement where there is room for give and take. Promoters very often own an advertising company. The advertising commission that goes to that company frequently ends up in their own pockets. It takes quite a while to know which promoters and what ad companies are connected. The same thing applies to ticket distributors that are connected with either Ticketron or another agency. Unless you've been doing settlements for a long period of time it would be difficult to pick up on those things. For example, Joe Blow will rent you his tarp for a stadium show, but he owns the tarp, so make sure you don't get overcharged for it.

"At the end of the 1975 Rolling Stones tour I went back to work on my normal accounts. Although I had a great time, I didn't really know if I wanted life on the road again or not. My mind was made up for me, however, when the Rolling Stones decided to tour Europe and requested that my firm give me a leave of absence to help them plan the tour. My firm gave me 6 months off and I went to Europe with Peter Rudge, then the manager of the Stones, the Who, and 38

Special. He was probably the top manager in the industry at the time, certainly the most creative. He knew how to make the most money for his bands and was obviously doing a great job because all his groups were doing well. Peter decided where and when the band would play, but I would then go to the promoter and 'do the deal.' This made the later settlements very easy, because I knew ahead of time the costs allowed in the deal.

"Tour accounting was only then becoming sophisticated. Today there are ways to resolve problems that arise along the way, but then there was never that much money at stake. Before the Stones, the average tour of Europe involved thousands of dollars, but the Rolling Stones were then getting hundreds of thousands of dollars. Even fluctuations in the exchange rate was a difference between a profit and a loss. Europe was a series of touring nightmares in those days. Some countries didn't even allow you to take money out of the country, like in Yugoslavia. It would have been nice if we were told ahead of time about that little problem. After two shows in Yugoslavia, I found myself sitting in my hotel room with a table piled high with Yugoslavian currency, but being told by the promoter I'd better spend it in Yugoslavia because if you cross the border with it we'd be thrown in jail.

"Mick Jagger came into the room about ten minutes later after having been told of our dilemma. He told me that they expected to get paid for those dates and the band would be waiting on the plane. I asked him if he had any ideas and he responded, that's your job and just walked out of the room laughing. I had no idea of what I was going to do. That evening by absolutely sheer luck, I had discovered the hotel's casino and played a few hands of blackjack. I cashed a few of my own dollars and got Dinero, the local currency. When I went to cash out they asked me if I wanted Dinero or Italian Lira. They had offered Lira because a majority of their tourists were Italian. A light went off in my head! Every fifteen minutes or so, I took a pile of Dinero to the window and bought about $10,000 worth of their chips, played two hands of blackjack, returned to the window and put everything back into Lira. The police at the airport were expecting me and went through everything I had until they found this giant bag of Lira. Taking out Lira was perfectly legal, so they let me go.

"When I went full time into the music business, approximately a year after the Stones tour, my initial staff consisted of me and a

241

bookkeeper. I was able to keep the Stones as clients. I needed other work and agreed to do a particular tour for a headliner who faded terribly. However, the opening act was a hit, Duran Duran. Joe Jackson was the next act that we signed and over the years we've been steadily adding some of the greatest bands in the business.

"Occasionally there is a difference in money at the end of the night. If you can't resolve the problem reasonably, you have to slug it out (so to speak). Many times it's a question of leverage and everyone has his own form of it. The promoter is holding the money; if you are either a heavy enough act or are backed by a strong agency, you can tell them that you're going to take future tours to another promoter. It's all a question of strength. We have the clout from representing a number of great artists, such as Keith Richards, David Bowie, Duran Duran, Julian Lennon, Depeche Mode, Europe and Joe Jackson.

"Tour accountants are generally compensated on a weekly wage. I was very well compensated by the Stones compared to the average tour accountant, but in the mid-70's accountants got paid anywhere from $300 to $500 a week. Today, they're paid anywhere from $1,000 to $3,000 a week and are usually bonused based on how well the tour goes.

"We have strict rules of ethics. The company policy regarding drugs and alcohol is very simple. It's not tolerated at any level, even socially. Given the level of trust that our clients put in the handling of large amounts of money there are no second chances. This is a hard and fast policy. I do not ever want to see one of my clients walk into a bar and find one of my employees even the slightest bit drunk. We are an entity unto ourselves and we don't compromise our position in any way whatsoever."

To young people thinking of forming a firm like Bill's, he suggests "Get the best financial and accounting background possible. That means that you will presumably graduate from a respectable school with a decent grade point average. Find yourself a national accounting firm (if not an international accounting firm) and pay two years worth of intensely boring dues learning what accounting really is. It's very important, for example, to know the difference between foreign currency exchanges, trading Francs for Lira, and facts like that taxes are lower in France to an American company than in Italy. And you have to know about the double tax treaties between various countries. Generally, you're not going to learn that in the music business, but only at an international accounting firm. Learn as much about international tax as you possibly can, get certified and pick up the phone and call me.

"The ultimate candidate for a job as a tour accountant on the road would be someone who went to college, got involved with a few local bands, promoted a couple of shows and got their accounting degree. That way you can go to a firm and say, I used to promote shows on campus, I know what a roadie does, I understand the buzz words — the lingo, and I'm a very good accountant. It's very likely that you will be hired.

"As a tour accountant you will sacrifice probably any social relationship you had going. It puts an incredible strain on any marriage. It's a very 'hurry up and wait' atmosphere on the road: you're waiting hours for a bus to leave or for a promoter to be ready to do a settlement. The positive side of the business is that there is a lot of money to be made if you are good at what you do. There is also an incredible amount of gratification in seeing people you enjoy working with succeeding very much because of your efforts. If you've come back from a tour that was expected to do mediocre business, but winds up selling out all over the country, you have a completely different sense of accomplishment, especially if the job you did in the settlements was an important factor in making good money for your firm and most importantly for the band. There's an immense amount of personal satisfaction that is unequalled in the corporate world."

HOW THIS BOOK
CAME TO BE WRITTEN

Lawyers who work in the entertainment business get into all kinds of situations. It's not all libraries and contracts nor is it all glamour and excitement. Lots of it is hard work and long hours. What it almost never is, however, is boring or, for that matter, unsatisfying. One of the situations I found myself in recently was facing a young writer who was interviewing me (about a famous star whom I represent) for an article he was doing about her. I had been interviewed before, of course, but this fellow's questions were interesting, probing and sensitive. I thought he was terrific and I was extremely pleased with the article itself when it was published in a national magazine. I didn't forget him.

When a good friend of mine, the head of one of the best stage sound and lighting and tour production companies in the business, Eric Todd, came to me with an idea for a book like this, I immediately thought of that writer, Frank Weimann. When Frank heard about it, he was enthusiastic and excited by the project. After a brief meeting in New York, we set out on our mission. In a matter of days we had contacted top professionals in the industry, many of whom Eric and/or I had worked with on various star-studded tours.

Everyone in this book is at the top of his or her field. Of course there are many others who are their equal and whose stories might have been just as useful and interesting, but there simply wasn't room in this first edition for all the wonderful people who take Rock 'n' Roll on the road. We are sure that all of you have attended concerts where the people in this book, without you ever knowing it, made it possible for you to enjoy an especially exciting evening with your favorite band or performer.

It may not have ever occurred to you that there were teams of people that put together those special nights for you. These teams include such unlikely Rock 'n' Roll members as travel agents, truck drivers, accountants and carpenters. You may never have thought that a career in any of those fields could make you part of the concert world. We hope this book will open your eyes to the possibilities and the opportunities that exist for exciting and useful careers in entertainment, even if you can't play the guitar. Here, then, is your BACKSTAGE PASS and good luck to you all from Eric, Frank and me.

ELH

BACKSTAGE PASS

Special Thanks To:

Lisa Aloisi, Richard Aloisi, Schroll Guerry Associates (for the cover), Otto Entertainment Graphics (for the use of their historic collection of backstage passes), Ricky "Rickster" Powell (for his camera, his eye and his photos), Nancy Hoffman, Harvey Sirota, The TypeWorks of Baltimore, Manhattan Design (for their cover suggestions), Susan Buyalski (for some great ideas), Suzy Stoller, John Holland, Nim Polanetska, Katy Valk, Vincent Grucci, Bob Carney & the staff at Meadowlands Arena.

Also, thanks from Eric to Abe, Andy, Bruno, Kasey, Steve and Ted (OSAH), the staff at BML, Francis, Mary and Sibby, Dr. A.H. Schwartz, B. Dempsky, R. Poznansky and J. Seigel.

Finally, thanks from all of us to friends, families, and all the wonderful industry colleagues who agreed to share their lives and experiences with us and with our readers.

The Authors

Backstage Pass: Special Services

Some of the participants in "Backstage Pass" may be available on a limited basis for speaking engagements before educational and community organizations. For further information write on letterhead to B.P.I., Box 745 Dept. 101, Belle Mead, NJ 08502.

Additional copies of "Backstage Pass" are available by writing B.P.I., Dept. 110 at the address shown above. Quantity and educational discounts are available to qualified organizations and educators.

Left to Right: ERIC M. TODD, FRANK WEIMANN and ELLIOT L. HOFFMAN
(Note simulated traditional authors' poses)

ABOUT THE AUTHORS

ERIC M. TODD is President of BML Concert Lighting and BML Productions of New Jersey, and currently manages CBS/Imagine recording artists "Danger Danger."

FRANK WEIMANN is a free-lance writer, author of "Everything You Ever Wanted To Know About Woody Allen" (Quinlan Press, 1989) and a literary agent with the Edward J. Acton Agency in New York City.

ELLIOT L. HOFFMAN is a member of the New York law firm Beldock Levine & Hoffman and President of Entertainment Corporation of America, producers of many tours of Yes, the Who, Asia and others.